D1591097

ACCIDENTAL ADVENTURES

The Extraordinary Travel Adventures of Two Ordinary People

Kathy Fronheiser

To Cyndi,
Adventures await!
Kathy Fronheiser

Accidental Adventures:
The Extraordinary Travel Experiences
of Two Ordinary People
Copyright © 2021 by Kathy Fronheiser

Published by
Far Off Lands Publishing
Allentown, Pennsylvania

All rights reserved.

No part of this book may be reproduced in any form or by any electronic or mechanical means, including information storage and retrieval systems, without written permission from the author, except in the case of a reviewer, who may quote brief passages embodied in critical articles or in a review.

Book cover design by bravoboy.
Interior book design by YellowStudios.

Paperback ISBN: 978-1-7330364-2-9
Library of Congress Control Number: 2021910726

Printed in the United States of America

For My Husband, Ed
The Love of My Life

CONTENTS

INTRODUCTION /
AUTHOR'S NOTES

WHEN I MET MY HUSBAND IN 1988, I told him that I dreamed of traveling the world. Ed has made that dream come true for me over and over. Writing about our memorable experiences is my way of thanking him. *Accidental Adventures* holds the tales of the many travels that Ed and I have shared during our years together. We started out camping in tents in nearby state parks during the early days, then took longer trips in an RV, and later expanded our travels to other countries by plane and rail. Since retiring, we've sailed around the world on cruise ships and loved every minute.

This isn't a travel guide and it certainly doesn't include all the places we've visited. Instead, it shares stories of our unintended "accidental adventures" that range from interesting and amusing conversations to getting lost to lengthy hospital stays in foreign countries. Some are just short anecdotes while others are detailed accounts. Many are funny, some are poignant, and a few are frightening, but all are true stories. Photos are included where possible but not for adventures where photography was not permitted, or for those that took place before digital cameras and smart phones. Sometimes the unexpected adventure took place before we realized that we should have taken a photo.

Our adventures also included relocating after our children were grown and on their own. We moved our household from Cleveland to Seattle to Denver to Germany, back to Denver, and finally to our retirement home in Allentown, Pennsylvania.

We traveled as often as we could and haven't stopped. Travel has taught us that kind people and fascinating adventures await us everywhere from our own neighborhood to the other side of the world, and we're always ready to explore them.

"Out there things can happen and frequently do
to people as brainy and footsy as you."

— Dr. Seuss, *Oh, The Places You'll Go!*

OUR FIRST
ACCIDENTAL ADVENTURE
WAS WHEN WE MET

WHEN PEOPLE ASK US HOW WE MET, they are often amazed and entertained by our story. Both of us had been married previously and were hoping to find love again.

I had been going out occasionally with my friend John who took me to dinner and concerts. He was very sweet but much older than me. Like 21 years older. Very nice man, but marriage was not in in our future. One evening at church choir practice, he handed me a copy of the March 1988 issue of *Clevelander*, a local magazine about arts and culture in the Cleveland area. It contained a listing of personal ads at the back. This was long before the internet. One particular ad had been circled. John said, "This ad was written for you. You should write this guy a letter."

The ad read, "Hopeless romantic, sensitive, caring professional, 44, enjoys quiet candlelight dinners, moonlight walks, sports, poetry and theatre; seeks trim white/Asian sensual professional female who desires to share life experiences. Photo please." It included a box number for responses. My immediate reaction was an absolute no. "Who knows what kind of person that is? I don't do that sort of thing. Arrange to meet a stranger? It's not safe." After some discussion, John convinced me to take the magazine home and think about it. He had met a woman through the magazine himself a while back. It didn't work out for him but that didn't mean it wouldn't work out for me.

About two weeks later I had a really bad day and sat down to write a letter to the guy who wrote the ad. Then I was afraid to mail it. Two weeks later after another bad day, my letter went into the mailbox. I had just wasted a stamp. A month went by and he didn't even call me.

Meanwhile, Ed's two older children who lived with him were hoping he would find a girlfriend. They gave him a gift certificate to *Clevelander* magazine for Christmas and helped him write the ad. After a month went by with no responses, he ran the ad again not knowing that the magazine held the responses and sent them together in one package. All of a sudden, he had 137 letters. Ed was one busy guy. A friend had told him not to invite any of these women out to dinner. Too expensive. Instead, meet them for coffee in the morning (have to dash off to the office), or for lunch (have to get back to work), or after work for a drink (have to get home to make dinner for the kids). He kept a folder in the back seat of his car with notes he had taken during the initial phone call with each candidate, so he could review them before he went inside to meet her in person. It was the only way to keep all these women straight.

Finally, he called me. As it turned out, we lived within walking distance of each other's houses. Our daughters went to the same school and sometimes walked together part of the way home. My daughter reminded me that we had run into Ed and his daughter in the grocery store a few weeks before. She said I had my nose in the store shelves while she talked to her friend and I never noticed him. Not only that, Ed and I were both working on master's degrees at the same college and had classes in the same building on the same nights. Surely, we had passed each other in the hall at some point.

We agreed to go out for coffee after class the following week. When I got home afterwards, my daughter was still awake. "I didn't like him at all," I told her. "He's too slick." When he called about a week later and asked me to have dinner at a jazz club, I decided to give him another chance and said okay. It wasn't like my social calendar had filled in since I last saw him. It was a much nicer evening. He seemed more relaxed and genuine.

The following day was Palm Sunday. He sent his children to my house with a beautiful flowering plant and an Easter card with a poem he had written himself all about springtime and hearts coming alive. I was hooked.

One year later on April 7, 1989, we were married.

OUR LOVE OF TRAVEL

SIX MONTHS AFTER WE WERE MARRIED, ED suffered a massive heart attack. He was incredibly lucky to have survived it. While he was recuperating, I gave him a book with pictures of beautiful mountains in North America. Ed was determined that after he recovered, he would climb the mountains in that book and the following summer he started doing just that. After climbing Mt Elbert in Colorado in 1992, he sent a photo of himself at the top to his cardiologist who hung the picture in his medical office. Ed became his star patient.

Nature and beautiful scenery have a calming effect on both of us, so getting away even for a day or two to see a new place or to spend time in a familiar one we love is always on our radar. In Colorado we didn't miss a chance to see blooming wildflowers in the prairie grasslands or the elk and bighorn sheep in Rocky Mountain National Park.

A man we met on one of the many trails we hiked recommended the Highpointers Club (www.highpointers.org) which promotes climbing to the highest geographical point in each of the fifty states and connects people who are looking for hiking partners. It turned out to be challenging and fun to log our progress toward achieving as many highpoints as we could.

Highpointing took us to places we never would have ventured to otherwise. Most of these trips were made before the internet and cell phones, so we relied on the club's published guidebook to take us to our destination in each state. The tricky part was, you could only take credit for a highpoint if you actually found and photographed the USGS bronze marker at the top. Not as easy as it sounds.

The discovery of highpointing marked the beginning of our many years of travel adventures together. As of this writing, I have made it to the top of 37 of state highpoints. Ed has completed 49 and was the 178th person to do so. Only Denali (Mt McKinley) in Alaska remains for him and that's a tough one.

As we took our RV around the country, we realized how different the regions of the United States are. The climate varies from north to south as well as east to west. Speech patterns and accents differ, even between neighboring states. The food people eat regularly in one state can be unheard of in the next. So many plants and animals are unique to a particular state or a particular area of the country. We continue to love learning about our country and the world.

The more we traveled, the more we discovered there was to see and do. Planning our travel is now part of the fun, especially when the framework of a trip is in place and I research and add lesser known, off the beaten path stops. In Washington DC we visited all the famous landmarks, monuments, memorials, and museums, and also included The Great Falls of the Potomac and Civil War Battlefields. One summer we followed the pioneer journey for 2000 miles on the Oregon Trail from Missouri to the End of the Trail Interpretive Center in Oregon City, Oregon.

I've always been fascinated by people in other parts of the world and how they go about their everyday lives. While working for the Department of Defense I realized that government jobs exist all over the world. Imagine how much traveling we could do if we lived and worked in Europe! When I was offered a position as Deputy Chief of Medical Management for the US Army in Bavaria, I jumped at the chance. We spent three years there and quickly learned that living overseas is very different from visiting as a tourist, but we loved it.

After we retired, we began to appreciate the advantages of cruising. Unpack once. Travel in comfort from place to place while you sleep without having to navigate unfamiliar roads, train stations and airports with your luggage. Make new friends and learn more than you ever dreamed possible. Our cruises have ranged from a week in Alaska to a month in the Mediterranean to sailing around the world. In 2018 we took a six-month world cruise from Miami to Miami on Oceania Cruises and loved it so much that we booked another one the following year for eight and a half months on Viking Ocean Cruises from London to London.

As our mode of travel evolved, so did the technology we used. We advanced from paper maps and guidebooks to cell phones and GPS. It was much easier to get lost years ago before smart phones and apps became common.

Over the years I've kept journals with photos of our trips and enjoy looking through them as I remember all the accidental adventures that Ed and I shared.

Dear Reader, I hope you enjoy them too.

LOST IN TRANSLATION

LANGUAGE HAS ALWAYS INTERESTED ME. MY FAVORITE subjects in school were French and German. Ed speaks German as well and we both know some Italian. We've picked up a few phrases in several languages, but don't consider ourselves fluent in anything.

People sometimes ask me why I'm not afraid to go to a country where I can't understand anyone. There is no reason to be concerned about this, I tell them. English is widely spoken around the world. Not absolutely everywhere of course, but usually it's possible to find someone who knows a little. If not, hand drawn pictures, gestures, and friendly smiles go a long way as you will see in the following accidental adventures.

TAXI DRIVER IN WARSAW

To visit Poland while working in Germany, we took a week off and flew to Warsaw with a plan to take a train directly from there to Krakow. According to the information online, it was possible to take the light rail from the airport to the main train station. We found the kiosk for light rail tickets, but none of the instructions were available in English.

A young Polish man who spoke some limited English offered to help us get our tickets from the machine. The station at the airport was not easy to get around in and we reached the right track just in time to see the light rail to downtown Warsaw pull out. The sign said the next one would leave in 45 minutes. Waiting for it meant we would miss our train to Krakow. We had already purchased our tickets online and they were only good for the late afternoon train. A taxi to the main station was our only option. Outside the airport entrance we found the taxi stand and climbed into the one at the head of the line. Not only did the driver not speak any English, but he also didn't understand any variation of the word train station in French, German, or Italian. I finally said, "Choo! Choo! Chuga, Chuga, Chuga." and then he laughed and nodded his head. He got us to the train station in plenty of time.

The train trip to Krakow was surprisingly elegant. Our first-class tickets included a hot meal and beverages, not common in other European countries. We were served a delicious pasta dish in relaxing seats and enjoyed the ride without encountering another English-speaking person during the entire journey.

SEARCHING FOR COLOMBIAN COFFEE

I couldn't leave Cartagena without buying some good Colombian coffee. When we came upon a lovely old building with a picture of a coffee cup hanging above the entrance, I went right in. The place was much larger than it looked from the outside. We walked around a large courtyard and past a museum entrance. Off in the corner was a little coffee shop that served all kinds of coffee drinks but didn't appear to sell bags of coffee. I took a closer look and saw three bags of coffee beans on display at the side of the counter. There were as many people working as there were customers drinking coffee. No English was spoken here but they were very nice. The semi-translated menu on the wall was a work of art.

Using my minimal Spanish speaking skills I tried to ask if they sold ground coffee, since all the bags on the counter were whole bean and I didn't have a grinder at home. It took a while to get my point across, but one guy finally understood and pointed to a grinder behind the counter. I gave him my most enthusiastic nod and he started grinding. The other two looked strangely at my American cash which had been accepted at other shops in Cartagena. When I pulled out my Visa card, however, they beamed. As I signed the receipt, I was stunned to see that my two pound bag of pure Colombian coffee came to less than $10.

SEARCHING FOR BUTTONS IN
MANILA, PHILIPPINES

On our second day in Manila, we took advantage of the shuttle bus from the cruise ship to a shopping mall. We needed to replace a button that Ed had lost from the snazzy suit he bought in South Africa. I cut off the remaining button and took it along so we could match it. This place had seven levels and over a thousand shops and restaurants. Surely a mall this big would have a fabric store or craft shop that carried buttons.

We started our search at the electronic kiosk by the door. It listed stores by name and location but not by category, so we gave up and tried the customer service counter. About 20 people crowded the counter without forming a line so I stood to the side while Ed worked his way up to the front of the group. When he came back, he said the woman told him to go to the National Bookstore and he repeated the directions she gave him. I said, "Are you sure she knew you wanted buttons and not books?" He said he had pointed to the buttons on his shirt when he talked to her. And so we started out, determined to find buttons one way or another by the end of the afternoon.

Words cannot describe the size and scope of this mall. The layout was filled with all kinds of turns, Y-shaped intersections, and corners. By some miracle we were able to find the bookstore, which did have some yarn and embroidery thread but no buttons. I showed the button to the woman behind a counter and asked her where I could find buttons. She just kept saying "We no have. We no have." Then I tried a young woman at the checkout who directed us to the Mini-Me store. Upstairs, turn right, go across to the other side. Something like that. Anyway, we found it. That store had little sewing kits with one shirt button inside.

Ed thought we might have better luck in the department store. We asked a clerk near the entrance there who said no, they didn't have buttons or a fabric department, but she suggested we try the tailor shop upstairs by the food court. It took a while to zero in on the tailor, only to find out that it was just a pickup and delivery point for the actual tailor who worked offsite in some obscure location that we couldn't quite grasp.

A clerk in the H&M store told us to go to the men's department in the department store which we hadn't tried. There we ran into someone who was actually helpful. She found a drawer full of odd buttons but none came close to the size of the one we needed. Then she took us to the alterations department. It sounded promising. There were three guys with sewing machines in a big room. All three of them denied any knowledge of buttons.

This place finally wore us down. We could not go on any longer, buttons or no buttons.

When we got back to the ship, I emptied my pockets and realized that somewhere along the way, I had lost the second button from Ed's jacket.

CONTINUING THE SEARCH FOR BUTTONS IN KOTA KINABALU, MALAYSIA

The last stop on our full day tour was a place known as the Filipino Market. Half of it was full of fresh produce and the other half displayed handicrafts. It had the narrowest aisles I'd ever seen in a market. Two people could not pass each other. The stalls went on and on but they were almost all selling the same jewelry and wood carvings. I went out of the building on the opposite side and was surprised to see that next to every entry door, there was a man sitting at a sewing machine. Aha! Maybe here I could finally find buttons. Ed couldn't wear his suit without them.

The first man didn't speak English and didn't respond to my attempts to communicate, so I moved to the second one. He seemed to understand what I wanted, but he said no. No buttons. The third one slowly opened a drawer at the side of his sewing machine and I held my breath. He brought out a box of buttons. Then another man came along who spoke some English and tried to help. I held up two fingers and kept saying two. Two buttons. Two big buttons. Another man approached and shoved a box of sunglasses under my nose. Then another one tried to get me to buy one of the belts hanging from his arm. A crowd was starting to build around me but I just kept saying buttons. I only want buttons.

When the sewing machine guy plunked down one big button, I was delighted. It was perfect. But I still needed another one so they would match. Two buttons. I held up two fingers again. He gave me a different one, much smaller. I tried to tell him they had to be the same. He looked at me like he couldn't understand how anybody could lose two buttons from the same garment. I wanted to tell him that it wasn't very hard. I had just done it. He finally pulled out two the same. Even though I knew they were too small for Ed's jacket, I felt obligated to buy them anyway and ran back to the bus in the pouring rain.

Ed's jacket remained buttonless until after we came home.

FINDING A WATCH BATTERY IN MONTEVIDEO, URUGUAY

The goal for our free afternoon in Montevideo was to find a new battery for my watch. I had it replaced before leaving Denver at watch repair shop that I don't normally use. Big mistake. It only lasted four months. I had asked the guide during the city tour that morning to recommend a place that had watch batteries. He said I'd find one on Colon Street.

After lunch, we walked six blocks up Colon Street and didn't come to anything that resembled a jewelry store or a shop that might have batteries. I went into a drugstore to inquire. They had a numbered ticket system that I wasn't able to figure out, so I just waited until all the other customers were taken care of and then approached the counter. No English was spoken here but I really didn't expect any. I used all the hand signals I could think of and repeated the Spanish word "Dónde" while pointing to my watch. The woman behind the counter finally understood and motioned for me to follow her outside. With more hand signals she directed me down the street to a shop opposite at the next corner.

From a distance it looked promising. This place had clocks in the window. Up close it looked more like a secondhand store and the clocks weren't ticking. Used household items and broken figurines lined the walls inside. The tiny proprietor looked like she had worked there all the many years of her life.

I wanted to slip away but Ed convinced me to stay there and try, even though every shelf overflowed with old stuff. I kept saying "battery" with the accent on different syllables while pointing to my watch until she understood. She motioned for me to hand her my watch. I did so reluctantly. When she picked up a pocketknife to open the back, I held my breath. She pried it apart, popped out my old battery and fished a matching one out of a package from a tiny drawer in a small bench that wasn't much wider than she was. She had my watch running again in no time.

As of this writing more than 18 months later, her battery is still keeping my watch on perfect time.

SINGING IN THE STREETS IN SPAIN

Our first visit to Barcelona was in the winter when there weren't many tourists. This was just before the vote at the height of Catalonia's efforts to secede from Spain. On the way to the main station to catch the subway to our hotel at the end of a long day touring the city, we heard music coming from a park on the next block. The performers were middle aged men who really seemed to be having the time of their lives getting the crowd to sing along with them about Catalonia. We clapped to the music when others did and could clearly sense the pride and love of the land in their voices. People standing near us soon gathered that we were Americans and smiled and nodded at us whenever we looked around.

It was great fun to join in their patriotic celebration and to feel so welcome and accepted, even though we couldn't understand a word.

LADIES RESTROOM CONVERSATION IN BARCELONA

As we walked by the Barcelona Opera House, we noticed a sign advertising a performance of Romeo and Juliet scheduled for that evening. The ticket office was open, and we were able to get good seats at a senior rate. The orchestra had at least 50 pieces and the music was fantastic. The performance, however, was not the ballet that I had expected to see. It was more like modern dance with minimal scenery and basic set design. If this had been a story that I wasn't familiar with, it would have been impossible to figure out what was going on. No matter. It was still interesting to see the Spanish interpretation of this timeless love story.

Although we weren't as well dressed as many others in the audience because we hadn't planned on this and didn't have time to go back to the hotel and change, we fit in well enough. The entire time we were there, I only heard Spanish and Catalan spoken around me, especially in the ladies' room at intermission where everyone in the long line around me complained about the shortage of facilities. I just nodded my head and kept saying, "Si, si" which must have been the appropriate response since none of the ladies nearby looked at me strangely.

SPEAKING ENGLISH IN AUCKLAND, NEW ZEALAND

One wouldn't think that communication would be a challenge in a modern English-speaking country like New Zealand, but it was.

The aquarium in Auckland was highly recommended so we took a taxi to the other side of the bay to see it. The young woman behind the ticket counter asked me a short question that I couldn't understand. After asking her to repeat it, I thought the question had a word in it that started with M. I thought maybe she was asking if I wanted a map, which is typical in places like this so I said yes, I'd like a map. She repeated her question. I finally figured out she was saying, "Are you a Mum?" It was "Mum's Day" in New Zealand. I said yes and got in free.

CONFUSING FOOTWEAR IN HIROSHIMA

In Asia we had become accustomed to removing our shoes when entering temples and shrines. The Gokoku Shrine at the edge of the castle grounds in Hiroshima provided slippers, a pleasant surprise. I put on the pair that the guard at the door handed me while Ed sat down to untie his shoes.

When I started to walk, they felt very awkward even though they looked like they were on the correct feet. I wasn't sure about getting through the entire temple in them without tripping. Then the guard at the door pointed at my feet and he kept repeating "Two pair. Two pair." I thought that's right, one pair for Ed and one pair for me. He was trying to tell me that one pair was inside the other and I trying to walk around with two slippers on each foot. The guard helped me separate Ed's slippers from mine and walking became much easier. He was still smirking when we left the room.

On the second floor of the shrine in the drum tower, a man in uniform was demonstrating a special drum that was used to signal the time of day during the Edo period of Japan's history. An explanation on the wall in English described the rules. "Drumbeats in the morning and evening were used to signal the opening and closing of the castle gate, as well as the time for samurai to report for their duties. From time to time a drummer would receive a warning if the sound of the drum was too soft or if an error was made when signaling the time of day." It didn't say what happened to the drummer if such an error was made.

CONFUSING BUFFET IN AREQUIPA

While in the beautiful old city of Arequipa, high in the Andes of Peru, we looked around for a place to have lunch. We had learned that it's always best to stop in a busy restaurant. If there are plenty of empty chairs, it's likely because the food isn't good or it isn't very clean. The first place we stopped in didn't accept credit cards or US dollars and we hadn't exchanged our dollars for Peruvian money. So we left and found another restaurant that had a Visa sign in the window. I wasn't hungry because I had eaten breakfast but Ed had not, so we just bought one meal. This place was a buffet that had very confusing rules.

The cashier tried to explain the buffet in limited English but Ed couldn't quite make out what the guy was telling him. It seemed that the price he paid was only connected to certain items in the buffet but not others. It didn't help that he couldn't read the little Spanish signs next to each dish. It was impossible to figure it out. Finally a guy came out of the back to help Ed put his lunch together. Some of the food was hard to identify but he enjoyed all of it.

UNUSUAL FOOD COURT IN XIAN

The cruise line had arranged an overland tour to visit the Terra Cotta Warriors and the Great Wall of China, which started with an overnight stay in the city of Xian. Our local guide in Xian met us at baggage claim in the airport and she was one of the best guides we'd ever had. Her Chinese name was very difficult to pronounce. She told us her name means rainbow, so it would be okay for us to call her that. At first it felt a little strange to say, "Excuse me — Rainbow?" but we got used to it.

Rainbow must have assumed everyone would eat dinner in the hotel, so she didn't offer any restaurant information. In the city of Xian, lighting displays for Chinese New Year were spread out over several blocks near the hotel. For us, seeing the lights was more important than eating dinner and they were tremendous.

By the time we finished walking through the displays it was 8:30 and we were hungry. All the signs here were naturally in Chinese only, so it was difficult to identify a restaurant. We didn't see any storefront windows with tables and chairs and people eating inside. In a nearby mall, three people were working at an information desk but none of them spoke any English. One tried a translation website on her phone but it was pretty tedious, so I used my hands to convey the idea of eating food and she got it. She pointed to the building across the street and held up three fingers. On the third floor of the building across the street there was indeed a restaurant.

What an experience this was. People seemed to be lined up to purchase cards. While we were trying to figure out the system by watching, one customer who spoke English explained that we should pay 100 Yuan and get a card to take inside. Whatever we buy goes against the money on the card. When we come out, we turn in the card and either get money back or pay more, depending on how much we ate. It sounded simple enough.

The restaurant was huge. There were probably ten large odd-sized rooms, each with tables and chairs in the middle and food stations around the sides. Most of the food for sale was either something I didn't recognize or something I wasn't brave enough to try. We walked through about half the rooms and then saw a man cooking pot stickers on a grill. I held up four fingers. He shook his head and pointed to a sign on the wall that was of course in Chinese. I looked at him and shrugged. Then he smiled and put ten pot stickers on a plate and handed them to me. Ten must have been the minimum number one can purchase. Ed gave him the card and we got the hang of it.

A woman at another stand pulled some slimy white stuff out of a big pile, added a few other things to the plate, and tried to hand it to me. It looked like a jellyfish pizza. I smiled, shook my head, and wandered away. Two very nice women at a noodle stand helped Ed decide what to try. We got two plates of noodles, found a table, and sat down. Neither of us had seen a place to get beverages, or even a bottle of water. We returned to the noodle women and used gestures again to ask about drinks. They laughed and pointed around the corner to where a man was squeezing oranges, so we got two glasses of juice from him.

We were the only non-Chinese people in the entire restaurant. Once we got settled at our table, we realized the Chinese people were watching us, most in amusement. We did the right thing by smiling and nodding whenever we caught someone's eye. The only thing on our table was a container of chopsticks. I had used them in Hong Kong with some success and knew that asking for a fork would be pointless, so I dug in. The sauce that Ed got on the noodles turned out to be loaded with chili peppers so I just ate half the pot stickers and it was plenty.

We turned in our card and got some money back, then stopped in the restrooms which were clearly labeled and extremely clean. My throat had been very dry all day and I wanted to find some ice cream. A nearby ice cream stand only sold premade ice cream bars which would have been fine, but they were not self-serve and all the wrappers and the signs were in Chinese with no pictures. We had no idea what to ask for or how.

It turned out this place was connected to the card system, so we had to go back to the desk at the restaurant and get another card. A young woman we had not seen behind the counter before spoke a little English. Once she understood we wanted ice cream, she walked us back to the same stand and tried to help us select something. The problem was, but she didn't know the English words for any of the flavors. She asked for two out of the case, we paid, and went back with her to turn in our card. I took a picture of her with Ed and she gave me her cell phone number so I could text it to her. It went through quickly and she was very pleased to have a picture of her American customer.

The flavor she chose turned out to be dark green with some kind of seeds in it. It could have been seaweed flavor or maybe green tea. No idea. It wasn't very good, but it didn't matter.

At the hotel breakfast buffet the next morning, the signs were just as confusing even though they were translated into English.

MORE FOOD ADVENTURES

SAUSAGE IN COBURG

The town of Coburg was a short ride from our German apartment in Amberg, and we always took friends and family there when they visited us from the US. They enjoyed touring the large castle high on the hill, but our favorite part of spending a day there was the unique sausages only found in Coburg. A Coburger wurst is ten inches long and hangs way outside the tiny piece of bread you hold it with while you bite into the meat from both ends. The unique flavor comes from cooking it over a pine cone fire. Add some mustard and a stein of beer and you've got yourself a fine meal.

SALAD INGREDIENTS IN RAVELLO

During one of our many trips to Italy, we visited the lovely town of Ravello near the Amalfi coast in early December when very few restaurants were open. After walking through the villa gardens, we stopped in a shop to ask where we could find something to eat. The young woman directed us down a few narrow winding streets and eventually we found the little trattoria she had described.

Only a handful of locals were inside and it smelled wonderful. Mama worked in the kitchen while Papa talked to the customers in the dining room and took the orders. From our table near the doorway to the kitchen, we could see Papa going outside with shears and coming back in with fresh lettuce that he had just cut from the garden.

When Ed's salad arrived at our table, he noticed one of the lettuce leaves was wiggling. He lifted the lettuce and saw a slug underneath. He pointed it out to Papa, who was mortified. He took the salad plate into the kitchen and we heard Mama shriek. She came out and talked to Ed in speedy Italian about how sorry she was. He smiled at her and they became instant friends.

At the end of our meal she offered us free dessert and one of the choices was chocolate cake. Ed asked if she had made it herself. When she told him that she had indeed baked it herself that morning, he replied, "If you made the cake yourself, then that's what I'd like to have." Her grin was priceless and her cake was as light as a feather.

After we paid our bill and put on our coats, Mama came out of the kitchen and gave both of us a hug, planting a big kiss on each cheek.

FIRE UNDER THE TABLE IN ERCOLANO

Ercolano is the Italian town near the foot of Mt Vesuvius where the ruins of Herculaneum are located. Our favorite stop was just up the hill from the ruins, a small family owned restaurant that served the best pizza in Italy. We ate there several times but only once in the winter. On that cold wet December day the owner got us settled at the table, then went over to the large brick oven along the back wall. He picked up a metal bucket and scooped hot coals into it. I gasped when he slid the bucket under the table to warm our feet.

The heat sure felt good but I worried the entire time we sat there that the tablecloth would go up in flames along with our pant legs.

SANGRIA IN BARCELONA

The walking tour that I had printed out from a travel website before leaving home recommended stopping at 4 Cats Café on a narrow pedestrian side street in the center of Barcelona. A small stand with the menu on it stood just outside the door. On the menu cover was a hand drawn picture of two men on a tandem bicycle. Picasso spent many hours drawing while drinking tea at this café and he drew the bicycle picture at a table there. In his day it was a popular hangout for artists and musicians.

We weren't hungry but a glass of Sangria sounded good. We ended up with a pitcher. While sipping Sangria, we gazed around the room at the bohemian décor and stained glass windows behind the bar and imagined what it was like when Picasso held his first solo art exhibition here at the age of seventeen.

The Sangria was the best we'd ever tasted so we ordered a second pitcher. By the time we were ready to leave, Ed was plastered. I was fine, but the Sangria really hit him hard. I was afraid I'd have to carry him. The fresh air outside didn't help. He kept weaving away from me.

The next day, we tried to go back but 4 Cats Café was closed. A movie was being filmed there, and the doorway was blocked off with heavy black curtains. A small group of people in 1920s clothing hung around the entrance. Everyone involved seemed to be rushing around on various errands. I looked around for someone approachable to ask what the movie was but had no success. We never did find out what was going on there but every now and then I search online for a movie filmed in Barcelona in November 2017. So far, no luck.

INTERESTING LUNCH IN NAGASAKI, JAPAN

Large 7-Eleven stores were everywhere in Japan. We browsed through one of them and found an ATM, lots of snacks and fancy packaged sushi. The food looked so good, we decided it was time to find a restaurant for lunch. We had just walked through Nagasaki's Chinatown and wanted to avoid the places with hand-written menus outside.

We saw a group of young people go into a restaurant on the main street and gave it a try. The menu had no English but it did have pictures. I ordered some spring rolls that were very good while Ed tried an odd dish that seemed to be mostly rice with Italian seasoning, some tomato sauce and cheese on top. It was actually quite tasty considering it was an Italian meal prepared in a Japanese restaurant. When we left, our tall waiter bowed so low that I thought his head was going to hit the floor.

FOOD ON SAFARI

In 2006, Ed climbed to the top of Mt Kilimanjaro, an altitude of 19,341 feet. The hard climb up this mountain ends at the glacier on the peak, which has receded considerably since he was there. If the snows of

Kilimanjaro haven't melted completely by now, they will be gone soon.

The guide service he chose for the one week climb also arranged our safari for the following week. A week wasn't nearly enough time to visit all the parks in northern Tanzania, so we included some of the lesser known but more interesting ones.

By drinking beverages directly from the bottle without ice, brushing our teeth with bottled water, and using plenty of hand sanitizer, we were able to stay healthy. The advice we had read in guidebooks was good: If you can't peel it or if it hasn't been boiled, don't eat it. Our box lunches on safari usually contained a hard-boiled egg, some bread, yogurt from Switzerland and a piece of very tough cooked chicken which I tasted once and then avoided, and a banana.

The evening buffet at the lodges offered plenty of cooked vegetables and a meat dish labeled "steak" with a variety of sauces to choose from. It could have been steak of zebra or steak of goat. We never knew; it was all just steak. If it seemed safe to eat and we were hungry, we dug in and didn't ask.

Years later we splurged on two nights at Kichaka, a luxury private wildlife reserve in South Africa while our cruise ship moved between two ports. It was very different from the Serengeti but we enjoyed every minute of it just as much. Our package included all meals and the menus were quite unique. For dinner the first night, I ordered warthog fillet. It tasted a lot like pork only tougher.

Now if someone asks me, "Have you ever eaten warthog?" I can say, "Yes, I have".

TREATS IN THE MIDDLE EAST

An enjoyable part of traveling is trying new foods and Israel was no exception. I had never been a fan of Middle Eastern food, but in so many of the countries we have visited over the years the local food is often the best and worth trying. Maybe that's because it's usually fresh, not processed and contains no preservatives.

One day I ate a persimmon for breakfast. It tasted like a cross between an apple and a peach and it was delicious. I learned to love hummus and falafel but my favorite food in Israel and Jordan was dates. They hardly resembled the ones I bought at home. These were soft and sweet as candy. Foods that I once steered away from became favorites by the end of the trip.

JORDANIAN PRINGLES

We enjoyed browsing around the grocery store down the road from our hotel on our last day in Jordan. It was the only grocery we'd been in during the entire trip. The most interesting item there was Pringles. The label on Jordan's version of Pringles looked the same except for the name: Pringoooals spelled with three Os. The price was in pounds, so they must have been imported from Britain along with most of the other items for sale there, which were probably just for tourists. We didn't buy any but the name fascinated me. I had never seen a word spelled with three Os. My online search after returning home revealed that this is the product name for Pringles sold not only in the Middle East but in Eastern Europe and Iceland as well.

Most people in the Middle Eastern countries we visited bought their food in the marketplace and were probably not interested in Pringoooals.

EMBARRASSMENT IN A WEST YELLOWSTONE RESTAURANT

Over the years we've made many trips to Yellowstone National Park, and it remains one of our favorite places in the world. On one particular visit we were unable to get reservations inside the park for our entire stay, so we booked a room in the town of West Yellowstone just outside the entrance for a few nights to bridge the gap.

We had dinner in a sports bar across the street from our hotel at the end of a long day of hiking. One of the tortilla chips that accompanied my quesadilla fell off my plate onto the carpeted floor. I thought someone would step on it, grind it into the carpet and make a mess. I was the one who dropped it, so I should pick it up. When I leaned over to get it, I reached a little too far and my chair tipped over and hit the floor with a bang, sending me sprawling.

Ed had his nose in his cell phone and didn't know what happened until he looked across the table and couldn't see me. By then I was on the floor with the young man who had rushed to my side, asking me if I was okay and offering to help me up. I thanked him and brushed him away in embarrassment, then righted my chair and slid into it with my eyes down, certain that everyone was staring at me. We ate someplace else after that. I was afraid our waiter would remember me and refuse to serve us.

RUM TAX ON THE CARIBBEAN ISLAND OF GRENADA

Rum is produced in large quantities from sugar crops in Grenada. Our tour guide said the government collects a tax on rum that is produced at home, so people in small villages who make their own keep it hidden. If they know the tax officials are on their way, everyone in the village drinks as much as they can before the inspectors arrive so they pay as little tax as possible.

Our guide said everyone can tell what's going on in a place like this when they drive through because all the people are stumbling around.

FRESH FISH FOR DINNER IN VIETNAM

In Hanoi, our cruise ship offered a shuttle bus to a shopping mall that was supposed to be about twenty minutes away. We went with another couple and planned to walk around a bit and then have some dinner. For some reason, the area where we were dropped off was only five minutes away and clearly not the one described in the ship newsletter. It was a long strip center that had been built only two years ago and it led to an amusement park being constructed by the Chinese. It's close enough to the border of China that many come here on vacation. The whole area was kind of bizarre.

As we walked along this long brightly lit stretch of shops, bars, and restaurants, we watched restaurant workers lining up tubs of unidentifiable seafood along the sidewalks, ready for customers to order and have prepared for them. Some of it was piled high on plates and still wiggling.

A restaurant on the other side of the street looked better than most of the others we'd passed, so we crossed the street the way we had learned in Saigon. Just step off the curb and let the traffic go around you. It takes courage but it works.

We were beckoned inside by an English-speaking hostess. The deciding factor was a menu that was written in Vietnamese and English. Our men ordered steamed clams while we women played it safe with vegetable fried rice. Although our server didn't speak English, she got the men out of the chairs, and led them over to a wall of tanks and tubs of seafood so they could pick out the kind of clams they wanted, sold by the kilo. A kilo is a lot of clams.

While our dinner was being prepared, we sipped Vietnamese beer and watched others approach the tanks and select their seafood. One couple requested a rather large fish and stood by while the man reached in the tank, grabbed it with both hands, slapped it down on the floor and clobbered it on the head with a big mallet. I can still hear that whack. Seafood doesn't get any fresher than that.

The big table next to us held about 24 young people who were sharing steaming dishes and pots of all kinds of food. They were all talking and eating at the same time as the food whirled around their table. I asked the hostess if I could take a picture of them and she said no problem.

Soon they started coming over to our table, shaking our hands and taking pictures of us even though we couldn't understand anything they were saying. One guy opened a big flask that he carried with a heavy shoulder strap and proceeded to pour drinks for our two men without saying anything. They were hesitant but didn't want to be rude, so they drank it. We'd heard about a type of rice wine that was some kind of Vietnamese fire water. Ed can now say he's tried it and it tasted terrible.

Then this same fellow put his flask away, got out a big pipe and wanted them to smoke with him. This time our men said no thank you. It was awkward, but we paid our bill and politely slid back outside.

EXPLODING CASH REGISTER IN TONGA

Our cruise ship docked in Nuku'alofa, the capital of Tonga where 70% of the people in this South Pacific country live. We walked around on our own for a while but it was hotter than hot so we found a place to stop for a cold beer. It was brand new, clean, and the women who worked there were dressed nicely. We had the impression that all three women were new at the restaurant business. The one we ordered our Tiki beer from forgot twice that we had ordered it, so we watched the locals walk by while we waited.

In Tonga, men wear a long piece of cloth tied at the waist called a Tupenu, kind of a long wrap skirt. Many also wear a Ta'ovala, which is the traditional woven mat worn over the skirt by both men and women. It's considered formal attire just like a suit and tie in the western world. All government workers must wear one to show respect and authority. There are different kinds of Ta'ovala for different occasions.

Somewhere along the line, one of the women bumped into the open cash register drawer and the inside drawer just exploded. It blew cash and coins all over the place. We watched this scene unfold from our seats at the end of the bar. The women were so flustered, they didn't know what to do. One got down on the floor and went after the cash, while one tried to get the drawer back in place without success and the third one went for help. They finally got everything back where it belonged. It provided for some good entertainment. The Americans seated at the bar were all laughing but the three women were not.

DRINKING LIKE LOCALS IN BERMUDA

With some free time in the afternoon, we walked through the town of Hamilton, Bermuda, and saw a sign advertising a Double Dark 'n Stormy for $7. A Dark 'n Stormy is made with Goslings thick black rum and ginger beer served over ice. This was highly recommended by our guide during the morning tour who admitted he doesn't drink.

Once we determined that there was enough time to try one, we opened the door to the bar to find that it was actually up two flights of stairs. We stared at the steep wooden steps in front of us. Should we really risk going up two long flights of stairs to have this crazy drink and hope to make our way down again and get back to the ship without incident? Of course!

The bartender explained that some people sip the rum off the top first and other people stir it up before drinking it. One small sip was enough for me. I stirred. I enjoyed the drink a bit more than Ed.

To make our day complete, we met a gentleman who takes his Bermuda shorts very seriously.

GREAT SNACKS IN QUEBEC CITY

Quebec City is steeped in history and filled with impressive architecture. Five cruise ships were docked there the day we arrived, and the city was overflowing with 8,000 visitors.

After our half day bus tour of the city, we stopped at the best snack shop in old town: Mary's Popcorn. Countless flavors and free samples made for an irresistible place to shop. We bought a large bag of salty and sweet mix that was out of this world. Two blocks away, we turned around, went back, and bought two more bags, one for each of our stateroom stewards who took such good care of us.

When our ship returned to Quebec City after dropping off 450 passengers in Montreal and picking up 450 new ones, we returned to Mary's popcorn for more. It's irresistible!

FRIENDLY CAFÉ IN PARINTINS

The small town of Parintins along the Amazon River offered a folklore show called Boi-Bumba that was unbelievable. Difficult to describe, but the photography instructor on the ship called it a tsunami for the senses: elaborate costumes, masks, drums, singing, chanting, and dancing, all on a very crowded stage. Ed made some new friends after the show.

After the performance ended, we wandered through the market-place outside where you could buy your own elaborate costumes, masks, and drums. We weren't quite ready to go back to the ship, so we went into a little café nearby for a beer. Maybe café is too generous a word. It was a small open area with a few plastic tables and chairs in front. The stage crew from the show sat at two of the three tables and seemed surprised to see us. They probably don't get many tourists in this place.

Ed went up to the counter at the back and ordered two Antarctica beers. I can't explain why Antarctica beer is sold in the Amazon. When I took a sip of mine, I told Ed it tasted like water so he traded in his unopened can for a giant Schin beer. I'd never seen such a big beer bottle. It had to be at least 18 inches tall. He also ordered two bowls of soup which turned out to be delicious with lots of vegetables. The soup spoon had a tiny bit of paper towel wrapped around the tip of it which evidently served as a napkin because that was all we got.

After we finished and Ed went up to the counter to pay, I tried to make conversation with the young woman behind the end of the counter. She asked my name but when I said Kathy, she couldn't manage the "th" so I said my name was Katarina. She was good with that.

LEARNING THE RULES

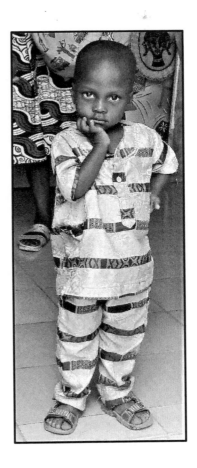

DELAWARE HIGHPOINT MOVED

Delaware was one of the easiest state highpoints in the United States to reach even though it's not the lowest. That distinction goes to Florida, and our trip there was pretty uneventful. At the time we visited Delaware, the highpoint was in the middle of an intersection which made it difficult to take pictures. This caused too many accidents involving highpointers, so a sign was erected at the side of the road. The Highpointers Club made this the official marker in the interest of safety. Years later after subsequent land surveys, a different highpoint was identified nearby that was two feet higher. We didn't go back to get this one. The highpoint that counts is the official one that existed at the time you were there.

PERMIT REQUIRED FOR CALIFORNIA HIGHPOINT

At 14,496 feet Mt Whitney is the highest peak in the lower 48 states. Only Denali (Mt McKinley) in Alaska is higher. The easiest route is 22 miles round trip and camping overnight along the trail requires a permit, which we didn't realize until we got there. Only a certain number of permits are issued per day and there were none left when we arrived. The ranger told Ed that his only option was to leave the ranger station at 12:01 am and do it all in one day.

Knowing it would be unavoidable to be hiking at least some of this trail in the dark, Ed had specifically scheduled it during a full moon. I dropped him off at the trailhead just before midnight under starry skies. The moon was so bright he could see without his headlamp as he traversed all 92 switchbacks along the open granite mountainside. When I picked him up around 3 pm, he said all those switchbacks made it one of the most boring trails he'd ever hiked.

MESSY EXIT FROM OUR CRUISE SHIP FOR JUST A FEW DAYS IN NEW YORK CITY

We had notified Viking when we booked our cruise that we planned to spend two nights at a hotel in the city while the ship was docked in New York for three days. We preferred to use our hotel reward points and stay in the center of Manhattan closer to the sights rather than spend our time trying to find the way to and from the ship. New York was our first US port after leaving London and was also a port where hundreds were getting off and hundreds of new passengers were getting on, so all passports had to be checked in person in the terminal. We were told to be ready at 9:00 am the day we docked.

A disorganized mess awaited us with staging areas all over the ship. It seemed like we spent an hour moving from one line to another. Then we were told to go to Guest Services and wait until the Customs and Border Patrol agents were ready for us. Then we were told we would be interviewed at 11:00 am. It wasn't like we were applying for citizenship or anything. We didn't understand any of this, but we waited.

Then we were told to be back on the ship by 9:00 am on the third day even though the ship wasn't scheduled to leave until 6:00 pm. We stood our ground on that and said unless they could give us a really good reason, we'd be back in the late afternoon. They made some phone calls and said late afternoon would be ok. Then we were told that once our passports were checked, we would have to get off the ship immediately and could not get back on until late afternoon on the third day as arranged.

We had scheduled a city tour for 1:00 pm and planned to take our bag on the tour bus with us, hoping to leave the tour somewhere in the vicinity of the hotel. We didn't expect to leave the ship until tour time. Now it looked like we would have to hang around the terminal for two hours until the tour started. More discussion and more phone calls. Then we were given permission to stay on the ship until our tour started at 1:00. At 11:15 we were escorted to the ship elevators where a Customs agent was leaning against the wall. He barely glanced at our passports and said we could go. That was our interview. We made ourselves comfortable in the ship lounge until 1:00 and finally left without any further issues.

It was worth the hassle. New York City was fantastic.

LOSING TRACK OF OUR CAR IN PRAGUE

Our favorite hotel in Prague was a small one in the center of the city. The first time we made a room reservation there, the website required a reservation for a parking space for guests arriving by car. We had heard many stories about car theft in the Czech Republic and were warned never to leave our car parked on the street. It could be dismantled and in Russia before you knew it was gone. So we reserved a hotel parking spot, entering our planned drop off and pick up times.

Upon arrival, the reason why they needed this information was obvious. The hotel was located on a narrow crowded street in the heart of downtown Prague. The hotel faced a small sidewalk, and next to the front door was an iron gate which led to a courtyard at the back for guest parking.

After we checked in, we were told to drive up to the gate and a man would open it for us. This gate was so narrow that we had to fold in the side view mirrors on our small sedan in order to drive through it. The guy was clearly annoyed with how slowly we crept through that gate. The courtyard was very narrow and the cars were tightly packed. As soon as we got out, he held out his hand for the car key. We gave it to him and went upstairs.

The window of our room looked out on the courtyard and we were shocked to see that our car was gone! It was too late to question the wisdom of handing over the key. All we could do was rely on the reputation of the hotel and hope that our car would return.

About an hour later, our car reappeared in the courtyard. The parking guy must have had access to an overflow lot somewhere. He was constantly rearranging cars, moving them in and out. He kept the cars strategically lined up very close together in the order they were needed which was always changing. He had a tough job, but he did it well.

Every time we left the hotel that weekend, we looked out the window as soon as we came back to make sure our car was still there. It became our favorite Prague hotel once we learned their parking system was safe and the guy who ran it knew what he was doing.

SHORT PERFORMANCE AT THE OPERA HOUSE IN BUDAPEST

On Thanksgiving weekend in Budapest, we saw a sign advertising the opera house performance of "The Nutcracker" and thought it might be fun to see the Hungarian version. We bought tickets the day before the performance and got there in time to enjoy the holiday decorations outside the theater.

Inside, we tried to check our coats but the woman behind the counter looked at us strangely. She didn't want to take our coats even though there were several on the racks behind her. She kept talking in Hungarian and of course we couldn't understand her. Finally, she gave up and found someone who spoke English. This young woman explained to us that the program had started, and it was already intermission. She demanded to know why we were so late. It seemed we were unable to read our Hungarian tickets correctly. We thought the tickets said the performance started at 8 pm, but 8 was actually the section our seats were in on the second level. She took our coats reluctantly and we went inside to enjoy the second half. It was very nice and we were sorry to have missed the beginning. Not spectacular, but traditional and sweet.

When it was over, we found the same woman downstairs and asked her where the restrooms were. She said the only ones in the theater were upstairs, and now that we had come down, we were not permitted to go back up.

We left the theater in search of an open bar where we could discuss our ongoing effort to learn the rules.

NO SEATS ON THE TRAIN FROM POMPEII

On a trip to Italy with friends years ago, we flew to Rome and went directly from the airport to the main station for our train to Pompeii. We had reserved rooms in a hotel near the station in Pompeii and spent the next day touring the ruins. The excavated area was huge and fascinating and we didn't allow nearly enough time there. Our train back to Rome was scheduled to leave at 6:00 the following morning.

The hotel staff was very gracious and had hot coffee with warm croissants ready for us at 5:30. We walked over to the station in plenty of time only to find that the ticket window didn't open until much later. We didn't realize that we should have bought our tickets the previous day when it was open. Others were waiting on the platform for the same train, so we got on, expecting to be able to buy our tickets from the conductor.

There were plenty of empty seats, so we settled in, not knowing that the seats were all reserved. As the train approached Naples, more and more seats filled up. We kept moving from one seat to another every time someone showed us their ticket with a reservation for the seat we were sitting in.

Our friends had not been to Italy before and they were getting extremely nervous. One said, "If they throw us off the train, I just hope they let us take our luggage with us." Her husband went out to the hallway next to the door between the cars and sat on their luggage just to make sure.

I was lucky. The man who had reserved the seat that I was in kindly offered to join his colleague in the next car, so I didn't have to move. Ed went in search of the conductor to get tickets and was gone for a very long time.

We bought our tickets just in time to get off the train in Rome. We had now learned that if we don't have tickets, it's best to sit in the dining car and slowly sip something until the conductor comes through.

SECURITY IN ISRAEL

All our adventures in the Middle East took place during a two-week guided tour of Israel and Jordan in February 2019. We'd never taken a bus trip like this before, but were confident that somehow, we would manage to get ourselves together early each morning, set our suitcases outside our hotel room by 7:15 am, eat breakfast, and board the bus by 8:00. Everything for our two week trip fit into two suitcases with some extra space for gifts and souvenirs, and we were on our way. As it turned out these two countries were so interesting that we were able to put our fatigue and jet lag aside and absorb all that we saw.

Israel is the size of New Jersey, and it holds nine million people. 90% of them live in the north, away from the desert. The road signs are in three languages: Hebrew, Arabic and English. Our entire week there was fascinating, exhausting and absolutely wonderful.

The overnight flight from Denver to Frankfurt, Germany was only about half full, quiet, and uneventful. Just as we arrived at the Tel Aviv gate in Frankfurt, police and security officials started roping off the area with yellow crime scene tape and telling everyone to move back to the main concourse area. No explanations. We stood around for about half an hour as fellow passengers asked us as well as each other what was going on. Nobody seemed to know anything.

Eventually, the yellow tape came down and we were permitted to proceed as if nothing had happened. We never found out what it was all about. A long slow line formed at the entrance to the Tel Aviv gate where the Israelis conducted their own security. Every carryon bag was searched while countless questions were asked of each passenger. It was a long slow tedious process, but no one complained.

At every one of the five different Israeli hotels we stayed in, we were given a sticker for each of our bags that had our name and room number written on it. Upon checkout, the bags were collected and assembled at the bus. One at a time, each of us had to point out our own bag, confirm we packed it ourselves and watch it get loaded. Then we could board the bus. Most people on the tour were very nice and easy to travel with. One refused to put the ID tags he was given on his suitcases, saying, "I don't like putting my name on things". He was persuaded by the guide to get over it.

The subject of Israeli-Palestinian conflict came up only once during our week in Israel. When we crossed into Palestinian territory to visit Bethlehem, someone on the bus asked our guide if we were entering the war zone. Our guide responded, "Do you mean Chicago? More people die in Chicago each year than here, so you are safer in Israel." I'm not sure the guy who asked the question bought the answer, but that was the end of the discussion about war zones.

TRANSITIONING FROM ISRAEL INTO JORDAN

On our way to the Jordan border, our Israeli guide gave us clear instructions. No photos were allowed at the border crossing. Everyone needed to make sure their luggage was moved from the Israeli bus to the Jordanian bus.

We were given blue visa slips when we entered Israel. At the end of the week we received pink visa slips to show the date we left. Fortunately only one other bus was at the border crossing at the same time as ours. Sometimes it takes hours to get through because there are so many people.

The other bus was filled with interesting people. The men wore Muslim dress, baggy pants, and fez-style head coverings. The women wore beautiful print two piece outfits trimmed with wide lace. I'd never seen dresses quite like these before. The top piece was very loose and the women walked with their hands folded underneath it. I wanted to talk to them but they weren't even talking to each other and I didn't want to seem rude. After coming home, I looked all over the internet and could not find anything close to what these women wore, so I have no idea where they were from.

On the Jordanian side, the men who took our luggage from the Israeli bus kept asking for our "group leader". At this point in time, we didn't have one. Our Israeli guide stayed on the Israeli side of the border and our Jordanian guide hadn't shown up yet. He had plenty of time. We had to wait there another two hours for six people to get VAT (Value Added Tax) refunds for items they had bought in Israel. Purchases totaling over $400 in one store are eligible for a tax refund so for the serious shoppers in our group, it was worthwhile.

Finally, our Jordanian guide appeared and we were on our way. In the zone between checkpoints, we passed several ravines with watchtowers and vehicles with huge machine guns mounted on them. At the Jordan entry point we stopped for another hour. Our guide walked down the aisle of the bus and collected all our passports in a plastic trash bag, and then he disappeared. We tried not to worry.

We were permitted to get off the bus but there wasn't much to see except lots of men hanging around not looking very busy. No women. A big open truck piled high with luggage went by and we hoped none of it belonged to us since it continued down the road until it was out of sight. Eventually our passports were returned and the bus got underway. Everyone's luggage miraculously found its way onto the bus.

Big sighs of relief all around.

TOURIST POLICE IN JORDAN

A man in uniform sat in the front seat of the bus and our guide explained that he was a member of the Tourist Police. We had one with us all the time during our week in Jordan. Each one worked three days and then had three days off. Jordan has had Tourist Police since 1996.

Someone asked if he was there to watch us to make sure we didn't do anything wrong, but our guide said no. This man was there to protect us in case someone bothered us or tried to get on the bus. We never felt unsafe or threatened in any way during our stay in Jordan, but it was comforting to know there was someone with us all the time to make sure nothing happened.

CONFUSION AT THE PUBLIC PARK IN THE MALDIVES

According to Wikipedia, 227,486 people live in the capital city of Malé on an island of only 3.2 square miles in the Maldives. I think the entire population was out riding their motor scooters the day we were there. There were very few cars and no lane markers on the streets. Scooters just zipped around each other wherever there was room. The riders ignored pedestrians and crosswalks completely. We came close to getting hit a couple of times.

Maldives is a Muslim country and this small island has over 20 mosques. Behind one of them was an old cemetery and a pile of prayer rugs but no people.

We headed down a side street and into a lovely park where a policeman told us it was a public park and we would have to pay to go inside. In our part of the world, public parks are free. The cost was $5 US per person for non-Maldivians. We really wanted to get a closer look at the enormous carved trees inside, so we paid.

A large round structure with a wide flight of steps dominated the middle of the park. From the top level, we could see an elaborate fountain below, but it had no water in it. A couple from the ship were sitting on a bench nearby. They had just caught the end of the fountain show and were waiting for it to start again. We hung around for a while, but nothing happened. Then Ed asked one of the roaming policemen what time the fountain was going to go off. He didn't know. A different policeman came over to us a short time later and said the fountain would go off at 4:00. It was only 11:30 so we moved on.

We passed a sign that might have been helpful if we had been able to read it:

The fountain-watching couple also told us that the park ticket was good for the National Museum too and they headed over there. We followed a short time later but this was not the case. Entry was $7 US. It was worth the price of admission just for the air conditioning. Several others from the ship were inside cooling off too. The museum wasn't very big, but it contained an interesting mix of clothing, turbans, chairs, and other furniture from the days of the sultans. I was particularly intrigued by the manual typewriter with keys in the local language of Thaana.

After the museum, we walked down a pedestrian-only street which was delightful. No scooters! We stopped for ice cream and then realized we had wandered around too much and lost our bearings. The buildings in the interior of the island were very dense and the streets were often quite crooked. We needed directions to find our way back to the waterfront.

The young man behind the ice cream counter looked at our map for a long time, then handed it back to me and said, "I will come to your table." He sat with us and studied the map again for a while. He finally marked the place where the ice cream shop was and also the fish market where we were headed next. It was clear that on this small island there isn't much of a need for map reading skills, but he did his best.

We stopped in a few shops on the way back, but everything was outrageously priced. A young man stopped us on the street and said, "Please come to my shop upstairs just over there. I make you good price. You go in other shops I see. When you come to mine, you will see my prices are good." It worried me that he had been watching us, but we followed him up a flight of very high and very steep steps to the second floor of a building. Part of me expected the door at the bottom to bang open, and big guys with guns to come out yelling but nothing happened. Maybe I read too many suspense novels.

The young man was right. His prices were lower, and he had very interesting merchandise. He handwrote the list of the items we were buying in the local language of Thaana, which consists primarily of indistinguishable squiggles. I wondered how they could read something that looks like nothing more than combinations of commas in all directions but then he could probably say the same about English cursive.

He listed prices and crossed them out, punched numbers in his calculator, and then discussed them with a man behind a desk. Ed negotiated some more, and they went back and forth. Finally we reached agreement and walked out with a bagful of very nice, reasonably priced gifts to take home.

The fish market had no fresh fish. It consisted mostly of long shelves of dried fish. We didn't stay long but stopped to watch a man spooning dark honey into big jars.

That evening on the ship, we talked to another couple who had been at the park not long after we were. The policeman told them the park was closed. They said they just wanted to walk through and were willing to pay. They were denied entry. We couldn't figure out the system but knew we were lucky to have been able to get in. Sometimes it isn't worth the effort to try to understand these things.

ILLEGAL PHOTOS IN BENIN

Benin is a very small country on the west coast of Africa. The day after our cruise ship stopped there, one of the lecturers on board told us he had been detained by soldiers in an area just down the street from the marketplace where we had spent the afternoon. It was an interesting area, so he walked around and took a lot of photos.

He wasn't aware that one of the photos he took had some soldiers in it. They stopped him and demanded to know why he was photographing them. He tried hard not to panic while they shouted at him but he was really afraid they would haul him away. He said he kept smiling and tried to explain he didn't realize they were in any of his pictures. They insisted he delete them and watched while he did so. They checked his photos again, and finally let him go with a warning never to photograph soldiers there again.

I'm sure he didn't.

HARASSED BY SOLDIERS ON THE TOUR BUS
IN KENYA

Our afternoon tour in Mombasa took us to Haller Park, a wildlife preserve that had been a huge limestone quarry until the early 1970s. When all the good stone had been removed, the owner planted trees and after 20 years of turning it into a native eco-system, he brought in African animals to live there.

It was miserably hot, and the guide said he understood that we were not accustomed to the weather there, so we spent as much time as possible in the shade. It was very kind of him, but it really didn't help much. I had learned to take a washcloth from our stateroom with me when going ashore so I could wipe my face with it. Kleenex was totally inadequate for the volume of sweat that poured down my face in places like this.

The traffic was horrible on the way back to the ship. On a divided four lane highway that was completely congested, a soldier stepped in front of our bus and held up his arm for the driver to stop. Another soldier started banging on a window toward the back of the bus, shouting in Swahili. We could see his angry face from our seats in the front of the bus. Both of them carried big weapons.

The driver opened his window and began a shouting match with the soldier in front who had stopped the bus. Then the window banger started pounding on the door, still shouting. The driver opened the door and he boarded the bus, yelling and waving his arms. Angry doesn't begin to describe this guy. The situation was getting scary.

Our guide had been cowering in the back of the bus but he finally stepped forward when the soldier started shouting in English. "He took a video! That man took a video!" We weren't sure which man he was talking about and wouldn't have said a word, even if we knew. He kept repeating his accusations while the guide tried to calm him down as he approached the man in question. The guide examined his camera and said, "He has only a little camera. He cannot take a video with this kind of camera." Good answer. The soldier looked dubious but stopped arguing and finally got off the bus.

We had been warned in most of the countries we had visited in this part of the world that we should never take a photo of policemen, police stations, military personnel, military installations, or anyone in uniform or any place associated with someone in uniform. Now we know what happens when someone does.

The bus was very quiet for the rest of the trip back.

CHARGING FINES TO KEEP PEOPLE HEALTHY IN SINGAPORE

As the guest lecturer on the ship said, "Singapore is a fine place. There is a fine for everything." This is a country that is so concerned about the health of their citizens that anything unhealthy is forbidden. We had been warned not to take tobacco of any kind on shore. It's illegal to bring in so much as a pack of cigarettes. Only once did we see an ashtray. It was on top of a trash bin where the few people who smoke must stand. There is a fine for carrying a lit cigarette around in public.

Singapore even charges a fine for possession of chewing gum. Supposedly this comes from an incident some years ago when vandals stuck used chewing gum on the edges of the subway doors. At the next stop, none of the doors would open and it caused a messy disruption of the mass transit system.

There were ads on billboards and on TV about the horrors of sugar: two people drinking bubble tea getting lectured about the amount of sugar in it being comparable to the sugar in an evil slice of apple pie. In a shopping mall, a fast food sign advertising charcoal black wafers caught my eye. Evidently burnt toast is considered acceptable.

In spite of all this Singapore is beautiful, easy to get around in, and we were sorry not to be able to spend more time there.

CHINESE BUREAUCRACY IN DALIAN

The Chinese authorities required us to carry a stamped copy of our passports with us whenever we left the cruise ship. Since Dalian was our last port in China, we had to turn in the stamped copy in person and have our original passports examined at the port building, which was a short bus ride away.

It was a miserable windy, cold, and damp day. We waited at the top of the gangway out of the wind until all the people waiting for the bus were allowed to board. No one knew why the Chinese authorities made everyone stand outside in line next to the bus for so long.

We wound our way through the port building, picked up our passports from the Purser's staff, stood in line to hand our passport and the stamped copy to someone in uniform who stared long and hard at our passports, the copies, and our faces before handing the passports back. After returning our passports to the Purser's staff, we followed the line back to the door where we were given a slip of paper that verified our documents were accepted. Then we went outside and got back on the bus. And sat. Even after the bus was full, we sat. The bus finally made its way back to the ship where we sat for another ten minutes before we were allowed to get off. Then we stood in a line outside for another ten minutes before we were allowed to board the ship. It was all so pointless that I wondered if this was the Chinese way of showing us Americans who really runs things.

MESSY EXIT FROM THE SHIP FOR A FEW DAYS IN JAPAN

The evening before we were due to arrive in Kobe for two days, we were told that Japanese authorities had not approved our planned overnight stay with another couple in nearby Kyoto. We couldn't believe they would tell us this at the last minute, especially when we had submitted a list of our planned nights off the ship for approval before the cruise started. Kyoto was a place we did not want to miss and we had reserved nonrefundable hotel rooms, as well as a private guide for the next day and a half. The Purser said he would appeal it but then he admitted there was no curfew the night we planned to be off the ship, so all this seemed a bit ridiculous. The problem was, it would be impossible to check into the hotel without our passports and they were all kept in the Purser's office. Since Japanese immigration would be boarding the ship early the next morning, we hoped for a discussion with a positive outcome and proceeded to pack an overnight bag.

First thing the next morning, we headed down to the Purser's office and were given the good news that Japanese immigration approved our night off the ship after all. We were given our passports with stern warnings not to get into any trouble or give the authorities any problems, as if we were teenagers. We promised to be good and dashed off the ship.

The directions I had printed at home to get us from the port building to the train station turned out to be from a different Kobe port than the one where we docked. Fortunately, the ship offered a shuttle bus that took us into downtown Kobe and dropped us off near the station. It took a while to fumble through the ticket purchase process but with the help of multiple locals we were able to buy tickets and find the train to Kyoto. It only took an hour to get there and the city was amazing. It was well worth all the hassle we went through to be able to spend two days there.

NO FOOD ASHORE IN PUERTO CHACABUCO

Chile was extremely strict about bringing any type of food ashore. Puerto Chacabuco required passengers to go through security when getting off the ship just to take a tour. Because Chile is locked between the Pacific Ocean and the Andes mountains, they don't want anything non-native coming in that might take root where it doesn't belong. Some people were stopped, their backpacks searched and their apples or whatever they tried to sneak ashore were confiscated. I have trouble understanding people who do this. No food means no food. We are guests in the countries we visit and need to respect their rules or stay home.

ASK FOR DIRECTIONS
OR STAY LOST AND
JUST KEEP WALKING

LOST INSIDE A CATHEDRAL IN MONTREAL

Our final stop on the Montreal city tour was the very impressive over-the-top St Joseph Oratory, Canada's largest church. It draws two million visitors a year. After having been there, I'd say they could all fit in it at once and they all came the same day we did. It was too big for anything more than one section of it to fit in a photo. We've visited a lot of churches in many places around the world but none came close to the size of this one. It included two huge sanctuaries on different floors, several chapels each the size of a large church, a museum, large gift shop, restaurant, and a whole lot of relics.

At least five levels connected by escalators and elevators at various places led not only to worship areas but also massive displays with thousands of crutches and canes left behind after their owners were healed in this basilica. Lighting a candle here required some significant legwork and good balance to get up and down those stairs.

When it was time to leave, we couldn't find our way out. Retracing our steps seemed like a good idea but we kept running into dead ends. Everywhere we went led farther away from the entrance and nothing looked familiar. I couldn't imagine how busy this church must be when there are services and events going on everywhere inside. Finally someone came to our rescue and directed us to the right set of escalators and we found our way to the door we came in. Even the parking lot was a maze but eventually we made it back to the right bus, exhausted but relieved.

DIRECTIONS TO LOUISIANA HIGHPOINT

One would not expect to need directions to find a state highpoint. After all, in the days before the internet we had a detailed map and a guidebook even though it was sometimes outdated and wasn't always detailed enough to get us where we needed to go. Sometimes we simply had to rely on information from someone who had recently been there. We found that some states advertised their highpoint and were proud of it. Others didn't post signs or mark their highpoint in any way. When we were really desperate, we stopped to ask for directions.

At the local Sheriff's Office in Bienville Parish, a short well-fed deputy behind the counter listened carefully as we asked him for the best way to get to Driskill Mountain. He sighed, took his hat off, wiped his furrowed brow and said, "Go down this here road out there and then you turn where the store used to be. But it ain't there no more." We thanked him for his time and left.

UNMARKED TRAIL AT NEVADA HIGHPOINT

Nevada's highpoint sits near the California state line in a hot dusty dry area filled with sagebrush and rocks. The roads leading to the highpoint were not paved and many were dead ends. In one area, the road was mostly just deep sand and we got stuck a few times. Our only way out was to dig deep holes behind the rear tires of the truck and fill the holes with rocks. I was afraid to pick up a rock without turning it over first, to make sure there were no unfriendly creatures underneath, and was nearly overcome by visions of snakes and scorpions. Once the truck started to move, we had to continue on far enough to find a place to turn around and try not to get stuck again.

Although we had left the campground early in the morning, this was turning into another highpoint with a late start at the trailhead. Returning the next day was not an option even if we could find it again. The trail was poorly maintained and difficult to follow even in the daylight, just like the road we had driven on to find it. When it turned into an unmarked steep climb over one boulder after another about halfway to the summit, I turned around and went back to the truck in order to give Ed a fair chance of making it to the top and back before dark. It was slow going on the way back because I couldn't pick up the trail again, but eventually I found the parking lot. I waited for several hours, hoping to see Ed walk out of the wilderness any minute.

Around midnight, the police showed up and talked with the people in the truck parked next to ours. A woman had become separated from their group and they believed she had hiked down the wrong side of the mountain. They couldn't find her. The police agreed to launch a helicopter search for her in the morning. I wanted to jump out and plead for the police to hunt for my Ed too, but I held back. I couldn't say for sure he was lost. He just hadn't come back – yet.

I cannot describe my feelings of hope an hour later when I saw a light flickering in the brush beyond the trailhead. It turned out to be Ed's headlamp. He had lost track of the trail coming back and ended up following the riverbank. He had slipped several times and tore a long gash in his thigh. All that mattered to him was that he made it to the top. We never did get the bloodstains from that gash out of the cloth seat in the truck.

EARLY RETURN FROM UTAH HIGHPOINT

Kings Peak was another long trek of 29 miles round trip which we planned to break up into three days. We backpacked in and spent the first night along the trail with no problem, except for drinking water. The iodine tablets we had brought to purify the water from the streams along the trail gave me a bad headache. On the second day we planned to hike to the top and back to the tent, then go back out on the third day.

Toward the top of the peak, I had to turn back at the steep boulder field. I just couldn't keep going. Ed continued on and reached the summit faster on his own. When he returned to our campsite, we agreed to pack up the tent and hike back to the car that afternoon instead of spending another night on the mountain.

Darkness fell sooner than we expected. Ed hiked ahead of me and I found myself getting farther and farther behind him. At one point the trail forked and I couldn't find a sign or determine which way he went. I sat down on a rock to decide which way to go, then got worried about mountain lions creeping around me in the dark so I picked one direction and started walking. Fortunately it turned out to be the same path Ed took.

By the time we reached the parking lot, we were exhausted and neither of us could remember exactly where we parked the truck. We wandered around but couldn't find it in the dark even with head-lamps. One car had a light on inside and it sounded like the guy was listening to a baseball game. Ed tapped on the window and talked to him.

It turned out there were two parking lots and we were in the wrong one.

TRYING TO GET AROUND IN HONOLULU

When our cruise ship docked in Honolulu overnight, the Hop On/Hop Off trolley that goes all around the city sounded like a good idea, but for some strange reason it was impossible to board. Several times we saw it go by but it was always empty and we never found a designated stop. Once Ed even ran up to the driver's window while it was stopped at a traffic light and the driver told him the closest stop was on some street the name of which Ed couldn't understand.

We gave up on trying to find the trolley and went in search of Chinatown on foot. Couldn't find that either.

LONG WALK IN SAN PEDRO

The Los Angeles port in San Pedro advertised a free trolley that goes around the city, so when our ship docked there, we searched for the closest stop marked on the brochure. The information we picked up from people in the area around the USS Iowa museum ranged from "The trolley only runs on weekends." to "The trolley doesn't start until noon." to "The trolley only runs in the summer." We kept walking.

Eventually we reached the center of San Pedro where a lovely little market was set up with arts and crafts on display along with fresh produce from nearby farms. At the far end were some stands with different foods and drinks along with some tables and chairs, and two men who sang and played guitars. We sat listening to them for a while, rested our feet, and sipped cold drinks.

Just behind the musicians was a beautiful Art Deco theater that advertised upcoming stage plays. Ed wanted to see the inside, so he rang the bell and a man came to the door holding a broom and dust-pan. He let us in and said if we had any questions, we should ask the guy standing around on the stage holding a coffee cup. The man at the door had no idea who we were but he didn't hesitate to let us in. This theater was like going back in time. It had been lovingly restored and well maintained. We really enjoyed walking through it.

Afterwards, Ed and I went to a Phillies Deli for some cheesesteaks. They were good, but not like the kind we find in Eastern Pennsylvania. After we ate, Ed said he'd like to go to see a movie. We had plenty of time and weren't ready to go back to the ship after five days at sea. The deli owner said there was a movie theater about a five minute car ride away.

We could have taken a $.50 local bus or called an Uber car, but that would have been too easy. We walked. And walked. And walked some more. San Pedro has some very nice neighborhoods with small tidy houses, beautiful blossoming trees, and lots of hills. I think we covered all of them.

When we finally reached the movie theater, I was so hot, tired, and thirsty that I didn't care what movie we saw, even if it was one in pro-gress. We sat through two of them and by the time the movies were over, we felt rested enough to head back to the ship. The walk was mostly downhill and shorter than the trip from town. By the end of the day, we had walked ten miles. Maybe next time we'll be able to find the trolley.

LOST IN GALAPAGOS ISLANDS

We booked a trip through a Galapagos travel service that runs a group of hotels and followed their instructions to wait for a driver to pick us up at the small airport on Baltra Island. We followed everyone else who got off the plane, retrieved our suitcase, and carried it over to the pier where we boarded a small ferry boat to cross a narrow channel to Santa Cruz Island. The airport workers tossed the luggage on top of the boat cover that sheltered the passengers from the sun. After the short ride, the same workers brought the suitcases back down and lined them up. Various forms of transportation were waiting to pick up the other passengers from the flight. We waited about fifteen minutes and eventually found ourselves standing alone on the pier with our luggage. There was no one else in sight.

Soon a taxi appeared and the driver asked us if we needed a ride. We explained that we were waiting for our transport to the hotel and showed him our confirmation. Cell phones were not common at the time but he had one and called the hotel for us. They told him to drive us over in his taxi and they would pay him directly since their driver said he was unable to find us. A lovely buffet lunch awaited us. We spent the afternoon on bikes provided by the hotel and gaped at the giant tortoises as we rode through the Darwin Research Station.

In the evening, we walked into town to watch the fishermen unload their catches of the day and fend off the sea lions who tried to get a share of the bounty. It wasn't long before we had wandered off the map and were lost in a part of town that we didn't recognize, surrounded by locals and stray dogs. A car horn and a man's voice calling, "Hello!" caught our attention. It was the taxi driver who brought us from the airport that morning. Seeing him again was like running into an old friend. He was on his way home, but he drove us back to our hotel and earned a handsome tip.

THE LAST BUS IN BUDAPEST

Budapest is a delightful city to visit when the Christmas markets are open, offering all kinds of crafts, gifts, ready to eat food in really big pots. and the most wonderful warm bread baked on rods over an open fire.

We spent our first day seeing the city sights from the Hop On/Hop Off bus which toured both sides of the Danube River. Our ticket covered the hilly Buda district as well as the flat Pest side of the city. In the early evening after consulting the schedule, we decided to catch the last bus of the day at the last stop on the route.

The problem was that although we were in the right area, it was impossible to determine from the map exactly where the last bus stop was located and we couldn't find any signs. We ended up climbing over guardrails, crossing a busy highway, and hiking up a hillside to reach a bridge where we hoped it would be. No luck. Exhaustion set in and my legs felt like they were going to fall off. It was pointless to continue hunting. A taxi seemed like a much better option but there were no taxis in sight. We kept walking.

After we finally located the sign for the bus stop and waited over half an hour, Ed called the phone number on the brochure. They agreed to send one more bus. When the bus arrived, it was empty and it didn't stop to pick up any other passengers. Evidently, they don't stick to the schedule much in the off season.

IN CORK, IT'S ONLY TEN MINUTES AWAY

We booked an independent tour of Ireland that included a local guide who met with us at our hotel in each city stop. The guide gave us information on what to see and do and explained how to get to the next city on our itinerary. For us, it was the perfect way to see an unfamiliar place without being herded around in a group.

We were told that the hotel in Cork was only a ten-minute walk from the train station. It was a nice day, so we decided to walk instead of taking a taxi. The map indicated we were on the right street, but the address numbers on the buildings were inconsistent and nowhere close to the one we were looking for. We stopped several times to ask for directions and each person said the same thing. Keep walking and you'll come to it in about ten minutes. Eventually we found it at the edge of town after walking for more than an hour.

There must be some sort of unwritten ten-minute rule in Ireland that prevents the locals from telling disappointed tourists how far they really have to walk.

FINDING THE SHIP IN DUBLIN

We had been to Dublin during the three years we lived in Germany, so at the end of our ship excursion we asked our guide to drop us off in the city center. We wanted to spend a little more time there on our own before returning to the port.

When we were ready to head back, we were about halfway between the shuttle bus stop and the port so we walked in the direction of the port and stopped in a pub for a light bite and a pint along the way. It was a good thing there was plenty of time because it turned out to be a lot farther that it looked on the map. It's amazing how often that happens.

Eventually we reached the port area, but it was very difficult to find a way to get through the fences. Just when we thought we'd found the right gate, there was a guy on the other side telling us to continue down to the road to the next gate to reach the ship. This area was filled with small roads that weren't on our little map and we almost missed the tiny sign that pointed to the cruise pier.

At the end of correct road, we came to a checkpoint with a guard who wouldn't let us through until someone came to get us with a little bus. The bus driver and the port worker who rode with him were happy to see us. Their job for the day was to sit in the little bus next to the checkpoint and wait for someone to come along who wanted to go to the cruise ship. Evidently there weren't very many that day. The driver said that last year someone died walking on the pier (he didn't say exactly how) and since then everyone has to be taken around by this little bus unless they work there. By the end of the day, we had walked six miles.

GETTING TO THE AIRPORT IN BELFAST, NORTHERN IRELAND

After our full day tour, we had planned to take a city bus from downtown Belfast to the airport for our flight to Edinburgh, Scotland where the ship would catch up with us three days later. While we waited on the pier for the shuttle bus to the city center, the security guard told us there would be no more shuttles that day. Protesters had blocked many of the roads and it would be best if we didn't go out again. He said today's protest was over abortion. Pro-choice people were clashing with anti-abortion people, and it wasn't safe to go into the city.

We explained our situation and tried to come up with a backup plan. Finally, the shuttle bus driver offered to take us as close to the city bus terminal as he could get. He was very kind. He dropped us off several blocks away with directions to reach it on foot, told us to be very careful, and wished us luck. We had no trouble finding it and got there before the airport bus pulled out. Good thing we left the ship with time to spare in case we had trouble somewhere along the way. We needed every bit of it.

FINDING PARK GUELL IN BARCELONA

On our second trip to Barcelona, we made an effort to see more of the unique architectural creations designed by Antonio Gaudi. His famous Park Guell is located high on a hill in the northern part of the city and we had heard it was worth seeing. We should have splurged on a taxi, but instead we took the subway to the nearest stop on the map.

Because the hills are so steep in this part of Barcelona, many of what appeared to be sidewalks on our tourist map were simply stairways. The views were spectacular, but it seemed to take forever to get to the top of the hill where the park was located. Another couple with heavy unidentifiable accents asked us the way to the park and we explained that we were headed there as well but weren't exactly sure of the way. Then we noticed a young Asian woman who appeared to be headed in the right direction, so we all followed her.

When we finally reached the plateau at the top of the hill, three men were playing Spanish guitars in a clearing. We could have listened to them all afternoon, but we still weren't sure exactly where we were or how to get into the park. By this time we had lost track of the Asian woman. It seemed that the only way out of this clearing was to go back the way we had just come up.

Then a small group of Americans appeared. They had been there before and knew the way to an obscure path that led to what I still believe is the world's longest stairway. The entrance to the park was on the opposite side of the long hill we had just come up, so we had to go all the way back down and around to the other side.

If the pictures of this park in our guidebook weren't so interesting, we would have given up. The directional signage was terrible. Thanks to the group of Americans, we reached the ticket office and bought timed entrance tickets without a wait. Then we found out that the place where you buy your ticket is not where you enter. Only if you bought your ticket online could you enter near the ticket office. Nothing about this was logical. A separate entrance that accepted the tickets sold at the park was in a different place that took a while to find. The park map was not at all clear either. Once we finally went inside, the great artwork and amazing colorful buildings made it all worthwhile.

After getting a bite to eat at a café near the exit, we began the very long walk to the subway at the south end of the park. At least it was downhill. At the main square I lost a $5 bet with Ed because I insisted that we were going the wrong way and I refused to walk any farther than necessary. You'd think I would have learned to believe him when he says he knows the right way no matter how wrong it sounds to me. He's built a nice little nest egg from winning bets with me about directions.

COMPLETELY LOST IN ROME

Before one of our return trips to Italy, we took a series of language lessons from a lovely Italian woman who taught them in her Denver home. She told us that if we needed directions while in Italy, we should ask three people. If two of them say the same thing then it was probably safe to go that way. Italians are not comfortable saying they don't know so they'll always offer directions whether they're accurate or not. We found this to be true.

On one of our trips to Rome several years ago before smart phones and GPS, we spent a full day at Ostia Antica to visit ruins of the old Roman seaport. It was similar to Pompeii and Herculaneum but not as well known. Following our guidebook instructions, we took the subway to a small train station at the edge of the city. After a short train ride, we had no trouble finding the ruins and spent the day walking through the entire area. It was well preserved and very interesting. On the way back to Rome, we took the right train but missed our subway stop to reach the hotel. Instead of going back into the station and riding back one stop, we looked at the map and decided it would be quicker to walk down the street about twelve blocks and we would reach our hotel. Big mistake.

We accidentally walked in the opposite direction from our hotel and ended up in an area that was off the edge of our map. We found ourselves in a residential neighborhood with different street names than the ones we were familiar with. After another hour it became clear that we were walking in circles. We started to see the same places a second time. People at sidewalk cafés stared at us. They knew we didn't belong there. We hesitated to go into one of those places and ask for directions or even ask where to find a taxi, so we kept walking.

In the distance at the top of a hill, I saw a big sign that said "Via Nomentana" with an arrow pointing to the right. All we had to do was make it over to that sign and we'd be on the same street as our hotel. As we walked, the sidewalk became narrower and narrower and then disappeared. We continued walking on the curb until we realized that we were on the entrance to the Autostrada freeway heading into a tunnel. Cars were honking at us but there was no room to turn ourselves around without stepping off the curb. It was tricky, but we managed to get back to the sidewalk and started looking for another way to reach Via Nomentana.

After another hour, we stumbled upon a transportation center that had about ten bus stops all in a line. Fortunately the bus stop signs in Rome list all the stops for each bus number, so we read every sign until we found a bus line that listed a stop we were familiar with. Then we waited.

When the bus came, it turned out to be a rickety old trolley with wooden benches. Only one seat was empty, so I sat down while Ed stood in the corner and anchored himself. Our legs were like rubber. Every time the trolley rounded a curve, Ed lost his footing and thrashed around until he could get himself anchored again. I couldn't stop laughing at him. I'm sure everyone on the trolley thought we were both drunk, but we were so happy to see familiar surroundings that we really didn't care.

When we reached our hotel, we were delighted to find that the small restaurant next door was still open. Pizza and cold beer never tasted so good.

FINDING OUR WAY BACK HOME IN OUR NEW HOMETOWN

The small town of Amberg is almost a thousand years old and the medieval wall with stone gates and towers still surrounds the center of town. Almost everything is within walking distance.

Not long after we moved to Germany, a friend from my office got a group of Americans together to have dinner at Brueckmueller Brewery during the bock beer festival. Bock beer goes back to the middle ages when the monks did not eat during Lent, but they were allowed to drink as much as they wanted. They brewed their own very strong beer during this time of year. It was filling and helped to offset the lack of food. For the festival, Brueckmueller brought in a great band that played some traditional beer drinking songs along with some American oldies.

Our American friends all left after dinner and Ed and I were the only ones who stayed. The remainder of our now empty long table was given to a group of young men who worked together at a metal factory down the road in Schwandorf. They didn't speak to us until I asked one of them in German if they were friends, relatives or if they worked together. After I broke the ice, they didn't stop talking and none of us stopped drinking. Ed was dancing on the tables before the night was over.

When it was time to leave, we paid our bill and went outside. It was a chilly night in March, our first time visiting this brewery and it was in a part of the town that we didn't know very well. Suddenly we had no idea how to get home. We thought we were sober until the cold air hit us. Ed was sure that home was one direction and I was sure it was the opposite way. Even though he was sure I was wrong, he decided it would be better to follow me rather than be left on his own. Ed was having a lot of trouble walking in a straight line.

We were both weaving down the sidewalk when we saw a police car approach. Logic should have told us that with all the beer that is consumed on any given night at this time of year, the police probably don't stop people for weaving down the sidewalk. Just to be sure, we hid behind a big tree until the police car went by. Eventually we came to the street that we would have reached a lot sooner if we had gone the way Ed wanted to go. I should have believed him. We slowly made our way home and up the three long flights of stairs to our apartment.

The shirt Ed wore that night was destined for the cleaners. When he picked it up the following week, he noticed it had a big rip up the middle of the back. He wished he had seen it before paying to have it laundered and pressed. It went straight into the trash. He still has no idea how it happened. It wasn't ripped when he put it on to go to the brewery. No regrets though. It was a fun night.

HOLOCAUST MEMORIAL IN ISRAEL – EASY TO GET IN BUT HARD TO GET OUT

During our tour of Israel, an entire afternoon was dedicated to visiting the immense World Holocaust Remembrance Center in Jerusalem. The most moving part was the Children's Memorial hollowed out from an underground cavern. There were no lights inside, but our guide assured us there were no steps and as we walked through, we could keep one hand on the wall. It was an emotional tribute to the 1.5 million Jewish children who were murdered during the Holocaust. A single lit candle was reflected infinitely in this dark space, which had the effect of millions of stars. As we walked through, the names of children, their ages, and countries of origin were read continuously. Everyone was respectful and very quiet.

Because we had visited concentration camp memorials when we lived in Germany, Ed chose not to go into the museum. I did, but about halfway through I just couldn't look at any more atrocity and left through the nearest door. Outside it was hard to get my bearings because the museum area was so large. After trying to follow the signs back to the main entrance without success, I stopped in a small bookstore at the same time as a Canadian woman who was also needing directions.

The woman behind the counter was quite snippy and made it clear that if people would just read the signs outside, they wouldn't need to come in to ask her. The Canadian woman and I went back outside and read the signs again but still couldn't find the right way. I decided to give the bookstore another try, hoping for a different person behind the counter. I couldn't come up with any better idea. The Canadian woman wandered off in another direction.

Just as I entered the bookstore for the second time, a man from our tour group was backing away from the counter. He was getting the same lecture I got from the same woman.

He and I agreed to find our way out of this complex no matter how long it took because we weren't going to ask that woman again. We tried to follow the signs when we were able to find one but ended up making several wrong turns on the way to the exit.

Eventually we made it to the parking lot where Ed and I stumbled upon each other and got on the bus.

LOOKING FOR THE PARTY IN CAPE TOWN, SOUTH AFRICA

On our last day in Cape Town, we were invited to a party in the city with about 200 of our fellow cruise passengers who were sailing around the world together. We rode in multiple buses and ours was the last one to head out.

After a short ride through the city, the bus driver pulled over next to a large parking lot, opened the door, and told us to "just walk over there". Ed and I were the first ones off the bus and we heard some people say, "Let's follow them. They look like they know where they're going." We walked "over there" into a restaurant and were greeted by a young hostess. Ed told her we were there for the party. She couldn't find a reservation and asked Ed how many of us there were. When he said about 200, she turned pale and speechless.

Just then, the bus driver appeared and told us to get back on the bus because this was not the right place. We had already figured that out. We went up the road a bit where a group of our hosts from the ship were wondering where we'd been.

SEARCHING FOR GELATO IN CARTAGENA, COLOMBIA

The beautiful old city of Cartagena was only a short ride on a catamaran from the port. As we passed the old city walls, our guide pointed out that these walls were used as the backdrop for the movie "Romancing the Stone" in the scene towards the end where Michael Douglas jumps into the water after the crocodile that swallowed the emerald. Several street scenes in the movie were filmed here as well.

Our guide offered one warning at the end of the catamaran ride. When you get off this boat many people will approach you and try to sell you something. Just keep walking. Do not look them in the eye. Do not say anything to them. If you do, they will follow you for the rest of your life. As it turned out, she wasn't kidding. We did as she advised and had no problems with anyone on the streets.

The colonial style buildings in Cartagena are beautifully preserved and very colorful. Many of the streets near the main square were pedestrian only and very crowded. The sun was terribly hot and many of the shops and museums weren't air conditioned so we didn't spend much time in any of them.

Instead, we went in search of Gelateria Paradiso, the best gelato shop in town according to the walking tour of the city that I had printed at home. It said, "Start at the clock tower and walk northwest". I thought the directions were simple enough to follow until I realized it was impossible to tell which way was northwest. Our map turned out to be pretty useless too. We asked a young woman in a shop how to get to Gelateria Paradiso and thought we understood her directions. We were wrong.

Very soon we were on streets with only a few locals and the sun was getting hotter. When we passed a bar advertising a free tapa with every beer, we decided to stop in, cool off and rest our feet. If it's starting to sound like we spent a lot of our time in search of a cold beer, that may be true but mostly in tropical climates where it was too hot and humid to do anything else.

Brazil was playing Serbia in the World Cup and the few people inside were enthusiastic Brazil fans. It was just a little place, but the server spoke English and was very friendly. The beer was cold and the tapas were tasty. We spent most of the afternoon there.

When the people at the other tables realized that we too were cheering for Brazil, they smiled and one person came over to ask where we were from. It was a great way to spend a hot afternoon. Before we left, we had to ask the server to show us on the map where we were so we could get back to the pier where the catamaran dropped us off. We found it with no problem.

DOLLARS AND SENSE
AND SOMETIMES NONSENSE

STICKER SHOCK IN TEL AVIV

On our first full day in Israel it seemed like a good idea to get some shekels to spend since we'd be in the country for an entire week. While Ed took care of checking out at the hotel desk, I found an ATM at the side of the lobby and got 400 shekels, equal to about $110. The hotel gift shop was nearby, so I stopped there and bought some stamps and postcards. Six postcards and enough stamps to send them to the US came to almost 100 shekels. Over $25! I was shocked but couldn't very well tell the man behind the counter to put all those stamps (three different ones for each postcard) back with the sheets he had just torn them from. He shrugged and said postage in Israel is very expensive. No kidding.

BANKS AND BANANAS IN THE CARIBBEAN

The island of St Lucia is the only country in the world named after a woman. On the way out of the capital city of Castries, our tour guide pointed out the First National Bank of St Lucia and told us that when the bank opened, it was possible to open an account with just one penny. They still call it The Penny Bank. Our last stop on the island tour was at the "Great View Banana Plantation" where they made banana ketchup and offered free samples. The flavor is difficult to describe. Not unpleasant but not exactly tasty either. They also sold banana cream rum liquor, ginger fudge, and coconut brittle along with several other food items unique to the island. A man in the parking lot was selling bowls and hats that he had made from banana leaves.

The bus stopped next to the banana fields and the guide pointed out one of the plants that had just produced a flower. The farmers cover each flower with a bright blue plastic bag until the bananas are formed to protect them from bugs and worms and to help them grow faster. They had exported huge amounts of bananas to the UK until their fields became infested with worms and all the fields had to be burned. Now they only ship them to neighboring islands until the crop recovers. Hopefully, they can make enough money selling banana ketchup and hats to tide them over until then but I'm not too sure about that.

BRAZILIAN SHOPPING ADVENTURES

The ship provided a shuttle bus from the port building to a marketplace in downtown Recife that had been converted from an old prison. Each prison cell was turned into an independent shop intended to be charming, but the building still looked like a prison inside and out even with all the flags.

We browsed around a bit and bought a few trinkets. After we left the marketplace, Ed wanted to see more of the city on foot. The streets were crowded, dirty, and in poor condition. I was reluctant to wander very far from the place where the shuttle bus would be picking us up but agreed to walk up the street a short way. There weren't any shops or cafés that we had any desire to go into, so we just made one big circle around the prison building.

A young man stopped us on the street and asked if we were from the ship. He was lost and a bit panicky. He showed us his ship crew ID, maybe because he was afraid we'd walk away from him. He said nobody here spoke English and he didn't know how to get back to the shuttle bus. We calmed him down and gave him directions. It wasn't far, but he had just gotten himself turned around. We saw him again when we got on the shuttle bus. He looked very relieved.

At the end of the day we learned that Brazil collects a 25% tax from any purchase made on the ship while in Brazilian waters, everything from merchandise in the gift shop to a glass of wine in the bar. We didn't pay this tax for the few things we bought in the marketplace so evidently it only applies to cruise ship purchases. I never did fully understand this.

TRYING TO PAY AND TRYING NOT TO PAY IN SALVADOR DE BAHIA

The largest church in this Brazilian city was the Cathedral Basilica built in the 17th century. It has a gold leaf altar that our tour guide said was really beautiful and he recommended we see it during our free time here. After our tour we tried to go inside the church but were stopped at the door by a ticket seller who only accepted Brazilian Reals. No credit cards. No American dollars. He said we could go down the street to exchange our money and come back. We certainly would have been willing to pay to enter, but the currency exchange had a high minimum and we didn't want to end up with a bunch of unused Reals after leaving Brazil.

We gave up and went to a sidewalk café that accepted Visa cards. A German couple sat down at the table next to us. They had ordered some kind of coffee concoction that looked very elegant. I had seen this type of coffee drink before and never knew what it was. When I learned from them that it was made with sweetened condensed milk, I was glad I didn't order it.

The women of Salvador de Bahia wore the most elaborate dresses I've ever seen to parade around the center of the city. Anyone who took their photo without paying for it was chased down immediately. Despite the size of their dresses, those women could really move.

FINDING A GUIDE IN NAMIBIA

Often when passengers get off a cruise ship, a crowd is waiting to sell their merchandise, a tour, or some sort of transportation. I talked to one guy who wanted $700 US to take us around the city of Walvis Bay. He had no clue what the exchange rate was. The one Ed talked to was much more professional and only wanted $80 US for the two of us to spend the entire day with him. He had just started his tour business two months earlier and was very accommodating.

Ed got into the car and the guide said, "Oh, did you want to drive?" Ed never noticed that the steering wheel was on the opposite side from American cars, and he had sat in the driver's seat. In Namibia, they drive on the left and sit on the right side of their cars.

SHOPPING IN KUALA LUMPUR

At the entrance to the central market, our guide gave us each a sticker to wear so we could use the restrooms without having to pay. He told us we would only have 20 minutes to shop because we couldn't be late to the restaurant for lunch. The market was more like an enclosed mall with multiple levels and all the shops were unique. We found some lovely items at great prices.

Ed bought a beautiful silk turquoise suit in traditional Malaysian style. He mostly just wanted the shirt but it was such a good deal that he bought the turquoise pants too. The suit came in handy for the formal Asian dinner on the ship. I even put his hair up in a bun for the occasion.

I found a loose fitting silk print blouse for the never-ending hot humid days for $7. The shopkeeper was willing to accept American dollars, but he had no change for my $10 bill. He said if I bought two blouses, they would be $5 each and then he would take my $10. Deal. I ended up with two almost identical blouses and both fell apart within six months.

NASTY PEDICAB DRIVERS IN VIETNAM

The large Saigon market that was within walking distance according to a guest lecturer turned out to be located a long way from the ship. We had plenty of time and managed to find our way on foot. The traffic was heavy and fast so crossing the street was quite a challenge. We tried stepping off the curb and letting the scooters and cars go around us, but here it was harder because Vietnamese crosswalks are totally meaningless.

The market turned out to be filled with interesting items. We spent about an hour there, bought some great gifts, and decided to take a taxi back to the ship. Two men talked us into a pedicab ride back to the ship rather than a regular taxi and it was hair raising. Even though we had agreed on $5 US each to take us to the port, the drivers of both pedicabs stopped several blocks from the port and told us to get out.

When Ed paid them the agreed upon amount, they both started yelling at us about wanting more money and insisted on being paid in local cash. They created such a scene that I was afraid more Vietnamese would join in the argument with them and we'd be in even bigger trouble. I gave one driver the only local money I had and told him to give half of it to the other one. He grabbed it, hopped on his pedicab, and pedaled out of sight. The other one continued to holler at us. It was horrible. Ed convinced me we should just walk away and not look back. The guy didn't come after us but kept yelling until we were too far away to hear him anymore.

No more pedicab rides in Vietnam ever again.

SHOPPING IN FRIENDLY HANOI

After dinner at a local restaurant in Hanoi, we ran into friends from the ship who had just bought some Oreos in a nearby convenience store. They loved Oreos and were thrilled to see them on the store shelf. The couple we had dinner with went in to get some also and came out with two packs. The store looked like it had all kinds of interesting things, so Ed and I went inside to look around. At the door, the clerk rushed right up to us with a pack of Oreos from China in each hand. Evidently the word got around that all Americans want to buy Oreos.

TONGA TAXI

Our day in Nuku'alofa, Tonga was hot and humid especially in contrast to the cooler weather we had just left behind in New Zealand. The sun just felt searing. We hadn't scheduled a tour so we just browsed through the market stalls by the port, bought a few gifts and picked up a map, then walked around the town.

I was about ready to go back to the ship on my own to cool down when Ed said he was going to walk out to see the blowholes. Well, those were on the opposite side of the island, and too far from the cruise pier to walk out there and back. I suggested we get a taxi and go together.

The driver tried to tell us about various points of interest on the way, but he didn't speak much English. We were able to understand that he had twelve children: nine girls and three boys. He and his wife work, along with the oldest boy and oldest girl but I wasn't clear about what jobs they had. I couldn't imagine how they survive here. Ours was the last cruise ship of the season.

The Blowholes of Tongatapu stretch along the southwest shore for three miles. Hundreds of holes in the coral rock here create enormous geysers from the crashing waves. They can go up to a hundred feet in the air as they roar down the coastline. I was so glad we didn't miss this impressive sight. Near the blowholes, some women had set up tables up by the parking lot with items for sale. I bought a necklace from one of them while Ed took a picture of the tiny piglet she had tied to the leg of her table. I jokingly asked her the price for the pig. She said, "You can just take him, but feed him well." We paid for the necklace and left the pig.

The taxi driver waited until we were ready to leave and then drove us back. We asked him to drop us off at the market and we could walk back to the ship from there. When Ed paid him the agreed upon $50 US he started to yell, demanding that we pay $50 per person, not $50

for the ride. As in many of these countries, the taxis don't use meters. You just agree on a price before getting inside, which we did. The ride was short and agreeing to $50 for both of us was already very generous. I understand that the people who live here need to survive, but this guy got so mean and nasty which really didn't help.

Ed finally gave in but swore it would never happen again, especially after our terrible experience with pedicab drivers in Vietnam. After this we started to carry a pen and paper with us to write down the agreed upon price for two people before getting into another meterless taxi.

CURRENCY EXCHANGE CHALLENGES IN SCOTLAND

The currency in Great Britain can be confusing because England, Scotland, and Northern Ireland use the British Pound, but The Republic of Ireland uses the Euro. They look too much alike for my taste. When our cruise ship was in the British Isles, it was hard to remember which currency to bring along when going out for the day.

A few years earlier, we had exchanged some US dollars for British pounds that we ended up not using because of a cancelled trip. Sometime after that, Great Britain decided to take their paper five and ten pound notes out of circulation and replace them with plastic notes to reduce the possibility of counterfeiting.

We still had three paper ten pound notes that no one would take no matter how hard we tried to spend them. Store clerks told us we could exchange them at a bank but we hadn't had enough time to find one and then stand in line. In the Inverness area of northern Scotland, the town of Invergordon had a few banks so it seemed like a good idea to take advantage of our free time there at the end of our tour and turn in the paper notes. Not so simple.

The first bank we went into consisted of a row of self-service machines and one guy at a desk in the back who popped up from his chair as soon as we walked in the door. He asked if we had an account there. I don't even remember the name of the bank. He said without an account he couldn't exchange the notes for us. He said there were a few other banks in town but they would tell us the same thing. Then he started explaining a convoluted process of going online, filling out a form and getting a verification number that we could bring back to his bank. The whole time he was talking, we were backing slowly toward the door. I really didn't like that guy.

Down the street at the Bank of Scotland, we had no trouble exchanging our paper notes for plastic ones. It felt like we had really accomplished something.

CANADIAN PENNIES

Canada had the same issue with pennies that Great Britain had with five and ten pound paper bills. Nobody wanted them. Somehow, we ended up with 40 Canadian pennies and the shops wouldn't take them. It didn't occur to us until after we left Canada that we could have just made a donation inside a church to include all our coins. We finally found a bank in Quebec that was willing to trade them in for dimes which lightened our load considerably. 40 pennies weigh more than you'd think.

FINDING CHRISTMAS DECORATIONS IN ARGENTINA

Ed has always loved hanging decorations for the holidays but we didn't bring any with us on our world cruise. When our ship docked in Ushuaia, we went out in search of a few Christmas decorations to put up in our stateroom and on the outside of our hallway door. The town had a lot of outdoor shops and some souvenir shops but none had decorations. Ed finally asked one of the store owners who spoke English where we could find holiday decorations. The guy gave us very specific directions up one of the side streets to a shop that sold home decor. She has decorations, he told us. We made it to the right shop, only to find it was closed for "siesta" until 4:00.

What to do? Have some local beer and pizza, of course. We stopped in a cozy historical restaurant built around 1912 that had Wi-Fi and stayed there until it was time for the shop to open. By this time we had learned to order one beer with two glasses until we determined how big the bottles were. In South America, they can be really big.

The shop turned out to be a gold mine for Christmas decorations. We carried our bags down sidewalks that were so steep they were more like stairways with irregular steps that were often hard to see. Ed almost tumbled headfirst in a place where he just didn't see a steep step. I grabbed his elbow just in time and spun him around right before he would have fallen. Whew!

FINDING NEW YEAR'S DECORATIONS IN MEXICO

Ed wanted to find some New Year's Eve decorations for the dinner party we were hosting on the cruise ship after leaving Cabo San Lucas. We invited five other couples to join us in the private dining room of the Italian Restaurant. He had brought some streamers and confetti from home but was convinced it wasn't enough. We went into countless marketplace shops near the pier but came up empty. Every time we asked where to find Año Nuevo party items, the answer was always the same. Walmart.

One guy showed us where to catch a local bus. He said the bus would say Walmart on it and would cost about $1 each. We didn't expect Walmart to be handwritten in white paint on the window in the list of several other stops but that's how we found the right bus.

We had used our singles for tips on the morning tour, so Ed gave the driver a $5 bill. He looked at it, turned it over a few times, then put it in his wallet. He took out a 50 Peso bill and gave it to Ed. We figured that should work for our trip back and we sat down. This bus was a wreck inside and out. Ed studied the map while I kept an eye on the streets to make sure we knew the way back.

The ride to Walmart took about 20 minutes. Only one other person rode the bus with us. The store was big, new, and in a shopping center with several smaller stores. It looked like the kind of place that would have party stuff.

The stereotypical Walmart greeter walked up to us and in perfect English asked how he could help. He walked us over to the party department, called the guy in charge of such things and after much discussion and hunting around, they both came to the conclusion that Walmart did not have any Año Nuevo stuff.

Our new best friend the greeter wasn't ready to give up. He led us over to a small store in the shopping center that he thought would have what we needed. They had plenty of party supplies but nothing for an Año Nuevo party. The woman in this little store suggested a place in downtown Cabo that might be our answer. The greeter marked on our map where to get off the bus and how to find this store. We shook his hand, thanked him, and left.

We were almost back at the bus stop when the greeter ran up and told us to come back with him. He was sure he had found what we were looking for. He led us to a small kiosk in the middle of the shopping center that had glittery hats and beads. It was perfect. We bought all they had and the greeter was so proud.

Thanks to him, our party was a huge success.

WORKING HARD AT SPENDING

The evening before our six month world cruise ended, we received a final statement from the Purser's Office showing that we still had a nonrefundable credit of over $2600 which would be forfeited if we didn't spend it onboard before 10:00 pm.

What a shock! We were not about to leave this much money behind but the only place we could use it was in the ship's boutique or the jewelry store. The only thing we could do was go speed shopping and buy as many overpriced items as we could without exceeding our credit balance.

Initially this was not as hard as it sounded because the prices were so high. I tried on some clothes and bought three basic items that came to $500. Ed kept track of our purchases and we found ourselves saying, "Is that all we spent? We still have to spend another $1000?" We were frantically running back and forth from the shops to our stateroom to make sure we had kept an accurate count. We even had to buy another suitcase to put all our new stuff in.

By the time the shops closed, the credit balance in our account was down to 81 cents. The last thing we did was to get one more final statement from the Purser's Office to make sure we didn't mess this up. It would have been terrible to find a bunch of charges on our credit card for stuff we didn't really need to buy in the first place. We breathed a sigh of relief when it all turned out okay and we could start laughing about it.

By the time we got everything packed up, we were exhausted. Our suitcases had to be outside our door by 10:00 or we would have had to take all of them off the ship ourselves. The crew members collecting bags were right around the corner when we put ours out.

TAKING CHANCES AND OTHER RISKY BUSINESS

SHARK DIVING NEAR CAPE TOWN

When our cruise ship docked in Cape Town for three days, Ed was ready to check another item off his bucket list. He was all set to go diving with the sharks on a tour that left the city at 7:00 am. I went along to take photos from the deck and stayed out of the water.

The dive company sent an email the day before we were scheduled to go saying they would pick us up at 3:30 am instead of 7:00. Bad weather was expected to move in during the day and it would be necessary to get back to shore before it got too windy. I'm all about safety especially on the water and this sounded risky to me. What if the bad weather moved in earlier than expected? I called the tour company to make sure of the pickup time and they assured me it really was 3:30 am and that everything would be fine.

Somehow, we managed to get up at 2:30 to make sure we'd be at the entrance to the port area before 3:30. I was shocked to see that the van was full and we were the last ones to join! The people who got picked up earlier than we did probably never went to bed. It was a 2 ½ hour drive to Gaansbai where we had breakfast before heading out to the boat with all the gear.

The cage hung off the side of the boat and held four people at a time. When a shark got close, a crew member yelled, "Down!". Everyone in the cage ducked below the surface of the water to see the shark coming toward them. It's impossible to describe how massive these creatures are.

For Ed it was every bit as exciting as he had hoped. For me this was the ultimate adrenaline rush I could imagine and I didn't even go in the water. The best souvenir was the video the company made of his dive. He watches it and relives his adventure over and over.

RIDING ELEPHANTS IN BALI

Our independent tour guide picked us up at the Bali port for the amazing experience of riding an elephant. On our way to the elephant camp, he said we had time to stop for coffee if we wanted and of course we said sure. It turned out to be a mini coffee and tea plantation where they roast their own coffee beans in a pan over an open fire and grind them by hand. Free coffee and tea tasting were included, so we shared a tray of twelve little cups of different flavors.

The shopkeeper offered to make me a cup of Luwak coffee, also known as Civet coffee or Weasel coffee. This is the coffee Jack Nicholson drank in the movie "The Bucket List". They have five civets on site that eat, digest, and leave whole beans in their droppings. It always sounded disgusting, but I decided to try it anyway. When would I have another opportunity? The shopkeeper prepared it in an elaborate one cup brewer and served it in a delicate china cup. Lovely presentation but I didn't like the taste.

As we drove into the elephant camp, we knew we had picked the right place. It was beautiful. Because we didn't have all day to spend there (all aboard time was 3:30 pm), we took care of the paperwork as soon as we arrived. The total cost for the day for both of us was $150, which included transportation from the port in a private car, a half hour elephant ride, insurance, and lunch. We were asked to order lunch before riding so it would be ready when we returned.

It was easier than I expected to get on the elephant thanks to the wooden platform at the top of a flight of steps. The mahout explained that our elephant, "Eppy", was 23 years old and had no children. He has worked with her and only her for seven years. He told us that he sleeps at the camp with her three nights a week and called her his second wife. She knew a lot of commands and was very gentle. It was hard to take photos during the ride because it wasn't exactly smooth. We rode past some lovely rice terraces and a troop of monkeys.

Our lunch was ready when we returned from the ride and was served outside on a shady terrace. It's amazing how you can work up an appetite after just a half hour on an elephant.

NO GANGWAY IN NEW ZEALAND

After an early dinner on the ship, we had time to walk into the town of Tauranga for a bit since all aboard time wasn't until 7:30 pm. On the way out of the port area, we asked the security guy who checked IDs at the entrance to the pier if he could recommend a good place to stop for a local beer. He mentioned a few but neither of us could understand the name of the beer he told us to drink. New Zealanders have a unique way of speaking. They seem to twirl their words so much that we couldn't understand them even though they were speaking English. I never did catch on to their accents.

It was a short walk into town. We tried a place that was advertised as a brewery but it was very small and there weren't many people in it, so we moved on to another one. The second place had the most beautiful restroom I'd ever seen in a bar.

All of a sudden, we realized what time it was. We hurried back to the ship, told the man in the booth how good the beer was and then stopped dead in our tracks. We couldn't see the gangway. We still had ten minutes before all aboard time. Surely, they wouldn't pull up the gangway before everyone had reboarded. Then a dock worker told us not to worry. The gangway had been moved to a lower deck because the tide had gone out. It was hidden behind a small building and we just couldn't see it from where we stood. The security officer who checks ID badges on the ship came outside at the top of the gangway and waved.

They didn't sail without us after all.

HOT COFFEE ON THE SHUTTLE BUS

We spent our second day in Namibia on a tour bus to see the landscape farther away from the coast. The scenery was fascinating and we had an excellent guide. When we returned to the cruise pier, the shuttle bus to a nearby shopping mall was getting ready to leave. We got off our bus and directly onto the other one.

We walked the entire mall, bought some snacks for our cabin stewards, and made it out to the parking lot with one minute to spare before the last bus back to the ship was scheduled to leave at 3:00. We were the only ones on it. Our grocery bag had an interesting message printed on the side.

The shuttle bus driver was wearing a shirt that said "Flying Coffee Pot" with pictures of winged percolators on the back. I had to ask him about it. He said the company used to have a coffee shop at the airport but it closed and he started a shuttle service instead. He said they tried serving coffee on the shuttle, but it didn't work out too well. I believe that. Things are wild enough in that part of the world without trying to keep hot coffee out of your lap.

STRANGE TOUR IN BERGEN

I came very close to booking a private guide for a three day tour in Norway until I saw this note in the description: "Special Notice: Due to Norwegian legislation, this tour includes payment for an overnight stay in a tent at our remote island in the Osterfjord. Notice that you don't need to utilize this, as this is solely to comply with the outdated Norwegian transportation law. In case you DO want to utilize this part of the tour, please notify the local supplier at the time of booking and a tent will be provided for your use. A $1500 security deposit must be paid for the tent. You will have to put up the tent yourself and make your way to the island on your own."

We booked a fjord tour that included a hotel stay instead.

NOT BUNGEE JUMPING FROM THE SKY TOWER IN AUCKLAND

Four people we knew from our cruise ship in 2018 went bungee jumping off the top of the Sky Tower in downtown Auckland. When the guy working on the landing platform noticed that the six of us who were standing around the bottom of the tower were waiting around and looking up, he invited us inside the fence of the landing area and allowed us to go up the stairs to the platform. There we could watch on a large TV screen what was happening on the launch platform 576 feet above as each person got ready to step off the edge.

Ed really wanted to jump with them but couldn't quite talk himself into it. The next day, he wished he had gone. He talked about it for weeks afterward.

SECOND CHANCE TO BUNGEE JUMP

On our second world cruise in 2019, Ed was determined not to miss bungee jumping in Auckland again. As it turned out, anyone over the age of 75 could jump for free, so he didn't even have to pay. This time he wasn't nervous at all. Several the people from the ship came to watch and cheer him on. We all stood at the side of the landing platform and watched him come down with a big smile on his face. He ended up with a great video and a T-shirt to prove he had made the jump.

Ed didn't stop glowing for days. He said he felt five years younger.

CLIMBING THE WRONG HIGHPOINT IN OKLAHOMA

It was already late in the day when we reached the area around the Oklahoma highpoint. Despite the lengthening shadows, we made a quick decision to go for it and hope to get back down before it got dark. The description of the approach in our old guidebook sounded easy, except that it was necessary to cross private ranchland to reach the trailhead.

Ed drove our pickup truck very slowly through a herd of cattle and parked it at the foot of the mesa as directed in the guidebook. Thorny bushes, heat and humidity combined to make a miserable hike to the top. Ed had just reached the edge of the mesa when he spotted a rattlesnake poised to strike. Instead of moving away or warning me, he said, "Get the camera out of my backpack. Quick!" He took a photo and we ran.

The USGS marker was nowhere to be found. Then I pointed out a nearby mesa that was higher than the one we had just climbed. Ed consulted the map and conceded that we had indeed climbed the wrong mesa. We hurried down and hiked up the other one, found the marker, and took our photos. By this time it was really getting dark. Ed insisted we would save time by angling down the side of the mesa off the trail instead of returning the way we had come. It was definitely shorter but we had to cross hillsides thickly covered with cactus plants with long nasty needles that were impossible to avoid.

By the time we reached the truck, our legs were covered with bleeding scratches and it was pitch dark. To avoid being seen by the rancher whose land we had trespassed on without taking the time to ask permission, we drove slowly back to the main road without headlights, hoping to avoid getting too close to any of the cattle and giving him a reason to get his shotgun out. We arrived back at the campground without incident and considered ourselves lucky. We later learned that after our guidebook was published, a new approach to the Oklahoma highpoint had been constructed on the other side of the hill making the hike to the top shorter and easier. Once again, we did it the hard way.

WRONG TRAIL AT MONTANA HIGHPOINT

Granite Peak in Montana is over 12,000 feet high. It's considered among the most difficult climbs in the US not because the trail is long but because of the icy rock climbs and steep ridges toward the top. Ed was usually able to find someone to team up with through the Highpointers Club for the tougher climbs like this one. He had arranged to meet a small group from Michigan at the trailhead early in the morning, so we parked our RV at a nearby campground the night before.

When we reached the trailhead, Ed realized it wasn't the same one where he had planned to meet the group. The trail names were very similar and he had printed directions to the wrong one. It was too late to drive to the other one and still catch up with them. My heart sank when he told me he was going to go anyway, especially when he said he'd be able to meet up with them if he spent the night on "Froze to Death Plateau". It took all the courage I had to drive away and leave him there but he insisted. I cried.

The climb was every bit as difficult as described, but Ed was able to find the group and they all made it back down safely. He has no desire to go back.

TREACHEROUS HIGHPOINT IN IDAHO

Borah Peak in Idaho is also over 12,000 feet high and requires more skill and fortitude than I will ever have. We camped in our tent overnight at the trailhead and Ed left very early the next morning. When I went outside the tent after he left, I noticed fresh bear scat nearby that wasn't there the night before. I took my sleeping bag inside the van and went back to sleep.

Ed expected to return about eight hours later assuming he had no problems at a place ominously called "Chicken Out Ridge", a very narrow path with steep drop-offs on both sides. Add that to the mountain's location in the "Lost River Range" and I had plenty of worrying to keep me busy for the rest of the day.

After he returned safely, we drove into the nearby town of Arco for dinner. Ed ordered a steak with a baked potato. Neither of us had ever seen such a big potato. It hung off both sides of his very large plate. Now we know why the Idaho license plate says, "famous potatoes".

DARK PLACES IN ARIZONA

During the climb up the Arizona high point, we became acquainted with two young men who asked if we wanted to join them afterwards in exploring a nearby cave. It was not a commercial one, they said, and few people knew about it. Instead of questioning the wisdom of this, we said sure. We had flashlights and it was only mid-afternoon. It amazes me now to think about all the "what ifs" that never crossed my mind.

The cave was only about a mile long and easy to get into, but there were places where the ceiling was so low that we had to crawl while holding our flashlights. We made it to the end and came back out while it was still daylight. That was when Ed discovered that he had gone through the entire cave wearing his sunglasses! One of our new friends remarked afterwards that Ed always likes a challenge.

UNDERWATER IN A YELLOWSTONE CREEK

During one of our many trips to Yellowstone, Ed planned a long hike on a steep trail. The description in our trail guide convinced me that this one was beyond my skill level, so he went by himself even though he knows it's never a good idea to hike alone.

At one point the trail crossed a fast running creek, swollen from recent rains. A bridge made from a few logs looked easy enough to cross but Ed's foot slipped, he lost his balance, and went over the edge into the water.

He wasn't injured but his boot got stuck between the logs so he was upside down under the surface of the water still wearing his backpack. His stomach muscles were strong enough to bring his upper body high enough to catch a breath, but he wasn't able to stay above the surface long enough to get his foot out. The water was cold, fast, and very frightening. Drowning was becoming a distinct possibility as he was losing strength.

The only thing he could do was get his backpack off and throw it as hard as he could onto the shore. Without the weight of the pack, he was able keep his upper body out of the water long enough to untie his boot and loosen his foot. He managed to pull himself out of the creek, put on his boot, retrieve his pack, and make it back to the trail, shaken but alive.

Ed still says that of all the adventures in his life, this one was the scariest.

CAUGHT ON A MOVING BRIDGE IN DELFT

During a visit to Amsterdam, we took a short train ride to Delft and tried to squeeze in a stop at the famous blue and white ceramics factory there at the end of the day. We were pressed for time and hoped to get there before the factory and shop closed at 5 pm.

Like Amsterdam, Delft has many canals. We had to cross a bridge over one of them to reach the street that led to the factory. Just as we approached, gates with flashing lights came down across the walkway. Waiting for the bridge meant we might not make it to the factory before it closed. A bicyclist came up from behind, went around us, past the gate, and across the bridge. Since the bridge still hadn't opened, we tried to run for it thinking it would split in the middle. As long as we reached the other side of the split before it went up, we'd be okay.

As it turned out, the bridge rose in one piece, starting from the opposite side. The Dutch people walking nearby stopped to watch in amazement as we tried to outrun the bridge. Just like in the movies, we jumped from the end of the rising bridge to the pavement and ran around the gate. It was a short jump but harrowing, nonetheless. We probably would have gotten a ticket if there had been a policeman nearby.

We reached the factory in time to buy a beautiful blue and white tulip vase, which is now my favorite.

BUS RIDE BACK TO DAR ES SALAM

Our trip to Bagamoyo in Tanzania was a full day tour that included lunch at a private lodge on the beach. Several people on our tour wanted to dip their toes into the Indian Ocean but the tide was so far out that it would have taken forever to reach the water and return. This made the beach more interesting because we could walk right up to the anchored wooden boats and look around inside. Time was built into the schedule for swimming but this was just not possible. It was terribly hot and since everyone was just hanging around in the shade, the bus took us back to the ship early.

Nine vans holding about 15 passengers each traveled out of the port area and back in a caravan with a police escort. At major intersections, policemen held up the traffic while we drove through red lights so we wouldn't have to stop. In many places, the pavement changed to dirt and rock, then back again. Ours was the last in the line of vans. Our driver often straddled the lane lines to prevent other vehicles from getting in between the vans and causing trouble. In the front seat next to the driver, a big guy with a radio (and probably a gun) kept watching everything around us. Someone from the ship staff rode in each van as well. I'll never know how those vans made it through all the traffic but we arrived back at the port unscathed and safe.

HIKING AT MASADA

I have been fascinated with the story of Masada ever since I saw a miniseries about it on TV back in 1981. Ruins of this ancient fortification sprawl across the top of an isolated plateau in the Judean desert overlooking the Dead Sea. It was built by King Herod and became the refuge of the last survivors of the Jewish revolt in 74 AD. When the Romans closed in, the remaining 960 Jews chose death rather than wait to be killed or enslaved. Because Judaism prohibits suicide, they drew lots and killed each other in turn down to the last man so that only one would have to take his own life. The Jews destroyed everything before they died so that when the Romans reached the top, there would be nothing left.

Most people who visit Masada take the cable car to the top of the plateau to see the ruins. Not Ed. He wanted to hike the switchbacks along the side of the hill to the top - about an hour and a half up the Serpentine Trail, the same one the Jews used over two thousand years ago. While Ed hiked alone, I rode up with the group to tour the ruins of Herod's palace with its mosaic floors and frescoed walls, the cisterns, and the remains of the orchards and houses.

Through our headsets, our guide kept Ed updated on where we were, so he could find us when he reached the top. There were a few others on the trail, but he was the only one from our group who hiked up. Our guide kept saying, "Ed, if you can hear me, we are at the cisterns"... or "Ed, we are in the palace". I heard a guy behind me say, "Does anybody know who Ed is?" After I turned around and explained, some of the men in our group said they would have hiked too if they had known they could do it. Only my Ed does things that others assume are not possible.

BAD LUCK AND GOOD LUCK IN MEXICO

A very nice elderly Swiss lady stayed in the stateroom next to ours during the entire six-month cruise. She told us that her sons were very much against her taking this trip and warned her not to get acquainted with any men on the ship because they would only be after her money.

She took an excursion to a black sand beach in Cabo San Lucas and left her sandals in the shade while she went into the water. After swimming, the sand was so hot that her feet were burned and blistered by the time she got back to her sandals. This poor lady could hardly walk to the medical center on the ship where they treated and bandaged her feet. She went back for multiple wound treatments and walked with a cane for a few weeks. It was terribly painful.

About a week burning her feet, she played Bingo with us. Evidently, the Swiss don't play Bingo. She had never played in her life and we had to explain to her how it works. She ended up winning two of the four games and walked away with over $300!

WHERE THE WILD THINGS ARE

KANGAROOS IN TASMANIA

The best part of our day in Hobart was the visit to Bonorong Wildlife Sanctuary. It's not a zoo. Bonorong cares for injured and orphaned wildlife with the goal of returning animals to the wild when they are able to manage on their own. Several different animals were being cared for there, but we spent most of our time with the kangaroos. Before we got off the bus, a naturalist came on board and explained how to pet a kangaroo (rub the chest) and how not to pet a kangaroo (don't touch the head or back).

There must of have been at least fifty of them hopping all around us. Small dispensers filled with free kangaroo food were everywhere. What a thrill it was to have kangaroos eating out of our hands. I couldn't believe how gentle they were. They seemed to have no fear of people at all. I could have stayed there for hours.

SNAKES AT NORTH DAKOTA HIGHPOINT

The day we climbed White Butte I was in no mood for another hot dusty hike. That day bagging another peak was more than I could summon the energy to do. About halfway up, I sat down on a rock and told Ed to pick me up there on the way back. He pointed to the row of holes in the hill right behind me and said I could wait there if I wanted, but those were snake holes so I'd better keep my eyes open. I reached the top before he did.

CLOSE ENCOUNTER WITH A BEAR IN ALASKA

Our first trip to Alaska was a two week tent camping trip arranged through a company called Camp Alaska, which is no longer in business. We brought our own sleeping bags and the tour company provided tents, food, and transportation in a 12-passenger van. The driver was also the guide and cook. We rode from Anchorage as far north as Denali National Park, east to Paxson and back to Anchorage. It was a wonderful trip.

At Denali, our group set up the tents along the river in a commercial campground just outside the national park. In the middle of breakfast, a huge black bear meandered toward our campsite. Our guide instructed us to grab our food and get up the riverbank to the main road as fast as we could. Ed insisted on taking pictures of the bear while I ran off with our food. In each photo he took, the bear was bigger and closer.

From the top of the bank we could safely watch the bear roam around the campground scaring other people. Two women in the campsite next to ours had brought a small dog and left a bowl of dog food outside their tent which attracted the bear. They scrambled inside their tent, zipped it shut, and held the dog to keep it quiet. The bear sat down against the side of the tent, right on top of one of the women laying inside while it ate all the dog food. They were lucky the bear didn't tear its way into their tent looking for more, but eventually the bear finished up the dog food and wandered away.

TINY BLACK ANTS IN BASSETERRE, ST KITTS & NEVIS

After a tour of the city, our bus headed up into the hills to the Fairview Great House where we learned about the history of the colonial mansion and the families that lived there. We had 45 minutes to walk around but it was very hot and humid. We found a place to sit in the shade at the top of the hill at the back of the property, which was lovely until I felt some nasty pinches on my ankles and looked down to find them covered with tiny black ants. Ed too. They bit right through our socks. We jumped up and started hopping around, slapping at our ankles. People from outside the plantation house were looking up the hill at us, probably wondering what we were doing. We must have looked like a pair of Bavarian Schuhplattler dancers.

Three days later they still itched.

WILDLIFE TOUR WITH NO WILDLIFE

Dominica is known as the nature isle of the Caribbean with many waterfalls, hot springs, lakes, mountainous rainforests, volcanoes, and beautiful views. Instead of touring these things, we took a whale and dolphin cruise, since it was toward the end of our six-month cruise and we hadn't seen any of these sea creatures so far on the entire trip.

Sadly, this excursion was no different. It turned out to be a $90 per person boat ride five miles out to sea where we sat watching for whales and dolphins that never appeared and moved around about every ten minutes and sat some more.

Rum punch was served just before we returned to shore four hours later. They should have started serving it earlier. People wouldn't have complained so much. Even though the descriptions of these tours always include a line that says wildlife sightings are not guaranteed, I couldn't help feeling disappointed.

SURROUNDED BY BISON IN YELLOWSTONE NATIONAL PARK

At each entrance station in Yellowstone National Park, visitors receive a written warning about wildlife danger. It states that visitors must stay at least 25 yards away from bison. "Bison can run three times faster than humans can sprint and are unpredictable and dangerous." This advice is easy to follow when viewing bison from a distance. It's a lot different when you're out hiking and they meander toward you.

On a short hike in early fall, we were approached by a herd of bison moving slowly but directly toward us. During all our many hikes in Yellowstone, this had never happened. Not wanting to provoke them but desperately wanting to distance ourselves, we kept moving along the trail, hoping they would change direction. No such luck. They kept coming.

Keeping a close eye on the bison we angled over toward a large fallen tree and sat down, hoping to appear as nonthreatening as possible while we waited for them to clear out of the area. Instead of continuing on, some stopped to nibble grass, some decided to lay down to rest and several just stood and stared at us. They were close, they had young ones, and they were very, very big.

I'm not sure how long we sat there, but I spent most of the time comparing the distance between me and the nearest big tree to the distance between me and the nearest bison. I tried to remember how far it was back to the car in case one of us got gored. Every now and then, Ed recommended we just sit there a while longer.

Eventually the herd moved on peacefully and so did we.

CHICKENS AND GARDENS IN TOBAGO

There wasn't much to see on this Caribbean island, but in the town of Scarborough a woman at the tourist information booth in the port building gave us a map and directions to a botanic garden about four blocks from the port. Chickens and roosters wandered around in the streets uninhibited by the traffic. There didn't seem to be any that met their demise in the middle of the road so evidently drivers here go around them.

Ironically, she said we should turn left at the KFC. Sure enough, there was a large portrait of Colonel Sanders on the corner. He looked really out of place in Tobago but the KFC was doing a good business.

Everything was uphill on this island. The garden was more like a city park but it was shady and we enjoyed the occasional breeze. Two women sitting on a bench near the entrance called to us and one walked over to greet us. She explained that they are both paid by the government to tell us about the various trees in the park. She looked relieved when we said we were happy to wander through the park on our own and went back to her bench in the shade. There were even more chickens and roosters in the park than on the streets. Apparently, they liked the shade, too.

As we were leaving, the other woman asked if we would please sign her register. She forgot that we had signed it on the way in, even though we were the only other people there. This woman loved Ed's long white ponytail and kept calling him "Cool Boy". Then she showed us the bags of cocoa balls she had for sale – solid pure cocoa. I bought two. They smelled so good and could be used that same way as ordinary cocoa powder. Although my clothes smelled like chocolate by the time I unpacked, it was okay. We had some great hot cocoa at home that winter. A little bit went a long way.

MONKEYS IN THE BOAT

Panama City is the only capital city in the world that has a rainforest inside it. We had a quick tour of a small part of it on the way to our jungle boat tour on the Chagres River which flows into Gatun Lake in the middle of the Panama Canal. All the ships going through the canal travel across this lake. I loved being required to wear my life jacket.

We stopped at various points around the islands in the lake hoping to get a glimpse of local wildlife. Our guide explained that there are seven kinds of monkeys in this area and we would likely see three of them. There are also 127 kinds of snakes, 11% of which are poisonous but don't worry, he said. We would have no snakes coming into the boat. I was more concerned about an iguana taking a flying leap into the boat when we were close to the shore.

Before we reached the island where the three different types of monkeys live, our guide warned us that we should never smile when the monkeys were around. Showing teeth is a sign of aggression in the monkey world and we would likely get bitten or scratched if we smiled.

We could hear the howler monkeys before we saw them. They sounded like big dogs. Big mean dogs. They have bright streaks of shaggy reddish-yellow hair on their backs. The tamarin monkeys were smaller with gray faces but they didn't look any friendlier. The capuchin monkeys were the smallest of the three. Several of those climbed onto the boat. Nobody smiled.

CLOSE ENCOUNTER WITH A BIG SNAKE IN BRAZIL

Because the Amazon was so fascinating and we might never be back, we booked a 4 ½ hour rainforest hike in the protected Tapajos National Forest near Santarém. The ride to the park took about 45 minutes on a small bus without air conditioning and the roads deteriorated as we went. We had a driver, tour guide, local park guide, and another local guy who seemed to be responsible for making sure we were all okay. I couldn't exactly tell what his job was.

Not far from the park entrance on a bumpy dirt road, the park guide started yelling at the bus driver to stop. The three local guys dashed off the bus while the driver stayed with us. The windows were small and there were none across the back of the bus so we couldn't see what was going on. We just heard a lot of yelling in Portuguese.

Then the guide called out, "Come! Come! Everyone off the bus!" We looked at each other. Was it an ambush? Wildlife? The bus was old and it was a long drop from the bottom step to the ground, so it took a while for everyone to get off.

We hurried toward the back of the bus to see the three guys standing next to a massive boa constrictor with a stick in its mouth. It was enough to stop me in my tracks. This thing was enormous. After all of us got a good look and took some photos, we crept back toward the bus as this huge creature slithered into forest.

The two guides led the hike while the third local guy stayed at the back of the group to make sure no one got lost or left behind or got swallowed by a boa constrictor. One of the guides carried a giant machete and hacked away at vines and branches that tried to overtake the trail.

The forest was so dense and the path so narrow that if you didn't keep up with the guide, you'd be lost in no time. Good thing we had that third guy along to keep us together. It would be easy to lose your sense of direction if you wandered off the path.

I kept my eye out for that big snake the whole time we were hiking but didn't see it again.

CAIMANS IN THE DARK

At our last port along the Amazon we signed up for a night tour that started at 8:30 pm called "In Search of Caimans". The closer we got to the departure time for this tour, the more I wondered what possessed me to agree to go out in a tiny canoe in the dark looking for a reptile that could bite my arm off.

To make matters worse, we received a letter the night before saying that the tour operator had been monitoring the low water levels in January Lake where we were headed and determined that the large boats would only be able to take us to the point where the lake and the river meet. From there, we would be transferred to small, motorized canoes to continue with the tour. It didn't say exactly how small these canoes would be. I was nervous.

The large boat picked us up on the pier right next to the ship at dusk and the cruise out to the lake was lovely. Then the guide explained that the place where we had to change boats was in the middle of the river. I had expected a dock someplace where we could get off one boat, walk across and get on the other one. No. We did this while both boats were loose and moving around. Some people just stayed on the big boat rather than attempt this.

It was a long drop from the deck of the big boat down into a canoe that only held eight people. Once in the canoe, we had to climb over benches to the farthest one, flip the back of the bench up and then sit down and hope the whole thing didn't capsize. I was not happy about having signed up for this, but it was too late to turn back.

There had to be at least 70 people on this tour. Once each canoe was full, it motored away into the darkness. The guide sat at the very front of the canoe with a strong flashlight scanning the grassy banks. With hand signals, he directed the driver at the back where to turn, when to slow down, and when to stop.

Occasionally the canoe pulled all the way into some tall grass and the guide actually got out and walked around barefoot holding his flashlight. Most of the time he returned empty handed and we moved on to conduct our search on another grassy bank.

Once he came back carrying a young caiman. He put a rubber band around the snout and tried to pass it back and forth so everyone could hold it and take photos. I was among the less enthusiastic about this especially when he said this young caiman would grow to a length of seven feet. What if this little fella's mother saw her child being taken and jumped into our canoe after it? The canoe sat low enough in the water that it was surely possible. I tried hard not to think about this. The caiman's back legs were much longer than the front ones and all four legs scrambled around looking for land. Up close it looked like something from "Jurassic Park". After everyone had seen enough, the guide took off the rubber band, and slid it back into the river so it could go back home.

At one point, I saw something out of the corner of my eye jump out of the water and into our canoe. It smacked the lady behind me in the face. She screamed, "It's still in the boat! I don't know what it is but it's still in the boat!" Some people thought it was a frog, and some said it was too dark to see anything. I thought it was a fish of some kind, but then it didn't smack *me* in the face. The guide said not to worry, it was probably a sardine. Well, I've only seen sardines in a can and this was a whole lot bigger. He said Amazon sardines can be eight or ten inches long. Jumping sardines? Whatever it was, somehow it found its way back into the water and eventually we all settled down. I really had the willies after that.

Getting out of the canoe was harder than getting in. None of us had any sense of dignity left after we allowed ourselves to be pushed from below and yanked upward onto the deck of the big boat. I felt a lot better once all the canoe business was over and we were back on the cruise ship again.

MORE CANOES

The morning after the caiman search, we left early for a "Meeting of the Waters" tour to the place where the dark Black River and the light brown Solimões River converge but don't mix together. It was like a straight line was drawn in the water, dark on one side and light on the other. I had never seen anything like it.

This area is part of the Central Amazon Conservation Complex, a UNESCO World Heritage Site that includes the majority of the ecosystems in the Amazon. It is home to pink Amazon dolphins, caiman, electric fish, manatee, otters, abundant birdlife, and innumerable other species but we didn't see much in the way of wildlife. Giant green and pink, tray-like lily pads also grow here. Didn't see those either.

My heart sank when I realized we would have to go through the big boat-little canoe routine again. The only difference today was that our little canoe was red instead of green, and we'd be doing this in the daylight. The rest was a repeat of climbing over the benches, eight people to a canoe. Water levels were low everywhere so there was no getting around it.

We saw a lot of houses on stilts along the shore. The guide on the boat explained that the people who live in the houses on the river have to move from the main level to the top level of their houses as the river rises during the wet season. Eventually they have to leave until the water goes down far enough that they can move back into the top level. He wasn't clear about where all these people go when that happens. When they come back to live in the top level, they find anacondas and fish in the lower levels. The hillsides along the river continue to erode, so eventually the houses fall away. It never occurred to me that there are so many people in the world who live like this.

Maybe because I knew what I was in for, getting into the little canoe didn't seem as hard this time. Maybe the daylight had something to do with it. Before our canoe motored away from the big boat, I watched one of the guides trying to explain to the remaining passengers how to get down into their canoe. They looked skeptical and I couldn't blame them.

I began to relax when I saw a man moving his canoe along with a pole. I thought the water couldn't be very deep if he were able to do that, right? Our canoe caravan made its way slowly through the ribbons of color and down the muddy Solimões River. Then I noticed that the dock we were approaching was way too high for anyone to reach from our canoe. At least we were aiming for a semi-solid structure next to a building instead of another floating boat. Most of us needed help making it onto the dock. It was all very undignified.

Inside the building on the dock was a gift shop, some restrooms, and a small bar. The local people working there waited until it looked like everyone bought all they were going to buy, then one of them led us up a long rickety wooden walkway propped up on slender stilts. From there we walked into the forest to where the giant lily pads were.

This walkway was pretty high off the ground and needed some serious reinforcement. It swayed and creaked as we walked, but we just kept going and tried not to think about how many people it could safely hold. Nobody told us that we had missed lily pad season and there weren't any left. No wildlife. No birds.

Getting back into our canoe afterwards was either easier or I was getting the hang of this. On our way back down the river, we saw two small children running down a hill on the nearby shore toward the canoes. Then a motorboat appeared out of nowhere and my first thought was we're being attacked by Amazon pirates and the children were a distraction so that we would slow down. Two of the canoes in front of us did slow down. As the children got closer to the river, we could see that the girl held a sloth and the boy carried a big snake. The guys in the motorboat had an anaconda and one of them was collecting money from the people in the other canoes who took pictures of the anaconda and the children.

All of the wildlife in this area are protected and not to be disturbed. We had seen uniformed men in military boats boarding private boats earlier in the day. If the Brazilian authorities had come by, they would have arrested not only the guy with the anaconda, but also the drivers of the canoes for stopping. Our canoe went around all of this and kept going. Our guide said the Brazilian authorities were always on patrol in these waters looking for illegal wildlife activity so they're pretty serious about it.

We made one more climb from the canoe up into the big boat and headed back to the cruise ship. By this time I was ready to start sailing back toward the Atlantic. Maybe the colorful parrots and toucans that I had hoped to see here live in a different part of the Amazon that we can visit on another trip. We sure didn't see any of them here. I'm still very glad we came. It's an amazing part of the world.

KOMODO DRAGONS IN INDONESIA

Seeing Komodo dragons in the wild is one of those things that could be terrific or terrifying, depending on your individual experience. They only live on this island. No place else.

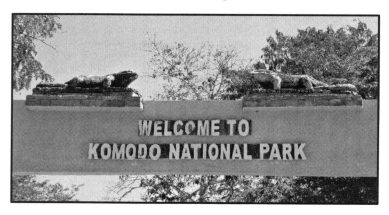

The ship provided a great deal of information about this island before we arrived. No one could go on shore independently. It was only allowed with a tour guide. Anyone wearing red or anyone with a cut or open sore was not allowed off the ship. Once we were assigned to a guide, it was not permitted to leave the group under any circumstances.

On shore we were organized into small groups with one guide at the front, one in the middle and one at the back. Each guide carried a pronged stick in case one of the dragons got too close. I wondered how effective a stick could be against a ten foot reptile weighing 150 pounds but I didn't ask. Komodo dragons eat almost anything including Timor deer, water buffalo. and each other. They also build very big nests for their eggs.

After about 45 minutes of walking, we reached the watering hole where about ten massive reptiles were hanging around. The guide drew a line in the sand with his stick and said, "Do not cross this line." Everyone instinctively took a step backwards. The dragons were not very active because it was midday and very hot. However, we were warned that one could take off in an instant without warning. We didn't stay long enough to find out. After everyone took their photos, we returned to the village.

A small outdoor bar had been set up near the pier so we stopped for a nice cold beer. The people who live on this island are descendants of convicts that were sent here in the 1800s. The villagers are mostly fishermen, and they also raise chickens and goats. The dragons are known to help themselves to these food sources. A friend from the ship talked to the bartender who showed her a video he had taken the previous day of a dragon that tore out of the jungle and grabbed a deer by the leg. The dragon ate pieces of the deer while it was still alive.

SAFARI IN TANZANIA

Words are not adequate to describe the abundance of wildlife in Africa. The itinerary we chose for our safari week in 2006 enabled us to have our own jeep and driver who was also our guide, so when we wanted to spend an hour watching a massive herd of elephants stroll by or enjoy the baby lions resting against the tires of our jeep in the shade or allow ourselves to be hypnotized by zebra stripes as hundreds of them surrounded us, we could do so as long as we reached our next lodge before dark. At Lake Manyara thousands of flamingoes made the lake look pink from a distance. Near the border of Kenya we caught the end of the wildebeest migration that turned the landscape from light tan to dark brown from the sheer number of these animals.

One day we passed a starving lioness near the side of the road. She had broken her leg and could no longer hunt. Her ribs stuck out under her scraggly fur and it was clear she would soon die from lack of food or become food herself.

One evening on our way to the lodge our driver spotted a bleeding man lying near the road. He told us to stay in the jeep while he went over to him. The man was a government tracker who had caught some poachers but he was attacked by a lion before he could arrest them. Deep claw marks were clearly visible through his torn shirt on the side of his body. Another jeep with two men in it stopped shortly after we did. Our driver helped them get him into the back seat and they took him to the nearest town.

Our guide kept reminding us that we must stay inside the jeep unless he said it was okay to get out.

LEMURS AT NOSY KOMBA

The ship excursion to see the lemurs of Madagascar was sold out when we tried to sign up so when the woman at the excursions desk called to let us know of a cancellation, we were thrilled. Then she called again later in the day to tell me that she had picked up a bag of almonds for us to feed to the lemurs because we had waited so long to get on the tour. She said the lemurs were very much accustomed to people and we would get better photos if we fed them.

We had read descriptions of several different independent tours to see the lemurs and the ship tour sounded like it would be the safest and least strenuous The tour description explained that we would take a tender boat to the pier on the island of Nosy Be. We would then go down some steps to board the individual boats to Nosy Komba. Please note, the description read, that the guides here do not speak much English; the pier is wooden, the steps are slippery and some steps may be missing; arrival in Nosy Komba will be a "wet landing" as there is no pier. We will climb over the side of the boat into the water which will be up to our knees and slog over to shore, then walk 700 meters through the forest to the sanctuary. Should be exciting, we thought.

While I was reading the above description, a travel program about Nosy Be was on our stateroom TV. The announcer said the island is home to various species of spiders and snakes of "remarkable dimensions". It's probably good that we were going directly to the sanctuary and not hiking very far through the big forest here. We didn't want to come back with any bites of remarkable dimensions. This island is also home to the "elephant bird", the largest bird that has ever lived, according to the announcer. I had never heard of an elephant bird but planned to take a photo if I saw one.

Unfortunately the port on Madagascar had to be cancelled due to strong headwinds and heavy currents. We'll never know how exciting this tour would have been. Ed and I got over our disappointment fairly quickly and decided to take a tour at the next port in Zanzibar to a forest where red colobus monkeys live. At the time it was the next best thing to seeing lemurs. When I went down to book it, the woman at the excursions desk told me that she ate the almonds.

AGGRESSIVE DEER ON MIYAJIMA ISLAND

Miyajima is considered one of the three most scenic spots in Japan and was easy to reach by ferry boat from Hiroshima.

The big attraction on the island is the bright red Torii Gate 200 meters offshore. It was built in the year 1168. At high tide, it looks like it's floating. The historic commercial center of the island is small but filled with charming shops and interesting street food.

Miyajima is also home to a strange breed of small and mangy looking deer. We watched one try to eat a tourist's lunch. The woman kept pushing it away and it kept coming back. They are not timid like most deer. In fact, the warning on the front of the brochure about the island said: "ATTENTION: The deer on Miyajima are wild. They may eat paper and cloth. Please pay attention and keep an eye on your belongings - especially tickets and souvenirs as the deer might eat them." These deer were everywhere and they weren't shy. We saw several of them during our time on the island and after watching one try to bite its way into a lady's purse, we can confirm that the brochure was very accurate.

JUMPING CROCODILES

Our boat trip to see the jumping crocodiles in Australia's Adelaide River was a 90 minute bus ride out of Darwin. Crocodile warnings were everywhere around here. The ship newsletter warned us not to walk on any beaches even if there were no crocodile warnings. They can come out of nowhere really fast and they eat people. Quickly.

Along the road, the driver pulled over so we could see some of the birds. The jabiru standing nearby had yellow eyes, knees that were backwards, and a pointed beak that was so sharp, it could stab a crocodile in the neck. It looked big, even from the bus. The guide told us more stories about people getting eaten by crocodiles than I could count. In the wetlands visitors center, a display of headlines from the local newspaper made me wonder if they were all true.

The crocodiles here can grow up to twelve feet and even longer. They also have lots and lots of pointed teeth. And I thought the Komodo dragons were scary.

The Adelaide River was very wide but there were no other boats around. Too many crocodiles evidently. Our boat ride started out with lots of warnings. Wherever you're sitting now is your seat for the entire ride. No moving around the boat. No sticking hands and feet between the bars on the sides of the boat. No leaning over the rails. If a croc jumps out of the water and grabs your hand, you'll be lucky if all it does is pull your arm out of the socket. Otherwise, it will pull you under the water until you drown, then drag you ashore until it's hungry enough to start eating. Believe it or not, people still tried walking around the boat and were hanging over the rails to get photos until the guide threatened to end the tour and take the boat right back to the dock.

It's hard to imagine, but these guys made the Komodo dragons look small.

MORE AUSTRALIAN WILDLIFE

During our first visit to Sydney, we booked an independent wildlife tour. Our guide, Liam, picked us up at our hotel at 11:15 in the morning. The tour wasn't scheduled to end until around midnight which gave us a chance to see the nocturnal animals as well.

Our first stop was along a country road to watch a "mob" of kangaroos hopping around in the wild. They went about their daily business without paying much attention to us. Liam was a wonderful guide. He made sure we had our fill of kangaroos before we piled back into the van.

Everyone was excited about seeing koalas and Liam assured us there would be many of them in the nearby eucalyptus forest. He parked the van and we walked up and down the dirt road scanning the treetops while our guide trekked into the forest and back out again. No koalas.

We trudged back to the van, hanging our heads in disappointment. Then, just as we were driving out of the forest, Liam hit the brakes and shouted, "There's one!" He turned the van around, parked it and we couldn't get out fast enough. I have no idea how he was able to see it up in the tree but we were delighted that he did. Liam explained that koalas have strong, razor-sharp claws that can cause severe injuries. Koalas can't tell the difference between a human leg and a tree trunk and can tear your leg to shreds with those claws. They can also bite tremendously hard. Although they may appear docile, they are capable of lashing out very quickly when threatened so we needed to stay quiet and not make any sudden moves just in case.

The group had no luck with platypus or wombats but saw some wallabies and possum later in day. Believe it or not, the highlight of this terrific tour wasn't the wildlife. It was the stars. Before we left the area for the drive back to Sydney, Liam pulled over so we could get out and look at the sky. It was magnificent. The Southern Cross and Milky Way were crystal clear. It will be a long time before I see stars like that again, if ever.

GLOW WORMS IN WAITANGI

The glow worm cave is on Maori land in New Zealand and everyone who works there belongs to the same Maori tribe. Our tour group numbered around 25 and every fourth person was given a lantern to carry. I made sure to stay right behind a lantern carrier. My night vision is terrible.

Glow worms are actually the larvae stage of flying insects that are similar to mosquitos. They thrive in dark, damp places and spin a sticky silk attachment that serves as a hammock allowing the worms to hang from the cave ceiling. The glow comes from a chemical reaction powered by their protein rich diet. It attracts tiny insects that get caught in the silk and become dinner.

The Maoris consider this a sacred site, so no photos beyond the entrance were allowed. We took as many as we could until our guide said no more pictures. The cave was full of ramps, stairways, and ladders. When we reached an area with a low ceiling, the guide told everyone to turn off the lanterns. It was like standing under a canopy of stars. The worms are the size of a wooden matchstick but all you can see is the blue glow of the tail. Some glows twinkled and some were steady. I stood in awe gazing at the ceiling until my neck hurt.

Nature is amazing.

WILDLIFE IN DUNEDIN

Dunedin was the last stop in New Zealand on our world cruise and I hated to leave this lovely country so soon. Warm, welcoming people, lots of beautiful scenery, and clean free restrooms. We spent the day with our guide Jane from Elm Wildlife Tours and four other people.

I had never heard of Dunedin before this trip but learned that it is the home of the first university in New Zealand, established in 1869. There are 140,000 people in this city and 25,000 of them attend the University, which is the largest employer here. It was settled by the Scottish, which is reflected in architecture and some say in the weather as well. It's one of the few places in New Zealand that has a kilt shop, a pipe band and haggis ceremonies.

We drove out to the Otago Peninsula to visit the only mainland breeding colony of royal albatross in the world. They can only be seen on a guided tour with a small group using timed entry tickets to the steep hillside nesting areas.

Albatross can fly at speeds of 75 mph with a wingspan of almost ten feet, twice the spread arms of the average person. Because their wings are so big, they need a lot of wind in order to fly very far. Late in the day we caught a glimpse of one in the air. It was magnificent.

Four albatross nests were visible, one with a newly hatched chick. These birds mate for life and have an amazing life cycle. Females lay at the most one egg a year. Parents share incubation duty over a period of eleven weeks. Hatching takes three days, then parents take turns feeding and sitting on the chick for several months. The unbelievable part of this is how big the chick gets. At seven months old, the chick weighs 20 pounds! The average adult albatross is 22-26 pounds. Our guide passed around a life sized stuffed chick. It was heavier than any toddler I've ever lifted. We even got a peek at one of the chicks when the mother stood up for a second to rearrange herself.

Afterwards Jane was waiting for us in the van with our box lunches which we ate on our way to our next stop, the sheep farm. The tour company had an arrangement with a sheep farmer who grants the tour groups access to his private beach. The wind along the coast is so strong that the trees grow sideways.

There are 100,000 black swans in New Zealand. I think we saw most of them on the way to the farm along with many spoonbills and oystercatchers. I have no idea how many sheep this farmer had, but it could have easily exceeded the number of black swans in New Zealand.

At the farm, we transferred to a four wheel drive jeep for the last part of the drive through the mud. A long rough stairway led down to a rocky beach where we visited a colony of fur seals. There were more seals than I could count and they paid no attention to us. Jane lured us away with descriptions of sea lions, yellow-eyed penguins, and blue penguins on the next beach. We had to go all the way back up to the top of the cliff, take a short ride in the jeep and go down another trail with more stairs. I was so glad I wore my heavy hiking boots.

Blue penguins typically spend their day in the sea and come ashore at dusk. The sheep farmer built nesting boxes for them. Some use the boxes and others prefer to dig their own burrows for their eggs. Only one of the four burrows we passed on the trail was occupied.

Down on the beach, huge sea lions were napping. It was such a unique experience to have this vast beach all to ourselves with wildlife that had no fear of us. One even waved as we walked by. Even the birds didn't skitter away. We crossed the beach and climbed another stairway to the area where the yellow-eyed penguins were nesting. By this time my legs were getting rubbery.

At the top, a small wooden structure enabled us to peer into a hollow under the trees to catch a glimpse of a yellow-eyed penguin chick. These are the rarest of the world's 18 species of penguins and they are found only in New Zealand. They are very shy so we had to stay quiet. A camera focused on the nest below gave us a great view but the nest was empty. Jane suspected that the chick had grown large enough to fend for itself. At that point the parents stop coming back with food so the chick will get hungry enough to leave the nest and find its own food. She spotted it under the brush and said it appeared to be okay but was probably apprehensive about leaving the nest alone.

When it was time to head back, Jane gave us the bad news that there was no way to reach the jeep from here, even though we were close to the top of the cliff. We had to go all the way back down to the beach, across to the trail we had come down, and hike back up again. We took our time and stopped for conversation along the way. Jane was so knowledgeable and clearly loved her work. It was a joy to spend the day with her.

During the ride back, Jane asked twice about stopping at a pub for a beer before returning to the ship. It would have been fun but we were all so tired and Ed and I couldn't remember what time we were supposed to be back. Good thing we declined. The gangway was pulled up five minutes after we boarded.

WALKING AMONG THE PENGUINS IN THE FALKLAND ISLANDS

Bad weather is common in the Falklands. They only have about 70 days of sunshine a year and we were lucky enough to get one of them. We had booked a wonderful independent full day tour to ride in a 4 x 4 jeep to Volunteer Point where thousands of gentoo, magellanic and king penguins live. I could hardly wait to get started.

Only about 3,000 people live in the Falklands, 75% of them in Port Stanley which feels very British. Once we left the city, the roads were no longer paved. They went from asphalt to packed dirt to sandy dirt to no road at all. The last half of the ride was off road and beyond bumpy, but it was great. The people who drive for the tour company use their own jeeps and travel out to Volunteer Point in a caravan. At least one jeep usually gets stuck somewhere in the bog so they all have winches.

Ed rode up front with our guide and driver while I rode in the back with a woman we knew from the ship. Our guide told us there have been times when a cruise ship anchors in the bay, sends small tender boats full of passengers ashore and the weather changes so drastically so fast that they can't get back to the ship. When this happens, people in Port Stanley open their homes to accommodate as many as they can, feed the stranded passengers and give them a place to sleep until the tenders can return. Sometimes it can take a couple of days until it's safe again.

The journey to the penguin colony involved driving twelve miles through the bog with no marked road. The drivers make this trip almost every day as long as there are tourists who want to go but I have no idea how they knew the way. There must have been landmarks that I couldn't see. Each driver had an old CB radio (no cell phone reception out there) and they talked to each other frequently along the way. As bumpy and bouncy as this ride was, it was delightful.

Before we could walk near the penguins, we dipped our shoes into a foot bath to prevent carrying anything into the fields that might harm them. It looked icky but it wasn't very deep.

And suddenly, there they were. Thousands of them! Everywhere! Words cannot describe what a thrill it was to be surrounded by wildlife like this. The whole experience was magical. They weren't shy and didn't hesitate to come close to get a good look at us. Some were building nests while others sat on the eggs they had recently laid. Some parents were giving swimming lessons.

The king penguins were really interested in what Ed had to say. It looked like he was conducting a training class and one student stayed afterwards to ask a question.

Groups of penguins waddled down to the edge of the sea and it appeared that they really wanted to go in but were hesitant. Then one of them spotted a hungry sea lion looking for his next meal. After some lively discussion they decided to head back to shore. It was like watching a National Geographic film only we were really there.

If I had to make a list of the most memorable experiences of my travels, this would be right at the top. It was one of the best days ever.

GIFTS FROM MOTHER NATURE

FLYING UMBRELLAS IN IRELAND

It was a wet windy foggy day when we visited the Cliffs of Moher and there were very few visitors. Our private driver handed us an old umbrella that he kept in his trunk. He said we'd have to hold onto it tightly but if it got away from us, well, it wouldn't be the first umbrella to fly over the cliffs.

Not only did we see an umbrella or two go over the edge but we also watched a few plastic ponchos get shredded by the wind and fly right off the backs of a group of shrieking tourists.

POT OF GOLD AT THE END OF THE RAINBOW

Urquhart Castle on the banks of Loch Ness is one of the most visited castles in Scotland. Loch Ness has more fresh water in it than all of the lakes in England and Wales combined. That's a lot of water.

During our visit, the weather changed throughout the afternoon from sunny to drizzly and back again with multiple rainbows in different parts of the sky. I'd never seen so many rainbows in such a short time. One rainbow completed a full arc over the lake. Our guide said he'd get the scuba gear out of the bus if anyone wanted to go after the pot of gold at the end of that one.

Nobody took him up on it so maybe it's still down there.

DROUGHT IN SOUTH AFRICA

In 2018, the water shortage in Cape Town was severe. Before visiting, I had read an article online about landscapers, car wash workers and others who had lost their jobs because there was no water available for these services. Experiencing it was quite different from reading about it. In public restrooms, gray water was used to flush the toilets and the sink taps were all turned off. Signs encouraging use of hand sanitizers were everywhere but many restrooms didn't have any. Billboards along the roads begged people to limit their showers to two minutes.

I talked with a young woman in the city about the water situation and asked her when it had rained last. She thought for a minute and said she couldn't remember but she was sure it before Christmas. That was on February 8.

BLOWING DUST IN JORDAN

Our guide in Jordan explained that the Kings Highway and the Desert Highway were once caravan routes that were used to carry goods and spices from the port in Aqaba to Amman and to settlements along the Dead Sea.

During the month of May, the winds really kick up along these highways. Visibility gets so bad from blowing sand that tour buses can be delayed as much as eight hours. Good thing we were there in February.

SNOW AND ICE ON THE GREAT WALL OF CHINA

The Great Wall extends 5,500 miles and has over 7,000 lookout towers. It was started by the same Emperor Qin who was buried in Xian but most of the wall was completed during the Ming Dynasty between 1368 and 1644, partly for defense and partly to collect taxes along the Silk Road. It is an engineering marvel.

When we boarded our flight in Xian after seeing the Terra Cotta Warriors, the weather was warm and sunny. By the time we landed in Beijing, it was winter. A sandstorm from the Gobi desert blew through the day before which cleared the smog from the air in the city but also caused the temperature to drop 45 degrees. The weather continued to get worse as our bus took us higher through the hills toward the wall.

Because of the snow and ice at the top, the tram we had planned to take was closed but our guide was able to convince the operator to open it for us. We bravely ventured out on icy steps and walkways at the top of the wall. Many people just rode the tram up, stuck their heads out to look at the wall, took photos and rode back down again. Not us. We had to venture out a little farther. It's hard to describe what it was like to stand on the Great Wall of China. We couldn't just turn around and go back down right away. Ed set out on his own and walked farther than I did. It was steep, uneven, slippery, and snow was blowing into our eyes. Visibility was very poor and it was getting dark. Despite all of that, it was fantastic.

We were the last visitors to come down on the final tram of the day and we really didn't want to leave. The guide waited for us and we walked down the street together to the restaurant reserved for our group's cocktail party and elaborate Chinese dinner. Many people grumbled about the miserable experience at the Great Wall, but we wouldn't have traded that cold snowy night for anything.

BAD WEATHER IN EAST CHINA SEA

After our cruise ship left China, we had the roughest weather we had ever experienced. Stacks of seasick bags were placed all over the ship along with crystalized ginger and plenty of ginger ale. The ship was so big and felt so secure that I wasn't nervous at all. I had complete confidence in the captain and crew. As I sat in the lounge on Deck 10 which is comparable to the tenth story of a building, the waves were hitting the windows. It was even rougher in the evening with winds over 50 mph.

Good thing we didn't have a juggler scheduled for that night's entertainment.

PASSING BY WHITE ISLAND

As our ship cruised along the coast of New Zealand, we heard an announcement that we would soon be passing White Island, where several people had recently died while hiking around the crater when the volcano erupted unexpectedly.

Someone asked the General Manager who was on the outside deck with us if the ship could get closer so we could see it better. He called the captain but was told that getting any closer to the island would not be safe and he wasn't willing to risk it.

The volcano was still belching with lots of smoke and ash in the air. It really looked eerie and almost sinister.

FLOODS, FIRES AND DROUGHT ALL IN ONE DAY

After our cruise ship left Tasmania, passengers received the bad news that we would not be able to stop in Melbourne as scheduled. A bad storm off the east coast of Australia would cause our ship to have to slow down so much that we would be very late arriving in Sydney unless we headed directly there.

Sydney was the end of a segment so arriving late would cause disembarking passengers to miss their flights home and delay the boarding of new passengers. The captain had no choice but to skip Melbourne and arrive in Sydney one day early. We wouldn't avoid the storm completely but we would at least be sure to reach Sydney on time this way and would stay for three days instead of two. Hours of strong winds, heavy seas and very rough weather followed this announcement.

Before leaving home, we had scheduled a full day independent wildlife tour for February 11, starting at noon. This was the same tour we took the previous year and we enjoyed it so much that we wanted to do it again. A few days before the Sydney schedule change, the ship announced a passenger event at the Sydney Opera House, also for February 11. Once we learned about our arrival in Sydney one day earlier than planned, we moved the wildlife tour to February 10. It was scheduled to leave at noon and return to the city around 10:30 pm which enabled everyone to see the nocturnal animals. We could still attend the Opera House event the next day. It sounded like it would work out perfectly.

The next day the wildlife tour company sent an email saying that the weather in Sydney was so bad they would have to cancel the February 10 tour. We were disappointed but the tour would not be safe because of heavy flooding and winds that continued to blow down trees. As it turned out, it was a good thing it was cancelled. We didn't arrive in Sydney until noon which would have been too late for our pickup. We would have missed the tour anyway. At least this way we were able to get a full refund.

The previous year in Sydney, we had eaten in a German restaurant in The Rocks neighborhood. We were able to find it again and the owner of the restaurant told us he wasn't even able to open the day before because this area had flooded so badly. The warehouse across the street that had been converted into shops also flooded and most of the stores were still closed. A lot of serious water damage there.

On top of all that, wildfires were ranging in the mountains nearby as well. We thought our mountain tour the following day would be cancelled but learned it was still possible to visit the areas that weren't burning and weren't affected by the storm. We headed up into the Blue Mountains, an area the size of Hong Kong that encompasses several national parks. The entire area had the most bizarre mix of weather. The bus took us through a new five mile tunnel that had floods on one side while the other side had wildfires, and the city we had just left still suffered from drought.

Our guide told us that the main reservoir that provides Sydney with water was down to 45% before it finally started to rain. Even though the level had come back to 70%, the city still charged fines for using a hose on your lawn. Only watering cans were allowed and only on vegetable gardens. No car washing. No flower beds. It was too hard to predict when it would rain again so the water they had needed to be conserved.

CROSSING THE INTERNATIONAL DATE LINE AND THE CHALLENGES OF TIME ZONES

Traveling has a way of messing up one's concept of time, especially when our cruise ship was in Asia where it seemed we were constantly moving our clocks back and forth. I had various conversations with different people about how the whole International Date Line thing works and quickly learned that I wasn't the only one who was confused. Interestingly the date line is not determined by international law and it isn't straight so that it doesn't divide any country or territory unnecessarily. The daily newsletter on the ship contained a full page explanation, but by the time I was done reading it, I was more mixed up than ever. When we crossed the date line in 2018, we had two May 23rds.

During our second world cruise in 2019, we traveled in the opposite direction. On that trip January 20 was actually a non-day. We skipped it completely when we crossed the date line. The Cruise Director said we should be well rested because we went to sleep on Sunday night and woke up on Tuesday.

Each country is free to decide the date and time zone they want to observe. That explains why our clocks were going back and forth so much in Asia. We had to be on the same time as the port we were heading toward, or our tour schedules would be all messed up.

As our cruise ship approached India, we were instructed to move our clocks forward one half hour. I had never heard of this. Whenever we changed our clocks, it had always been a full hour at a time. A tour guide in Mangalore told us that the half hour time zone business is

India's way of thumbing its nose at Great Britain. It's been this way since India obtained their independence. All of India is one time zone. China is also all one time zone even though it's big enough for six US time zones.

We later learned that there are other time zones in the world that are offset by 30 or even 45 minutes instead of a full hour. All this time zone business got straightened out when we were back in international waters but it sure was confusing.

As we sailed around the tip of South America, it got colder as we traveled south and warmer again as we came north, the exact opposite of home. During our winter when we were in the southern hemisphere, it was warm. We weren't accustomed to sweating in January. Although there weren't many time changes in South America, the sunrise and sunset times varied widely as we traveled.

We also learned that in 2011, Samoa decided to change their time zone by two hours. They shifted the dateline to the west and removed December 30 from the calendar that year. They did this to facilitate trade with Australia and New Zealand. Who knew that such things were going on in the world such a short time ago?

When we left the coast of Greenland heading toward Canada, we had exactly 12 hours of daylight and 12 hours of night: sunrise at 7:05 am and sunset at 7:05 pm. Somehow, I expected that sort of thing to happen at the equator. Evidently, I was wrong.

Ever wonder where the Pacific Ocean got its name? When Ferdinand Magellan crossed this ocean 500 years ago, he named it "Mar Pacifico" or "peaceful sea". The people onboard our cruise ship who were suffering from seasickness would probably disagree with the accuracy of this name but there it is.

MORE TIME CHANGE CONFUSION IN CANADA

At 2:00 in the afternoon on the day we emerged from the St Lawrence River, we changed our clocks one hour ahead to Atlantic Standard Time, the time zone of Nova Scotia. Previous time changes had always occurred during the night, not in the middle of the afternoon. It sounded like a good idea to avoid disrupting everyone's sleep, but it made the afternoon schedule a bit tricky. Neither of us realized exactly how this worked.

It happened on a sea day, so Ed planned to play bridge at 2:00 like every other sea day. Because the time changed at 2:00, bridge actually started at 1:00 so that when the clocks moved ahead, the group would finish playing at the usual end time of 4:30. By the time he got there, everyone in the bridge room had already been playing for an hour. Nothing worse than being late for a game of bridge.

It was the only time the captain tried to change the time in the middle of the day. It seemed like a good idea, but everyone on board got too confused. We never did it that way again.

CAUGHT IN A FLOOD ON THE WAY HOME FROM WORK

In September of 2013 Denver experienced three straight days of what the weather forecasters called "rain of biblical proportions". On my way to work the morning of the third day of rain, a large intersection that I normally drive through was already filled with high water.

Later that morning, my boss recommended that I pack up my laptop and work from home the rest of the day. The rain had stopped but more heavy rain was expected in the afternoon, so it was a good time to leave. Unfortunately the rain picked up again shortly after I left.

Because of all the high water I had encountered on the way in, I took a different route home. I was about halfway there when I drove through an intersection and saw water pouring down a hill from an apartment complex pond that was overflowing and filling the road in front of me. A raised median strip was on my left and a large pickup truck was in the lane to my right. I had nowhere to go but through the water. I didn't get very far when the engine stalled and the car wouldn't restart.

Soon water started coming in under the doors soaking my feet. The car still wouldn't start. I could feel it moving around in the water and it was only a matter of time before it floated into another car.

Traffic was lining up behind me. I put on the emergency flashers and gathered my belongings. When I got out of the car, the water was over my knees and still rising. My umbrella was useless.

I made my way to the sidewalk near a parking lot for the community college and called Ed. Luckily, he was still home. He left his car a few blocks from the college and walked the rest of the way. Two guys helped him push my car out of the deep water and into the parking lot. When we got home, I called the college security office to explain what had happened and told them we would come back to pick up the car when the rain stopped. No problem, they said. Come back and pick it up whenever you're ready. We probably weren't the only ones who had to abandon a stalled car that day.

In the evening, the car still wouldn't start. Letting it dry out until the following morning didn't help either so we had it towed. The mechanic said the mucky water I drove through got sucked into the engine through the air filter and the car was ruined. I was sick.

This car was a ten year old classic silver Jaguar, the only car in my life that I could say I loved and enjoyed driving. It didn't take long for the insurance adjuster to look at it. The engine was totaled but the body was in good shape, it had new tires, and even had full tank of gas. The adjuster said it was a model that would appeal to a collector and gave us more than we expected.

A co-worker drove me to the office the next day while Ed went car shopping. He found a car he thought I would like and picked me up after work to look at it. I was so upset. I didn't want a new car; I just wanted my Jaguar back. Tears were running down my cheeks as I walked around the showroom. The salesman took me to his desk, brought me a cup of coffee, and told me all about the old Jeep he used to have that he hated to part with. Finally I agreed to drive the car Ed picked out and we took it home. It turned out to be a very good car and I drove it for eight years.

Panic attacks and bad dreams about deep water continued long after this accidental adventure. High water on the road still scares me.

RAIN AT NEW YORK HIGHPOINT

Our very first state highpoint was Mt Marcy in upstate New York in the summer of 1990. It was also our first overnight backpacking trip. It rained.

The trail quickly became muddy and slick which slowed us down, and the skies darkened early. Flashlights didn't help us find the camping area we had marked on the trail map. We had to keep walking until we could find someplace flat enough to pitch the tent where the forest wasn't too dense. Finally we heard voices and then saw the flickering light of a campfire.

After we set up the tent and crawled inside, I took off my soaking wet shoes and socks to reveal nasty blisters on both feet. I glared at Ed and said, "Don't ever make me do this again". The next morning, sunshine, dry socks and bandages improved my attitude. We made it to the top and climbed many more highpoints after that.

FOG AT VERMONT HIGHPOINT

We managed to squeeze in a cluster of New England highpoints on a long weekend. The most memorable of these was in Vermont. The hike was only about two and a half miles, but it was a cold rainy day and Mt Mansfield was covered with dark clouds. The trail was often nothing more than slabs of rock resembling steps of varying dimensions that went on and on. This would have made for slow going on a dry day, but the rocks were muddy and slick from the morning rain. It bordered on treacherous.

Thankfully the top was fairly level but it was so foggy up there that we could hardly see each other let alone find the USGS marker. After much wandering around and constantly calling out to one another to avoid getting lost, we found the marker and took a picture that turned out to be mostly white haze.

Going back down was worse. One slip on those muddy rocks would probably have resulted in broken bones. It took us all day to complete the "short" highpoint of Vermont but we were happy to have done it without incident. This one is on the list of highpoints we aren't likely do again.

FIRE AT WYOMING HIGHPOINT

Like several of the western states, reaching Wyoming's highpoint is a long arduous trek. Ed always said Gannett Peak was the most beautiful highpoint, but it's also the most remote. Getting to the top of Gannett required a 54 mile round trip hike because the nearest road is so far away. Ed tried it twice before making it to the top on his third attempt. Each time he hiked with a different group of climbers.

The third group rented mules to carry their backpacks. The rancher who rented out the mules warned Ed and his climbing partners that it was the first trip out in the wilderness for these mules after the long winter and they would likely try to break loose and run back to the ranch. It wasn't long before Ed's hands had to be bandaged because they were covered with rope burns from trying to hold onto those mules.

High fire danger further complicated this climb. It was a tough decision to go forward with it because wildfires can be so unpredictable. Shortly after they started out, the trailhead was closed because of a nearby wildfire that was spreading fast. They were able to reach the summit, although it took longer than they had planned. On the way back out, smoke surrounded them. Dry trees and shrubs burst into flames in an instant, frightening the mules as well as the climbers. They were able to continue moving, keep the mules under control, and somehow, they managed it back to the trailhead safely.

Clearly Ed has more than nine lives.

LIGHTNING AT COLORADO HIGHPOINT

Our oldest son, Michael, died suddenly on April 14, 2001. His wife of 18 months said he had told her that when he died, he wanted to be cremated and his ashes scattered at the top of Mt Elbert, the highest mountain in Colorado. They were highpointers too. A few months after the funeral, our daughter-in-law, her brother, and our younger daughter accompanied Ed and me to take Mike's ashes up the mountain. The eleven-mile round trip hike was slowed by our heavy hearts and we reached the summit much later than intended. We gave our daughter-in-law a few moments of peace and privacy after she emptied the box of ashes into a hole, on top of a letter she had written to him and filled it in with rocks. The pain of losing him cannot be put into words. We wanted to stay near all that was left of our Mike for as long as we could, but we had to leave the summit to avoid getting caught in the afternoon thunderstorm that was moving in fast.

We had just started down when the air around us crackled with electricity. Our daughter wore metal barrettes in her hair and kept slapping the side of her head thinking she was surrounded by the buzz of mosquitoes. Ed's metal trekking poles attracted electricity so fast that he threw them down and ran. All of us except Ed had headaches and nausea from the altitude but we had to keep moving. He dashed back to pick up his poles by their cloth wrist loops and we hurried down the trail. The storm didn't last long and we escaped injury, rattled but unharmed.

Since then, Ed has climbed Mt Elbert on his own many times, always leaving a memento for Mike under those rocks at the top. The first time he returned to that spot, he stopped for a rest and a snack along the trail and found himself surrounded by at least 30 gray jays who ate crumbs from his hand and from the tops of his knees. Some believe that spirits can come back to earth through birds when the death of the body is recent. We'd like to believe that too.

STORMY NIGHT ON A SECLUDED ISLAND

A friend and I have taken many girlfriend trips together over the years, each one different and each one enjoyable. Fox Island in Resurrection Bay near the Kenai Peninsula sounded like a beautiful pristine and unique place to spend a night during our trip to Alaska. The island was only accessible by boat and offered eight rustic cabins situated on a narrow peninsula with the bay on one side and a freshwater lagoon on the other. The dining room served gourmet meals to overnight guests. Wildlife viewing opportunities were endless here. The island had some solar power, but no internet, TV, or phones. Just a small generator and a two-way radio for emergencies.

On a dark and cloudy day, we got off the daily boat with our luggage, excited about spending a night in such a beautiful place. We put our suitcases in the corner of the large building near the dock and enjoyed a wonderful meal with about a hundred other tourists who came just for the salmon bake lunch.

After lunch a young man approached and explained that we were the only guests who would be staying overnight on the island and a strong storm was expected to blow in that night. He couldn't be sure if the boat would be able to come back for us tomorrow. The chef was the only staff person staying the night. He would be in his room above the kitchen if we needed him. Did we still want to stay? We could leave with the tour boat now but we would have to decide quickly.

This was beginning to sound like a murder mystery where the people are killed off one at a time on a dark and stormy night. We decided the opportunity to stay here wasn't likely to come along again and surely, they have strong storms up here all the time. We watched the tour boat leave the dock and tried not to regret our decision.

Our congenial chef prepared a delicious gourmet dinner for us and the wine was even better. After dinner we opened a second bottle, played board games, and got silly. Back in our cabin I fell into a deep sleep while my friend stayed awake listening to the wind howl louder and louder, wondering how much more rain could fall before the cabin started to float away. She kept getting up to look out the back window where the lagoon was overflowing with heavy rain, then went to look out the front window where the waves were growing higher and coming closer to the cabin. She said she kept asking me if I was awake and when I didn't answer, she repeatedly checked to make sure I was breathing. She couldn't understand how anyone could sleep through this. I had no trouble.

It was still raining in the morning but the worst of the storm had passed. The chef cooked a wonderful breakfast and said it looked like the boat would be able to make in as long as the wind didn't pick up again. We were able to take a walk along the beach later in the morning after the rain stopped. When the boat arrived, we joined the daily tourists for another salmon lunch before departing. The people we sat with couldn't get over how remote and secluded this island village was. Neither could we.

SANDSTORM IN NEW MEXICO

In addition to state highpoints, we have enjoyed visiting many national parks, national monuments, and other preserved lands over the years. One of those unique places was White Sands National Park, filled with otherworldly dunes made of gypsum. We parked the car at one of the trails along the loop road and began to follow the markers along the path. Initially neither of us noticed the wind picking up but when we turned around to head back, it was strong enough to blow the sand over the trail, cover the path, and bury the markers completely. It didn't take long to lose our sense of direction in the approaching storm. We were afraid to move for fear of getting farther off the path than we already were.

Imagine our relief when we were approached by two park rangers who had noticed our car in the parking area and came looking for us!

SOGGY HIKE IN COSTA RICA

Our guide in the cloud forest was very welcoming and spoke excellent English. I laughed when he said most cruise ship passengers confuse Costa Rica with Puerto Rico because the capital cities in both are San Jose. Costa Rica has 120 volcanoes and five of them are active. Five million people live here, 70% of them in the central valley around San Jose. Costa Rica boasts an impressive 98% literacy rate. The Army was abolished 51 years ago and the money was transferred to education.

Our "Walk in the Clouds" started in the pouring rain with a stop at an enclosed butterfly garden. It's very hard to take photos of butterflies when they're flitting around, especially with fogged up glasses. I thought I had two good shots until Ed pointed out that the butterflies that I had photographed were dead and that's why they weren't moving. It was a wet hike but no one seemed to mind because our guide was so good. We crossed some suspension bridges, walked down a long hill, past a river and back up again. We didn't see any wildlife because of the rain.

Occasionally, the guide could identify a bird when he heard a specific call, and then he showed us on his phone what the bird looked like. That's as close as we got. It was so foggy we could hardly see the hummingbirds. We could hear the flutter of their wings and sometimes caught a glimpse of something flitting by and, but they were really hard to see.

On the ship that evening, we forgot all about the cold wet weather and enjoyed a deliciously extravagant buffet of chocolate delights prepared by our pastry chef who said a balanced diet is a chocolate in each hand.

ROUGH VOYAGE ACROSS THE IRISH SEA

In anticipation of the rocky crossing from Liverpool to Glasgow, the stateroom stewards pushed our balcony furniture over into one corner and put tape on all the drawers in the stateroom to prevent them from sliding open on their own. They even taped the shower door closed so it wouldn't come loose, bang around, and crack the glass. Dishes of crystalized ginger appeared at every dining venue and the bars kept running out of ginger ale. Lots of seasickness was going on that night. On Oceania ships, the seasick bags are by the elevators. On Viking ships, they're in the restrooms. Seems to me if you can make it to the restroom, why fiddle around with a bag?

STRONG WINDS IN CHILE

Puerto Montt was founded in 1853 after government-sponsored immigration brought Germans here to populate and develop this region. It sits at the edge of Llanquihue Lake which is still dotted with German villages boasting "endless delights, magnificent gardens and charming architecture from Old Europe".

Too bad we weren't able to see any of it. Most of the passengers were already in the theater waiting for their tour ticket numbers to be called so they could head down to the tender platform when the General Manager announced that we would have to miss this port. Because of high winds and rough swells, the tenders could not safely take us to shore. I had been out on our balcony briefly to check the weather and saw one of the tenders bouncing all over the waves, so I wasn't surprised. The ship was actually dragging the anchor along the sea floor because the wind was so strong.

We were a bit disappointed as we were planning to spend a full day at Osorno Volcano, Petrohue Falls and the town of Puerto Varas (one of those German villages with endless delights mentioned above). However, safety comes first. We later learned that one of the crew was injured on that bouncing tender boat.

NOT PARASAILING IN MEXICO

After watching parasailers during our stop in Bali, Ed decided he wanted to parasail. Every place that he asked about this after Bali either didn't offer it, or there was too much wind, or it was too far away to get there and back before the ship left. Some ports where he expected to find parasailing opportunities weren't offering it.

In Cabo San Lucas, he picked one of several places that advertised it but was told they had to stop taking people out because the wind was too strong. After a walk through the marketplace, we went back and asked again. This time, the guy said the wind had calmed down and he could go. Ed paid for him to go up and for me to just ride on the boat and take photos. A car would pick us up in twenty minutes, shuttle us down the beach to the boat and Ed would finally get to parasail. When we went back twenty minutes later, he called the boat again to confirm and this time the current was too strong and the winds were likely to kick up again so it was still a no go.

Maybe next time.

NOT SEEING THE PANAMA CANAL

On our 2018 world cruise, we learned that when transiting the canal from the Pacific Ocean to the Atlantic Ocean via the Caribbean, a ship actually travels northwest because Central America is so tightly curved. The Panama Canal has two lanes of ships with two sets of locks at each end of the canal. Most of the eight hour transit time is spent crossing Gatun Lake, located between the locks at 85 feet above sea level.

Unfortunately we saw very little of the canal, the lake, or the locks. It rained so hard while we were there that we couldn't see out the windows all day.

NO PANORAMIC VIEWS OR STUNNING SCENERY

As our cruise ship sailed around the southern tip of New Zealand, our schedule indicated that from 10:30 - 12:00, we would take in the "panoramic views and stunning scenery" of Dusky Sound. Then from 1:30 - 2:45 pm, we would take in the "panoramic views and stunning scenery" of Doubtful Sound, followed by the "panoramic views and stunning scenery" of Milford Sound from 5:45 - 6:30. Low gray clouds followed our ship all day with much of the magnificent scenery hidden from view. The naturalist onboard assured us during his commentary throughout the day that all this rain would make the waterfalls even more spectacular. The problem was we were never able to see them through the low clouds and fog. The weather worsened by late afternoon and we had to abandon the entire area.

The heavy rain also brought flooding to the rivers that flowed into the sound, carrying so much debris that the entire area had to be closed to all marine traffic. Several towns were cut off and people had to be rescued from floodwaters. Our panoramic views and stunning scenery turned into one big mess but we were safe and that was the most important thing.

LEARNING ABOUT THE EARTHQUAKE IN CHRISTCHURCH

The port of Akaroa is a very pretty small town located on the east coast of New Zealand, surrounded by beautiful scenery. It was about an hour and a half drive from there to the city of Christchurch.

Our tour bus driver had lived in Christchurch all his life and told us a lot about what it was like during the terrible earthquake of February 2011 when 187 people died and 10,000 houses were destroyed along with 1500 commercial buildings. A red zone was set up in the city center, closing it off for 2 ½ years because it was so unsafe. Ten years later, Christchurch is still restoring and reinforcing historic buildings.

The shaking actually started in December 2010. The big event was not a rolling earthquake, but a forceful jerking of the earth back and forth that caused houses to break in half or sink up to the windows as water seeped into the sandy soil beneath them. Over 25,000 people left the city afterwards, mostly to live in a place that was not earthquake-prone or to simply recover from the trauma of living through this catastrophic event. Children were especially affected. He said 30,000 people came from all over the world to help rebuild the city. Homeowners insurance covered individual losses so people could start over but it took a long time.

The government bought the land from people whose houses were destroyed and turned it into public parks. This prevented people from rebuilding on earthquake-prone land. Until the city could work through this process, people had no choice but to stay in their damaged houses. Roads were impassable. Water and sewer systems didn't function so they set up port-a-potties wherever they could. The driver said it wasn't unusual to see people wandering the streets at night in their pajamas looking for a toilet. What a nightmare.

So often when we hear of a disaster or a tragedy somewhere in the world, we think about how terrible it is, but only for a very short time and then we move on, forgetting what it's like for those who are living through the aftermath. One new building we passed had a large sign across the top that said EVERYTHING IS GOING TO BE ALRIGHT. It put a lump in my throat.

THE WAY THINGS
ARE IS THE WAY THINGS ARE

LIVING AND WORKING IN GERMANY

Because we enjoy traveling so much, we decided to find work overseas until it was time to retire. It took over a year to land a job in a part of the world where we wanted to live. When I finally received an offer to work as the Deputy Chief of Medical Management for the US Army in Bavaria, we moved to Germany where we lived for three years.

Although it was sometimes difficult navigating everyday life in a foreign country, we wouldn't trade those years for anything. As tourists, we don't think about things like where to get license plates for the car or how to set up internet service. As residents, we often relied on the learning experiences of other Americans who were already settled and knew how to do things.

The apartment we rented was large enough for all our belongings, but the appliances were a bit challenging. Our place was on the third floor and the building had no elevator, just a winding wooden stairway that was beautiful, but long. We had a small garage in the back.

The washer and dryer, located in the basement, were smaller than even apartment sized laundry machines in the US. The dryer had a reservoir to collect the water that was spun out of the clothes before it actually started drying with heat. It saved energy but the reservoir had to be taken out after every other load, carried up the basement steps without spilling too much of the water and emptied into the flower bed outside.

These machines could only accommodate very small loads. After a while I learned to start a load in the washer when I left for work in the morning, move it to the dryer when I got home at the end of the day and bring the dry clothes upstairs after dinner. That way I had to go down all four flights and back up only once for each load of laundry.

The kitchen had an induction stove that required magnetic cookware. After moving in, we had to find a store that carried cookware, then look on the bottom of all the pots and pans until we found a set that showed the right symbol for induction energy. It took some getting used to, but we came to appreciate that this type of stove cooks everything very quickly as long as we remembered to push two different buttons at the same time. Otherwise, it didn't work at all.

We learned the hard way that some of the electric items we brought with us were not designed for 110/220 V. Only 110 V. When Ed plugged the charger for his cordless screwdriver into a converter plug and then into the wall outlet, it sent out a sudden blue flash, made a loud bang and all the electricity in the apartment went out. The landlord showed us how to reset the breaker but warned us not to try that again.

We had two TVs in our house in Denver and brought them both with us, not knowing when we packed up what size our German home would be. Both TVs turned out to be 110 V only, so we had to buy another one in Germany that we could actually use. The two TVs we brought spent three years under the guest room bed in their shipping cartons. The only English TV station that the German cable company offered was BBC News. A person can only watch so much of that, so we mostly just used the TV to watch DVD movies. The internet service was fast and steady.

Renters insurance seemed like a good idea but it could only be bought from a specific type of insurance agency. We never fully understood German insurance system so it took a while to find an agent that offered what we needed. It wasn't easy. The one we found explained that in Germany, insurance works differently than in the US. It doesn't protect our belongings; it's more like personal liability and everyone has it.

The agent said, "If you go to the house of a person and you make a damage there, we will pay it." Fortunately, we never had to file a claim.

LATE LUGGAGE IN LONDON

We arrived at London Heathrow Airport under sunny skies to begin our 245 day cruise around the world on Viking. Our ship held 930 passengers and was scheduled to stop at 111 ports in 51 countries on six continents with overnights in 23 cities. There were 463 crew members from 43 different countries. Words cannot describe how excited we were.

The bus from Heathrow to the Greenwich pier had trouble getting close to the ship because of the protests against Brexit and against Boris Johnson shutting down Parliament. Many of the roads were closed.

After a long slow roundabout drive, the bus got as close as it could. Cranes and construction were everywhere. Many of the buildings that went up very quickly in the aftermath of WWII are in need of reinforcement or replacement. Even Big Ben was getting some much needed cleaning and repairwork. The cruise line had representatives on every corner directing us on foot the remainder of the way.

Luggage tags had arrived in the mail a few weeks before our departure with our names and stateroom number so the bags could be unloaded from the bus and delivered directly to our stateroom on the ship. Nice idea, but three hours later we still didn't have the bags from the bus.

We had bought tickets online for a "Phantom of the Opera" performance at Her Majesty's Theatre the night before our ship was scheduled to sail from Greenwich. We had reserved a hotel room in Westminster so we could stay in the center of London after the show and return to the ship the following afternoon before sailing. I had packed a small overnight bag before we got on the plane, thinking I could just transfer that bag from the suitcase to the backpack and we'd be on our way. Silly me. No suitcase, no overnight bag. Fortunately, we had packed enough in our backpack just in case something like this happened, so we were fine. We took a sightseeing boat to Westminster from a departure point just down the pier from to the ship.

The show was well worth the effort. It was tremendous. The next morning, we walked from the hotel back to the Westminster pier to catch the tour boat down the Thames back to Greenwich with plenty of time to spare. Surely things would go more smoothly today.

While standing in line at the dock, we heard an announcement that the boat we were waiting for had engine trouble and the next sailing was cancelled. It would be 40 minutes until the next boat, which would then take another 90 minutes to reach Greenwich. We hadn't read any of the papers in our stateroom during the brief time we were on the ship, so we didn't know what time the mandatory safety drill was. We only knew that the ship was scheduled to sail at 3 pm and missing the mandatory safety drill is a very bad thing to do.

Since we were standing in the boat line for such a long time, we became acquainted with the couple in front of us. They had come to London from Devon just for the weekend. We had a nice long talk about our respective travels, then started talking about Brexit, which we've never fully understood. The man owned an import/export business dealing with fabrics and textiles. Many of his products came from Germany and he had been unable to get much specific information about what Brexit would do to the cost of his goods. In the meantime, he was building relationships with companies in the US.

The Gold Coach - 1897 Queen Victorias Diamond Jubilee
Buckingham Palace Mews   Richard Woolven is Lead Postilion

He gave me a copy of a photograph of his great grandfather who was a horseman during Queen Victoria's Diamond Jubilee in 1897. We had seen one of today's mounted horsemen outside 10 Downing Street on our walk from the hotel and he looked exactly the same as the one in the photograph.

It turned out that three other passengers waiting for the tour boat were also headed for our ship. One of them was confident that the safety drill wasn't until 2 pm and we'd be back in time. He was right about that and everything turned out fine.

DOING LAUNDRY ON THE SHIP

When the first sea day of our Viking voyage arrived, it was already past time to tackle the laundry. We had accumulated a big bag of dirty clothes during our road trip to take the car from Colorado to Pennsylvania before leaving the country. Laundry service was free on Oceania the previous year but Viking didn't offer free laundry until halfway through the world cruise so we did our own. The self-serve laundry was just down the hall from our stateroom. It had four washers and four dryers, and the machines were European style (small).

Another woman and I stood side by side reading the detailed instructions on the wall in the laundry room to learn how to use them. The trickiest part was pushing one button on the washer after the clothes were loaded then going around the corner to the soap machines mounted on the wall and pushing the right button over there that corresponded to the washer with my clothes in it, then going back to the washer to push a different button to get it started. If these things were done in the wrong order, the washer wouldn't start. It took five hours but I finished before the sun went down.

By the end of the cruise, I had provided instructions to more new passengers than I could count. One remarked that I should conduct an enrichment lecture on how to do the laundry.

INTERNET ISSUES

Internet service was included in our Viking cruise fare but we were unable to get Wi-Fi to work in our stateroom. I called Guest Services the day we left London and was told to use the Wi-Fi in the atrium areas because I wouldn't be able to get it in my stateroom. Three weeks later I found out from a fellow passenger that everybody has Wi-Fi in their stateroom and I needed to go complain. I did, it got fixed and the woman in Guest Services who gave me wrong information was reassigned. Sometimes the only option is to speak up louder.

HOTEL ELEVATOR IN ISRAEL

Our hotel in Jerusalem was built on the side of a hill and it was kind of upside down. The lobby was on the 6th floor and the dining room was on the 1st floor. Our room was on the 4th floor. We always had to stop and think before pushing an elevator button because going up to get outside was so counter-intuitive.

The hotel also had a dedicated "Shabbat Elevator". It stopped on every floor automatically to comply with the religious law requiring Jews to abstain from operating electrical switches (doing work) on the Sabbath. Our guide warned us that if we got on this elevator, it could take a very long time to reach our floor. As some of our fellow travelers found out, pushing the wrong button in the wrong elevator could make you very late.

Each hotel we stayed in during our trip to Jordan had a card placed under the glass on the nightstand or the desk in every room. The arrow on the card points toward Mecca so Muslim guests know which direction to face when it's time for prayers.

LOCKED IN THE RESTROOM IN BONAIRE

While walking through Kralendijk on this beautiful Caribbean Island, Ed and I stopped at a little retail mall to use the restroom. There was only one unisex restroom and I went in first. When I was ready to leave, I couldn't get the door unlocked. No matter which way I turned the lock and the knob, the door wouldn't open. I banged on the door and called to Ed, but he had wandered away. Panic started to creep in as I kept banging on the door, rattling the knob and nothing happened.

Then a lady who worked in one of the shops came to use the restroom and she had a key. What a relief it was to see that door open. She said they have this problem all the time and then she went in and locked the door behind her. Why they didn't just fix it was beyond me. By the time she came out, Ed had returned. I told him not to close the door all the way in case he couldn't get out and we couldn't find the lady with the key. I neglected to ask her where she worked. When Ed came out, I warned the young family that was waiting not to lock the door.

What happened after that is anybody's guess.

SURPRISES IN ST THOMAS, US VIRGIN ISLANDS

Our 2 ½ hour tour here was really just a drive up to the top of the mountain in the middle of the island to enjoy the views and visit the giant gift shop there. I must admit it was beautiful. The best part was the ride in the open air bus. Nice and cool!

Under clear morning skies we could see several of the surrounding islands that are not always visible. One of them was Tortola, where we had docked the previous day. A man in our group asked the guide how far it was. The guide said you could take a ferry and be there in 20 minutes. We were shocked. The man said, "It took our ship 13 hours and we can see it from here!" The guide said most of the ships just zigzag around because the islands are so close together. They leave these ports by sunset so no one has trouble finding their way back to the ship in the dark. I suspect it also keeps people from drinking too much rum and getting into trouble. Maybe the cruise line saves on port taxes that way too.

The guide said St Thomas was hit hard by Hurricane Maria in 2017 but managed much better than Puerto Rico because for years they had built big cisterns to collect rainwater in all the homes and buildings. Most of the houses here have an interesting water collection system in the front. Pipes from the gutters carry the rainwater to the cistern below the house. As much water as we slogged through during rainstorms on these islands, it would seem that people would be able to collect a lot of water in a very short period of time.

In contrast, Puerto Rico continued to rely on government infrastructure that was fragile at best and it failed them completely. He said many people committed suicide in the aftermath of the hurricane there because they could no longer cope with no water, no electricity, and no home. His stories were very sad.

About half the people on our little bus asked to be let off in the center of town at the end of the tour. The guide said it was over two miles from there to the ship and we should plan to take a taxi. We got off the bus, looked around town for a while and then walked back to the ship. It really wasn't that far. I think the guide had a lot of friends who were taxi drivers. Too bad it rained and Ed's umbrella broke.

FINDING A RESTROOM IN KUALA LUMPUR

Our full day tour of Kuala Lumpur started out slow due to unusually heavy traffic. Kuala Lumpur had some really fancy air conditioned buses. What should have been a 45-minute drive from the port to the first stop ended up taking over two hours, so everyone was ready for a restroom break when we reached the city.

We stopped at the National Monument built in tribute to the soldiers who died during the communist insurgency in the 1950s. The area was surrounded by beautiful gardens and some very clean looking public restrooms which were inexplicably closed. The guide said these restrooms were always open. This had never happened before and he didn't know what to do. Some people on the bus were getting very cranky about this. He told us the only other place he knew of nearby was a restaurant at the top of a long hill, so we joined most of the 32 people from the bus and started up the path.

The restaurant was a jumble of plastic chairs and tables outside with some containers filled with what looked like chicken in the process of breading and a kitchen too dirty to describe. A long line of us marched single file through the kitchen and down some steps at the back to the "toilets". The cook was waving his arms and yelling but there was no stopping this group once we had zeroed in on the location of the restroom. Another man ran down the steps to get us to turn around and leave but everyone ignored him. It was quite a circus.

There were only two small unisex restrooms and neither one had a working light, so we had to leave the doors propped open a bit in order for each person to be able to see while inside. Given the condition of the kitchen, it was probably better that we couldn't see much. Anyway, men and women took turns one at a time using both rooms and the line moved along. Fortunately it was a good group and everyone was very courteous.

We started to trickle back down the hill to the parking lot, only to find that the bus was gone! The few people who had chosen to remain behind while the others went off in search of the restaurant restroom had no idea where the bus went, or where the guide went either. Somebody finally found the bus and came back to get the rest of us.

By this time, we were really behind schedule and never did get caught up. In the afternoon we got a glimpse of the famous Petronas Towers and some interesting apartment buildings where residents are required to plant lush greenery on their balconies to reduce carbon dioxide and increase oxygen. Great idea.

Like many big cities around the world, Kuala Lumpur has a crime problem in some areas. We were always careful with our belongings, but it never hurts to be reminded of which might happen.

WAITER WITH BRACES

On our cruise ship, we were often served by a waiter from the Philippines who wore braces on his teeth. I asked him how he maintains them when he's away on the ship for so long. He said he would go home for a while at the end of the cruise but when the ship stops in Manila, he planned to "run very fast to his dentist to have his braces checked". He said the dentist told him if they feel loose, he should drink something cold and if they feel too tight, drink something hot.

Maybe regular orthodontic visits aren't as necessary as I thought.

STATEROOM REPAIRS

After our ship picked up new passengers in Los Angeles, we began to hear a lot of door slamming going on and not just the hallway doors. Bathroom doors, closet doors, and balcony doors too. Our quiet hallway neighborhood was no longer quiet. Late one day, Ed was on his way into the bathroom when the door handle came off in his hand. It struck us both so funny that we couldn't stop laughing. We assumed it was the vibration from all the door slamming that made our bathroom door handle work itself loose. I called Guest Services and they promised to send someone up right away. It was fixed quickly.

Early the next morning, I heard loud banging coming from our balcony and I thought, what are those people doing now? I opened the drapes and saw that the divider between our balcony and the next one over had come loose, was swinging in the wind, and hitting the balcony furniture. Ed tried to fix it, but it required a special tool. I called Guest Services again, not realizing that our stateroom stewards, Pablo and Rafa, kept this special tool handy. Pablo came and had it fixed within five minutes. When I saw Rafa later he said in his heavy Filipino accent, "They call me from down the stairs and I send you the Pablo."

FUEL TANKER PIRATES

It was no surprise that we needed fuel when we reached Togo at the end of our transatlantic crossing. We assumed the ship had taken on fuel while we were on shore during the day, but when it was time to sail away, the Cruise Director announced that the ship would move out into the bay, anchor, and be refueled by a tanker ship. This process was going to take about four hours and it was already getting dark. The whole thing seemed kind of strange.

I woke up in the middle of the night and assumed that the bright light in our stateroom was coming from the balcony light that must have been left on when the balconies were cleaned earlier that day. The light was actually coming from the tanker ship that had anchored right next to our side of the ship. But there were no fuel hoses in between. A few guys were walking around on the deck and two guys were in the window of the bridge, but nobody on the tanker looked very busy. We went back to bed.

The next morning, it was announced that we would refuel at our next port in Benin because we never got any fuel from the tanker. The crew on the tanker wanted more money for the fuel than the amount that had been agreed upon with Oceania and our captain refused to pay. The tanker crew must have thought we were in desperate need of fuel after just having crossed the ocean, but we had enough to make it to Benin and got fuel on the dock there the next day.

Nobody was going to try to take advantage of our captain and get away with it.

PIRATES IN SÃO TOMÉ AND PRINCIPE

This area of West Africa has a problem with sea pirates, just like Somalia does in East Africa. The captain of our cruise ship sent a letter to each stateroom about five days before we reached this area announcing that a mandatory Piracy Drill would be held the following day for all passengers. The letter included a code word that would come over the PA system if we had an actual pirate emergency. If we heard that word, everyone must darken their staterooms and stay in the corridors away from any windows until told it was safe or until other instructions were given.

The Captain's letter also tried to reassure passengers that the pirate attacks that had taken place were against commercial vessels that were at anchor or traveling at very slow speeds. He said our ship was faster and more maneuverable than other ships and we had more security staff. Lookouts would be in place on decks all around the ship as well as on the bridge. During our transit through this area, we should expect to encounter fishing boats. However, if they got too close to our ship, or sailed directly toward us, the Captain may choose to take steps to "keep them at a distance", such as weaving from side to side or changing course.

The day after the drill, the outside decks where the lifeboats were kept had been closed off with a sign that said fire hoses were being set up there and access would remain closed until we were safely past the pirate danger area. This whole thing reminded me a lot of the movie, "Captain Phillips".

São Tomé was a shallow port, so the ship anchored outside the harbor and we rode in on tender boats. There wasn't much to see so we didn't stay long. As the tender boat reached the ship on the return trip, I watched a man in an old rowboat lingering around the very back of the ship, looking at everything. I was sure the driver of the tender boat saw him and reported it but nobody mentioned it. This man could have been just curious, or maybe he was looking for an easy way to get onto our ship. It was hard to tell.

Later, as we were eating lunch on board, we saw a motorboat with about ten ragged looking men in it, one standing and pointing at different sections of the ship. It kept going back and forth along the side and got really close. A police boat came alongside, talked to them for a few minutes, and then left. The motorboat full of men left with the police but returned after a few minutes riding back and forth again.

These guys really looked like trouble. They were standing up in their boat, waving their arms and yelling. Some nets were piled around in the boat, but anything could have been underneath. I'm happy to say that we departed this area without incident, but it certainly was an eye-opener. I never expected to find pirates in that part of Africa and hope it was as close as I ever get to them.

FAINTING ON THE BUSES IN MYANMAR

Our guide told us that until recently, none of the public buses in the incredibly hot humid city of Yangon were air conditioned. I couldn't imagine it. So many people were fainting from the heat on the buses that the city passed a law requiring all public buses to be air conditioned. Weak air conditioning units were installed on the tops of all the city buses. Most of the local people who rode the buses didn't understand the concept of air conditioning, so they kept opening the windows letting in all the heat. People there are still fainting on the buses.

DRINKING WATER AT THE GRAND PALACE IN BANGKOK

The stunning Grand Palace is an enormous complex of elaborate buildings in the heart of Bangkok and it was fascinating. It had been the official residence of the King of Siam; royal ceremonies and state functions are still held here. We had to take our shoes off every time we entered a building and then find them again when we came out. The place was packed.

At the end of our long tour, it was so hot when we came out of the palace gate that our guide made everyone stand in the shade until a guy came on a bicycle with a box of cold water bottles strapped to the back. The guide gave each of us a bottle. It looked like official Grand Palace drinking water. He said we would stay there until everyone drank at least half of our bottle so none of us would faint on the way back to the bus. He had seen this happen to Americans several times and he no longer takes a chance that it could happen again. No one argued with him. Cold water never tasted so good.

CLIMBING OUT THE BOAT WINDOWS IN BANGKOK

On our second day in Bangkok we toured the city from the river. Afterwards our boat dropped us off at a pier next to a modern mall. This pier was used by many different kinds of boats and was staffed by a guy whose job was clearly to keep the boats moving in and out. The problem was that our boat was much higher than the pier. We expected a plank or gangway to be attached to the front of the boat as it was when we got on, but there was none in sight. The pier guy was running back and forth yelling at everybody to hurry and get off because we were holding up the other boats lining up to dock.

The only way to get off the boat was to stand on the benches and climb out through the open windows. Somebody behind me started counting the number of people who fell down after they wiggled through the windows and then landed flat on the pier like beached whales. Amazingly, no one was hurt. We just dusted ourselves off and walked into the mall like nothing unusual had happened. It was strange how we had become so accustomed to these things during our travels. Ed and I just looked at each other and said, "Oh well. Looks like we have to stand on the seats and wiggle out the side of the boat." The way things are is the way things are.

GETTING FROM HERE TO THERE

DONKEYS AND BUSES IN PETRA

The ruins of Petra stand at the crossroads of ancient caravan routes between Syria and Egypt, surrounded by deep gorges and enormous rock formations. It is believed to have been settled as early as 9,000 BC and was established as a regional trading hub in the 4th century BC by nomadic Arabs. The city was abandoned after the Crusaders left in the 12th century AD and rediscovered in 1812 by a Swiss explorer. The Treasury building was featured in the movie "Indiana Jones and the Last Crusade". It's an amazing place.

The walk from the visitors center to the ruins of this ancient city was two miles downhill which meant two miles uphill to get back out. It's possible to hire a pony cart to ride as far as the entrance to the old city at the Treasury and back. When those pony carts came flying past, there wasn't much time or much room to get out of their way.

Ed decided early in the walk that he was going to go on ahead of the group to give himself enough time to make it up to the Monastery and back. It was on a path off the main route through the city, above the Royal Tombs at the top of over 900 steps. Just getting to the tombs was quite a climb. He needed all the extra time he could get. Not many people made as far as the Monastery but Ed found someone to take a photo of him standing in front of the entrance.

Everything I saw in Petra fascinated me. I could have spent a week there. The canyons were spectacular. When I reached the restaurant where the group was told to meet for lunch, I saw no sign of Ed there or on the steep hill beyond which led to the Monastery.

I wasn't hungry but I bought a bottle of very refreshing lemon soda at the restaurant and started walking back, hoping to meet up with Ed later on the path. I hadn't gotten very far when I heard a young girl yell, "Excuse me!" I turned just as her donkey knocked me to the side as it ran down the path. I stumbled but didn't fall. It was the first time I'd ever been sideswiped by a hit-and-run donkey! It appeared that the girl's mother and sisters, each riding alone, were trying to get their donkeys under control without success as well. They disappeared in a cloud of dust.

Not long after recovering from that, I heard a familiar voice call out, "Hey Lady!" and saw Ed trot past me on a donkey. I called back to him, "Wait for me at the Treasury!" The man holding the rope attached to Ed's donkey told him that he had lived in a cave here until a few years ago. He asked Ed's age, then told him, "You're in good shape. You could get another wife."

I wish we'd had more time to spend here. Petra is a unique place in the world and we loved every minute of our visit. Each building held its own story and the people who live and work in this area were like none I'd ever encountered. It's hard to imagine how they survive in such a rugged environment.

It was a hard slow walk back up the hill. At the entrance, Ed and I split up and agreed to meet on the bus. I headed to the restrooms while he went to find a cold drink. The bus parking lot was still a few blocks away. Uphill. It was packed with buses, but ours was not among them. No Ed there either. Neither of us noticed on the way in that there were two bus parking lots. Our bus was waiting in the second one, which was not the one we parked in when we arrived that morning. Once I found the bus, I went back to look for Ed. He had turned a block too soon and was still hunting for the morning parking lot when I found him.

BOAT RIDE ON THE SEA OF GALILEE

After getting caught in a flood in Denver, I developed some serious angst about deep water and small boats. Cruise ships were no problem, but small rocky boats were another story. As much as I looked forward to visiting the Sea of Galilee when we were in Israel, I wasn't excited about seeing it from the very old wooden boat that headed toward the dock to pick us up. There were no life jackets in sight. I almost didn't get on.

Shortly after we left the pier, one of the men on the boat raised a flag for every country represented by the passengers. He told us that most of the people who come to ride on their boats are American but he was very clear that everyone is welcome and they have a supply of flags from many countries. They just don't use most of them.

Once we started out and it became clear that we weren't going to sink, I began to relax, enjoy the scenery, and watch the sun sparkle on the surface. That rugged old boat gave us a lovely ride around the lake and brought us back safely. It gave me a reason work harder on overcoming my fear of water.

STUCK IN THE MUD IN BRAZIL

After our cruise ship crossed the equator, we sailed south to the city of Belem, about 60 miles up the Para River in the lower Amazon. Sitting on our balcony as we cruised down the river, we could only see thick rainforest all the way down to the water's edge with just a few wooden dwellings dotting the shore. The river was very dark and muddy along here.

When we reached Belem, we were shocked to see skyscrapers and dense buildings along the waterfront from the opposite side of our ship. This city has 1.8 million people and I'd never heard of it until I saw it listed on the cruise itinerary. The view was amazing. A modern city on one side of the ship and a barely inhabited rainforest on the other. No bridge.

Our ship excursion left at 1:00 pm to go up the nearby Guama River to Acara Island, walk through the forest and visit an indigenous village. We took a small bag with bottled water, rain jackets and the camera. Because of the low water level in this area, the ship had anchored out in the middle of this wide river, and we took a tender boat to the shore. It took almost a half hour to reach the pier, much longer than normal tender rides.

The double decker riverboat was docked right next to the tender landing. It was pouring rain but at least the walk was short. There must have been at least 200 people on the tour. During the one hour ride to the island, each of the five local guides took turns speaking about Brazil, Belem, the Amazon, and the way of life here. We saw very little evidence of civilization along the way, but now and then someone waved to us from the front of a wooden house.

Just before the boat docked on the island, the guides passed out hard hats. They said we had to wear them because it was the season of ripening brazil nuts. If one drops from a tree and hits you on the head, it can knock you out. We heard one fall while we were in the forest and I believe it. They weigh a couple of pounds and they fall from a long way up. Ed chose to make a fashion statement with his and get some extra protection from the falling nuts at the same time. A few others took notice and did the same.

The dock building on the island had two levels with high ceilings. The boat arrived during an unusually high tide, so instead of stepping directly from the boat onto the dock, the guides set up a plank for everyone to walk down from the lower deck of the boat to the upper level of the dock building. It was the only way to get off the boat.

People really complained about having to walk on this plank. It was pretty narrow. The guides hung on to each person one at a time until we were all safe on the dock. Some elected to stay on the boat. I saw one man with a knee brace and a walker, and a woman with a crutch but there may have been others equally challenged. No one expected such a harrowing experience upon arrival, but as far as I know everyone who wanted to get off made it down the plank without mishaps.

We were divided into several groups of about fifteen people each and we followed our guide into the forest, making several stops to learn about the trees, plants, animals, and the people who live among them. Ours was an excellent guide and we learned so much from him. The trails were narrow and muddy. Taking too long for the right photo could mean getting easily separated or lost, so it was really important to keep up.

We spent some time at the beginning and the end of the tour at a small wooden house where a 76-year-old man lived. His family owns a lot of land on the island that has remained undeveloped. He was quite agile and showed off his ability to climb an acai tree that was probably 50 feet high. It only took a split second for him to slide back down. Then he picked up a tarantula and passed it around with an engaging toothless grin. At his home, green parrots sat around the front porch railing and a young man with an enormous knife slashed harvested brazil nuts with alarming speed.

Toward the end of the tour, a woman in another group insisted that her husband was lost in the forest. The guide for that group kept calling his name and retracing the paths, only to learn later that the man had found his own way back and was waiting on the boat.

We arrived back at the dock to find that the extreme high tide we had experienced earlier was now an extreme low tide. When we docked, the lower deck of the boat was higher than the upper level of the building. Now the upper deck of the boat was much lower than the lower level of the building. No one seemed to know what to do, except get another plank ready. It took a while to make sure everyone was accounted for.

Our four hour tour had already turned into well over five hours because of all the plank business and the extra time spent in the forest. It didn't seem like anyone, including the boat captain, realized that the delay in our departure would make such a difference in the water level.

We could hear the engines roar, but the boat was stuck solid in the muck at the bottom of the river. The guides were running back and forth with much yelling and arm waving between them and the people on the dock. First, they asked everyone to move toward the front of the boat, hoping that would raise the engine at the back. That didn't help. Then the guides asked if 70 people could please get off the boat to lessen the overall weight. They said as soon as the boat was free, they would turn it around, and these 70 could get back on. Ed and I stayed, but I think more than 70 got off. They probably figured this wouldn't take long so most of them left their belongings on board.

The boat still didn't budge. A few other small tour boats started to appear. Locals helped rope them together to try to pull our boat loose, but it only turned sideways. The back end stayed mired in the muck but now the boat was perpendicular to the dock and not close enough for anyone to get back on. By this time, everyone in the village had heard about the trouble and showed up to watch. Men were walking around the dock, getting on and off small boats or just standing around shaking their heads. Mass confusion doesn't begin to describe this.

Then we were told that another boat was coming to take us back to the ship. It finally arrived at dusk but it could only take 85 people from our boat. Ed and I didn't get in line fast enough, so we didn't make it off.

About 50 were left on our boat, which was the original one we arrived on, and over 70 were still on the dock. Our boat was still stuck and pointed away from the dock, so there was no way for us to get off unless another boat was brought alongside.

The three remaining boats that had tried to pull ours out of the mud were small and old. They couldn't hold very many people and they sure didn't look like they'd make it all the way to Belem. The guides said that we would have to wait for the boat that took the 85 people off to come back for more of us, but as time went on, that seemed less likely. By now it was dark. Electricity in this area was limited and there were very few lights. I didn't know how anybody would be able to find us.

Patience among the passengers was wearing thin. The guides had to keep repeating that they weren't permitted to use the available small boats so we would just have to wait. We assumed that only boats that had been inspected or were licensed could be used. This tour had one escort from the excursions staff who was communicating by radio with the ship. We never really understood a lot of what was going on, but all of a sudden, the guides said we were going to use the small boats.

They started clearing out the 70 people on the dock first; they had been standing or sitting on the floor all this time. No chairs. Before they could load, we had to go through our boat and help gather the belongings that those people had left on board when they thought they'd only be on the dock for a short time. The guides were passing things from our boat to another boat to another boat to the dock. It was unbelievable. I didn't hear anything about missing items, so evidently everybody got their stuff.

Around 8:30 or so, Ed and I finally boarded the last of the small boats. Again, we had to walk across a plank to board, then duck below an overhang while stepping down three really steep steps in very dim light. The man with the leg brace and the woman with the crutch went first and this took a while. I don't know how either one of them managed. I had trouble myself. The guides were side by side helping everyone down and in.

Then we waited while the guides went all through the dock building and the surrounding area to make sure no one was left behind, and we finally departed. I don't think anyone was keeping track of the number of people getting on and off the boats anytime during all of this.

Our small boat returned to Belem through different channels of the river that made for a shorter trip back. We sat shoulder to shoulder on narrow benches along the perimeter inside our small boat. I kept my eyes on the floor watching for leaks.

When we arrived in Belem, our small boat had to dock at the edge of the city because the tank didn't hold enough fuel to make it all the way to the pier we had left from that morning. From there, we walked through a large boathouse and down a dark street where a bus was waiting to take us to the main pier in the city center. The bus ride lasted at least 20 minutes, but it was a large, very plush double decker bus that had enough room for everyone. It was beginning to look like we'd actually make it through this. We still had a long way to go but at least we were back in the city.

Then the guide explained that once we got off the bus, we would have to walk a few blocks to the pier. Armed guards were waiting outside the bus to escort us and it was important to stay with them. More guards patrolled the pier. Again it amazed me that no one got lost in the dark during all this.

At the pier we expected to see the ship tenders waiting for us. Instead, we were loaded onto another double decker riverboat crammed with chairs. In the dark I couldn't see that mine contained a puddle, which instantly soaked the back of my pants. I was already a mess from the 89 degree heat, the 95% humidity and the mud. Now I had wet clothes. Some of the staff from the ship were on this boat, checking to make sure everyone had a proper key card. One of them used a counter to keep track of the number of passengers as we boarded. We had to wait a while to make sure no one got left behind at this point before leaving.

By the time we reached the cruise ship, it was 9:45 pm, almost five hours later than we expected to be back and most of us hadn't eaten anything since noon. Ten ship officers were waiting to personally

5

---

welcome each person back on board. The Executive Chef told us they had reopened the buffet and we should go upstairs to enjoy a good meal. What a day!

REACHING THE NEW HAMPSHIRE HIGHPOINT THE HARD WAY

The top of Mt Washington can easily be reached by car or by train. Too easy for Ed. He wanted to hike up. We didn't know until we reached the trailhead that the route he had selected was closed for maintenance. The easiest thing to do was take the closest alternate trail. It wasn't until we were well underway that we realized how steep it was. At one point the trail became vertical with a ladder anchored into solid rock. My vertigo and fear of heights in places like this nearly paralyzed me but somehow, I made it to the top. I wasn't willing to push my luck by hiking back down and facing that ladder again. Ed and our son took the same trail back while our daughter and I walked down the road until a family offered to drive us the rest of the way. Getting into a stranger's car in a national park was a lot safer in those days.

LEAKY CANOE IN ALASKA

Our oldest son went along for the first week of our Alaska camping trip, but he had just started a new job and couldn't stay for the second week. At a campground outside Paxson, the three of us rented a canoe at the campground office and went out on the nearby lake.

The canoe only had two seats, so Ed and Mike sat on the benches and rowed while I sat between them in the bottom of the canoe with my floatation cushion. We were a long way from shore when I noticed that my pants felt wet and I realized we had a leaky canoe. I bailed the water with the only thing I could use – the cap of my water bottle. It was too small to be effective, but I bailed with it anyway. We turned the canoe around and headed back, but by the time we reached the campground my pants were soaked.

A young Japanese woman from our group was in the camp office when we returned. She looked at me, pointed to the roaring fire in the fireplace and said, "Oh, Kathy. You must flame yourself."

DON'T LEAVE HOME WITHOUT GOOD TRAVEL INSURANCE

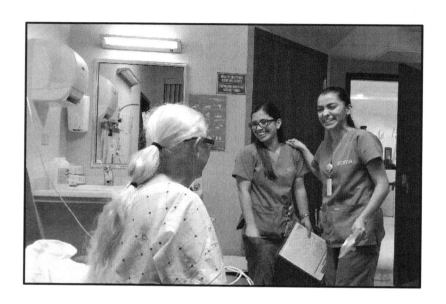

HOSPITAL STAY IN SAN JOSE

Our fourth trip to Costa Rica wasn't exactly a planned one. In December 2016 we boarded a cruise ship to take us from Ft. Lauderdale all the way around South America toward Antarctica and back up to Buenos Aires. We had also booked an independent tour of Machu Picchu while our ship docked in Lima, Peru for three days.

Before we left Denver, Ed was complaining about pain in his left shoulder. The doctor told him it was probably arthritis, gave him some medication, and told him he would feel better soon. It was okay to go ahead and make the trip.

Three days into the cruise, Ed developed a fever that reached 104.9 F. His arm was reddish purple, swollen and so painful that he could hardly move it. The Medical Center on the ship treated him with antibiotics but told him that he had a severe infection and needed to go to the nearest hospital. The doctor contacted our travel insurance agent immediately and made arrangements to have an ambulance meet us at our next stop in Puerto Limon, Costa Rica. I packed everything up and we prepared to leave the ship the next morning.

Initially, the ambulance driver refused to allow us to bring our luggage in the ambulance. It was terrible. Ed was suffering and needed to get to the hospital and I was having to get into a fight over luggage. With the help of one of the ship's crew as interpreter, we were able to get it all loaded and still have room for me. The medic spoke only Spanish, so we conversed using a translation app on our cell phones. Each of us entered what we wanted to say, hit the Translate button, and handed the phone to the other person. It took a long time to carry on a conversation this way, but the ride to the hospital was more than three hours over the mountains so there was plenty of time to get to know one another.

The travel insurance agent arranged for Ed to be admitted to a private hospital in San Jose, which was excellent. All the staff spoke English and the care was outstanding. The Emergency Room doctor told us Ed had a septic staph infection and would need surgery as well as lots of heavy duty antibiotics. His private room included a sleeper sofa so I was able to stay with him. The nurses were very professional, kind, and there were a lot of them.

By the time Ed was discharged a week later, he'd had two surgeries to clean out the infection in his shoulder and was treated for pneumonia because the infection had spread to his lungs. It had also settled in one of the valves of his heart. After the first surgery, he was taken to the ICU because his blood pressure was so erratic. He was very uncomfortable and unable to sleep. One of the male nurses noticed he was restless and braided Ed's long hair in the middle of the night.

Ed stayed in the ICU for three days. The survival rate for septic staph infections is only 50%. I shouldn't have been researching his condition on the internet while he was in the hospital, but I couldn't help it. It seemed that every time I left his bedside, another machine had been set up and connected to him while I was gone. In the evening of the third day, I returned from dinner and his entire bed was gone.

I thought it was over and frantically searched for someone who could tell me where he was. Someone had taken him for another MRI.

During the time he was in the ICU, I stayed at a hotel down the street. Every night at the hotel, all I could do was cry. The kind bellman at the hotel who helped me check in with my luggage understood how upset I was. Every time I saw him, he wanted to know how my husband was and asked if there was anything he could do for me.

Thankfully, Ed's condition improved and the doctor made arrangements with the travel insurance agent for him to return to Denver, which included sending a private nurse from Denver to accompany him to administer oxygen and monitor his vital signs on the way home. He needed to be in first class to minimize exposure to the other passengers because he was so weak, and the doctor wouldn't allow him to risk picking up any other germs. I called every one of the credit cards we'd brought along to get our credit limit bumped up as high as possible before Ed was discharged. Although the travel insurance covered his illness, we had to pay up front and file a claim for reimbursement. I had no idea how much the bill would be until we were ready to leave.

An ambulance picked us up at the Denver airport and took us immediately to the hospital where Ed stayed for another week with more IV antibiotics and lots of monitoring. After coming home, he still needed IV antibiotics twice daily for six more weeks, which I learned to administer. Over the next six months, he regained his strength and his health returned to normal.

We were very lucky.

SNOWMOBILE MISHAP IN YELLOWSTONE NATIONAL PARK

In 2001, we booked a package tour to see Yellowstone in winter and flew to Jackson, Wyoming with another couple. The roads in the park are not plowed in the winter. Guests are transported in and out of the park by "snow cats", specially made enclosed truck-sized, fully tracked vehicles designed to move on top of the packed snow and ice. The interior is cramped and noisy but that's part of the adventure. The snow cats share the road with wildlife, which seemed accustomed to the engine noise. Bison and elk wandered alongside us, finding it easier to walk on the road than through the deep snow in the forest.

A full day of snowmobiling awaited us on our second day in the park. We suited up and rode out on two-seater machines from Old Faithful under clear skies and sunshine. North of Madison Junction, the snowmobile in front of ours stopped suddenly and Ed swerved to avoid hitting it. Because I was seated directly behind him, I didn't see the swerve coming. I flew off the back of the snowmobile and landed hard on the ice with my right leg twisted sideways at a nasty angle.

When I stopped screaming and calmed down, I knew there was no way I could get back on the snowmobile. I sat propped up against the side of it, hoping everyone would just leave me to the wolves. The pain was beyond description. A woman stopped her snowmobile next to me and explained that she was a paramedic. She asked if I would let her straighten my leg. I thought, how much more could it hurt? She sent her son to gather some branches and then tied them to my leg with my scarf. She then promised to call the park ranger as soon as she reached a pay phone. This was long before cell phones were common.

The ranger finally arrived. I was glad to see him, but he arrived on a snowmobile. He radioed for a vehicle, and when another ranger brought one, he drove us to the west entrance of the park where we were picked up by a county ambulance. At the county line, we were transferred to another ambulance that took us to a small hospital in Rexburg, Idaho. The ER doctor there put a brace on my knee, gave me some crutches, and warned me not to put any weight on my leg until I saw an orthopedic surgeon upon my return to Denver. The goal there seemed to be to patch me up enough to send me home but not to identify the full extent of my injury or develop a treatment plan.

The hospital administrator just happened to be walking through the ER while we were there and was kind enough to drive Ed to K-Mart to buy some clothes. We only wore our snowmobile suits and long thermal underwear, intending to return to the lodge to change after our snowmobile ride but now we needed clothes. The administrator then drove us to the Best Western Hotel for the night.

Ed called the Snow Lodge in Yellowstone and gave the staff permission to let our friends into our room to pack up our belongings as we would not be returning. The lodge put our luggage on the next morning's snow cat back to Jackson Hole airport.

In the morning, Ed set about making arrangements to get us to Jackson for our rescheduled flight home. Rexburg had no public transportation services or taxis. The only rental car company didn't permit one-way rentals so we had no way to get to the airport. The young woman working at the hotel desk helped Ed as much as she could, but nothing came together. That afternoon she offered to drive us to Jackson in her own car if we would reimburse her for the gas and the time she would lose from work.

My injured leg bundled up in a brace prevented me from fitting into the back seat of her car, no matter how we tried. So she and Ed went to the car rental agency where he rented an SUV for her to drive round trip. She took us over Teton Pass in a snowstorm to get to the airport in time for our flight. She assured us that she raced snowmobiles every winter and was accustomed to driving through snowstorms. We arrived at the airport, safe and grateful. Ed deposited me into an airport wheelchair and took care of our plane tickets. This was back in the day when planes normally had some empty seats and reservations could be changed at the last minute without additional cost.

I had never been on crutches before and was terrified by the water left by snowy boots on the restroom floor in the airport. Every step with those crutches could have resulted in a nasty fall further injuring my knee but I managed not to slip. I collapsed into the wheelchair outside the restroom and Ed pushed me to the gate. My heart sank when I saw our waiting aircraft outside the window. Ice-encrusted steps were pushed up against the open door. Watching from the gate as our suitcases were being loaded onto the plane, I had no idea how I was going to get through the snow and ice and make it up those steps when it was time to board.

It's amazing how accommodating the airlines were in those days. The gate agent assured us that the plane wasn't full, and she would rearrange the seating to enable me to have the entire bulkhead row to myself, so I could put my leg up across all three seats. The flight attendant wheeled me outside and let me ride up on the catering fork-lift to get into the plane. When we arrived in Denver, Ed retrieved our van from the airport parking lot while I waited in a wheelchair. We made the last leg of the trip home much relieved and very grateful to all who helped us through this ordeal.

Multiple surgeries put my knee back together followed by months of physical therapy. It was fine until 2009 when I slipped in the office parking lot one morning heading into work and tore it apart again. This time repairing it wasn't possible. Workers Compensation covered a total knee replacement for me that included two weeks in a residential rehab center. I haven't had any trouble with it since.

After this incident we started buying travel insurance and have never traveled without it.

SURGERY IN THE BASEMENT IN AMBERG

During the time we lived in Germany, Ed had multiple medical adventures. Doctors in Germany are not easy to find. It seems like people just have to know where they are. In small towns they often practice in second story offices above storefronts that aren't clearly marked or they see patients at offices set up in their own homes. The Army Clinic where I worked was only available to civilians on a space available basis, and it was hard to get an appointment there. Eventually we learned the German system and submitted our bills to our federal employee health insurance which reimbursed overseas claims at 90%. It took a long time to get our bills and records translated and processed for payment, but it worked out okay.

By word of mouth we were able to find two internal medicine doctors who shared an office near the town hospital. Patients lined up outside the office every morning and were seen on a first come, first served basis starting at 8:00 am. Usually no more than five or six people were waiting for the office to open and everyone was always respectful of their place in line.

Ed had developed a hernia the second year we were in Germany. The doctor said he needed surgery and set up an appointment for him to see a surgeon the same day. The surgeon's office was a few blocks from our apartment in a very old building that was being renovated. Scaffolding and small cranes lined the street, so it was hard to find the right entrance. It didn't look like much from the outside.

Ed asked the surgeon if the hernia repair would be done at the hospital in Amberg. The doctor said no, he performs surgery down in the basement of his building and could do it the following week. After his appointment, Ed went downstairs to take a look but it was too dark to see much besides a hallway with some closed doors. He decided he had to trust that it would all turn out ok. What choice did he have?

The surgeon told Ed there was no need for me to stay and wait for him on the day of surgery. His office would call me when it was time to pick him up. I dropped him off in pouring the rain outside the building, wondering if we were doing the right thing. What kind of doctor performs surgery in his basement? Ed seemed okay when I picked him up and he took a nap after we got home. The surgeon called around 9:00 that night to see how Ed was doing and offered more pain medication if he needed it.

Ed would be the first to admit that this was a rather strange experience, but he developed great respect for the German medical system. You get what you need when you need it, nothing more and nothing less.

BEER IN THE HOSPITAL IN AMBERG

About six months before we returned to the US, Ed developed a kidney stone. He again went to stand in line at the doctor's office to wait his turn after it opened at 8:00 am. The doctor ran some tests in the office lab and after performing an ultrasound in the office, she confirmed he had a large kidney stone that would have to be removed. The office staff made an appointment for Ed with a urologist at the Amberg hospital for the same afternoon.

The urologist gave Ed a choice of having the stone crushed ultrasonically, removed with a scope or by incision. They agreed to try the ultrasound first. It didn't work. He spent one night in the hospital and returned the following week to try the scope. The stone was too big, got caught and wouldn't come out. The urologist inserted a stent and Ed spent another night in the hospital. He went back a week later, and the stone finally came out. This time, two nights in the hospital.

Amberg had excellent tasting drinking water, but it was filled with minerals. Urology was the largest department of the local hospital because so many people got kidney stones. The first time Ed was seen there, the admissions staff asked if he wanted to be treated by a regular urologist or the head of the department at a higher cost. Evidently in the German system, the patient pays extra for additional expertise. Since our American medical insurance didn't differentiate between doctors, Ed requested the head of the department.

German hospitals require patients to bring their own towels and pajamas. A hospital gown is provided in conjunction with a procedure but not on a routine basis. People wear street clothes while resting in bed and are permitted to go outside if they wish and are able. I saw more than a few walking down the sidewalk with their IV poles, some of them smoking. Quite different from our American system where most patients are too sick to be out walking around.

The urology nurse recommended that Ed drink beer to help flush everything out. She believed Hefeweizen worked best but another nurse came by to recommend Weissbier. They told us that several varieties of beer were available for purchase in the hospital gift shop. A friend who was visiting Ed at the time went down to get some, but the gift shop was closed. He went home and returned with a six pack. The three of us drank all of it.

SUDDENLY UNABLE TO WALK

A few months after the kidney stone, Ed woke me up in the middle of the night. He said he needed to go to the bathroom, but he couldn't walk. I thought he might have had a stroke, but it turned out he had a big red warm spot on the outside of his ankle and the joint was swollen. In the morning, Ed again waited in line at 8:00 am to see the doctor, who treated him for gout. He returned home with pills to take for three days and by then it should be better. It wasn't.

By the next morning, Ed's ankle had worsened, and this time he was able to secure an open slot at the clinic on the post. The Army doctor said it was either an infection or a blood clot but definitely not gout. She gave him a big bottle of antibiotics and told him to go to the Emergency Room at the Amberg hospital and ask for an ultrasound as soon as possible.

The Emergency Room was overflowing with critical patients, so it was a long wait. The doctor who read the ultrasound results told Ed he had psoriasis of the bone and gave him medication for pain, inflammation and an anti-viral. The doctor was quite irritated that Ed had seen three doctors within a week and was still suffering because he didn't have an accurate diagnosis. His ankle cleared up, but we never knew what caused it.

FALLING DOWN THE STAIRS IN HUNGARY

In 2006 while Ed was climbing Mt Kilimanjaro, I flew to Budapest to spend time with a German couple we had known for many years. I had reserved a third story walk up condo at a time share resort in Heviz near Lake Balaton where the three of us spent the week touring Hungary. It was a lovely townhouse with two bedrooms and two bathrooms.

On the second day, my friend got up early to make breakfast and slipped on the wooden spiral stairway heading down to the kitchen. She hit her back on the edge of a step and couldn't get up. I ran to the Reception building and asked them to call an ambulance.

Three paramedics managed to get her down the stairs to the parking lot. The ambulance had minimal equipment and a very old rusty stretcher. They spoke only Hungarian, so we had no idea where we were going or how long it would take to get there. I rode in the ambulance while her husband followed in their rental car. She was taken to the hospital in the nearby town of Keszthely where she remained for five days.

The Emergency Room was one big open area with clusters of people discussing patient conditions. No privacy policy here. The English speaking doctor showed us a fracture on the x-ray of her back. She needed to be admitted and immobilized.

She was placed in a room with three other women. No curtains, no chairs – just four beds. The hospital made a mold of a brace for her later that day. She was not permitted to get out of bed until five days later when the brace was delivered. It was like a suit of armor, covering her from shoulder to waist completely front to back with multiple fasteners on each side holding the front section to the back section. It was a complicated contraption to get her into and out of, but we managed. She wore it for six weeks and told me later that the doctor she saw after returning to Germany said it was the right treatment. Her back healed and she has had no problems since.

STOMACH BUG IN FLORENCE

Two days before we were scheduled to fly home from a trip to Italy, Ed developed some sort of intestinal bug. Public restrooms are not easy to find in Florence. When Ed needed a restroom stop, we went into a coffee shop and I ordered a cappuccino while Ed used the restroom. This sometimes resulted in my needing restroom stops also, but since Ed had to stop frequently anyway, it worked out okay. By the time we checked into the hotel at the Florence airport before our flight home the next morning, the bug had attacked me too, bringing on severe vomiting and diarrhea. Although it hit me harder than Ed, there was no way either one of us was in any condition to get on a plane the next day.

Our travel insurance agent contacted a doctor in Florence who came to our hotel room. He spoke excellent English, prescribed some medication for me, and explained that the hotel would send someone to the pharmacy to pick it up for us. He said I would feel better in a few days, but I had to be careful to start slowly with a few sips of water and in the evening, only a cracker or two.

Shortly after the doctor left, a young man knocked on our door and said he was going to get my medicine. He said 20 Euros should be enough to cover it, so that's what Ed gave him. When he returned, he was very precise about counting out the change and showing Ed the receipt to make sure we understood that he was honest.

The following day I felt well enough to start making plans to go home. The travel insurance agent said that it would be a few more days before our rescheduled flight would leave Florence and the trip would involve multiple plane changes. More options would be available if we flew out of Rome. The hotel shuttle took us back to the main station in the center of Florence where we caught the train and spent the next night at the hotel at the Rome airport. I was starting to feel a little better but very afraid to eat anything until we were back home again. This was not the kind of problem anyone would want to have on an airplane, especially a transatlantic one.

Fortunately, our trip home was uneventful.

NASTY BITES IN QUEPOS

Over the years, we have made a total of four trips to Costa Rica, each to a different area. The third trip was with friends over New Year's. We stayed in a small bed and breakfast outside Quepos that had a pool on the deck. One evening, after a sticky day of hiking and then a shower, we sat by the pool before going into town for dinner.

Living in Denver where the air is very dry, I was in the habit of coating my skin with lotion after every shower. It didn't occur to me that my lotion would be so attractive to the tiny bugs that hung around that pool.

The next day, the itchy bites on my legs became intolerable, especially around my ankles. The red welts turned into circles of bruising and I was afraid something was eating away at me from under my skin. At the next hotel, which was in Arenal, I called the travel insurance agent, established a claim, and asked for a recommendation for a doctor. This was a small town and they had no one on their list to recommend here.

Our friend said he had noticed a doctor's office on our way into town, and suggested we try it. When we finally located it, the doctor turned out to be a veterinarian. It was the only doctor we could find, but I refused to go in.

Later, the hotel gave us the name of another doctor and this one sounded more promising. We found him with no problem and he gave me an injection of antihistamine. The bites were much better by the next day. I didn't open that bottle of lotion again until after we returned home from the trip.

INJURED IN GALAPAGOS ISLANDS

On our second day in the Galapagos Islands, we took a short boat ride to Isabela island with our naturalist guide for an overnight stay. We left our big suitcase at the hotel on Santa Cruz Island since we would only be gone one night and just took an overnight bag. We checked into the hotel on Isabela Island and rode on a small boat with the guide across the channel. From the pier, the guide pointed to an area along the shore where we could see some small penguins. He warned us to watch out for the sharp volcanic rocks that covered that part of the shore. The rocks were wet, mossy, and very slick.

Ed had just told me to be careful when he slipped and fell himself, hitting his knee on a sharp rock. He lay on the rocks while I called out to the guide. Ed was unable to walk or even stand. The guide went to get help and returned with a few locals and a flimsy orange stretcher that looked like a relic from World War II. They managed to carry Ed onto the boat after pushing their way through a crowd of Asian tourists snapping his picture. The stretcher didn't fit, so they balanced it on the rails for the short ride back. It hung over on both sides and so did Ed, but he managed to stay out of the water.

Someone the guide knew brought an old rusty pickup truck to the boat landing and they put Ed on the stretcher in the bed of it for the short ride to the dispensary, a two-room building staffed with one man who had very few supplies. Some used plastic water bottles with handwritten labels for alcohol and peroxide stood on the counter alongside some bandages. That was about it. This man wiggled Ed's knee and told the guide in Spanish that he didn't think it was broken but would write down the names of some things that we could get for Ed from the pharmacy.

He walked over to a small desk, opened the drawer, and took out an old brown paper bag. He tore off a small corner of the bag, wrote three things on it, then handed it to me. The guide told me I could go to the pharmacy in the truck, so I followed the driver outside. The pharmacy was right around the corner. The driver showed me inside and wandered away.

The pharmacy consisted of a small storefront with a glass counter and some shelves along the back wall that were partially filled with items I didn't recognize. An elderly woman wearing a housecoat and slippers came out of the back of the pharmacy, scratching a headful of gray curls that needed combing. She was evidently the pharmacist. I gave her the slip of brown paper that the man in the dispensary had given me. She looked at it and muttered a lot. After placing three items on the counter, she handed me a pen and a small tablet, but I couldn't understand what she wanted me to write. I took the pen and put my name and address on some of the lines. She looked at what I had written and shook her head and sighed and glared at me. I couldn't understand anything she said but it was clear she was not pleased. She entered some numbers in a small handheld calculator and showed me the total. After I paid, I tried to tell her that I needed a receipt for the insurance, but she couldn't understand me any better than I could understand her.

While I was negotiating for my receipt, the driver reappeared and took the three items off the counter. I was finally able to get something from her that looked like it might pass for a receipt and when I went outside, the truck was gone. I walked back to the dispensary and the guide said Ed was ready to leave. He had only two of the items from the pharmacy. I told the guide that there were three things. Even though I had no idea what they were, it seemed important that Ed should have them. The guide explained that Ed really just needed two of them. "That third item," he said, "Well, it's a donation". Evidently the injured Americans who pass through are expected to keep the dispensary stocked.

The driver reappeared again and took us to the hotel. Earlier we had checked into a room on the second floor which Ed was now unable to reach so the hotel gave us a room on the first floor that faced the beach. The guide called our travel insurance company on his cell phone for me and I began the task of filing a claim.

While I was talking, the guide wanted to help and asked me to hand him the phone. He covered it with his hand and whispered to me about some classes he had taken. "I know what to say to these people", he told me. He started talking to the insurance agent about Ed's vital signs and his inability to walk. He told them they would have to send a plane for Ed. Then he handed me the phone. The insurance agent asked me if that man was a doctor. I simply said he came from the dispensary, which was true. There was no one else.

The insurance company reviewed Ed's case and the agent called back on the hotel phone to say that they would send a private medical plane to airlift him to Guayaquil on the Ecuador mainland. However, the Galapagos Islands are a protected World Heritage Site which required official approval for a plane to land on the island we were on. This took two more days.

Another group was coming to stay at the hotel, and they had reserved the beachfront rooms, so we had to relocate again. The other members of our group came by one at a time to say goodbye and they moved on to the next leg of our trip without us.

I walked into the village and bought a deck of playing cards from a little store on the main street, so we could pass the time. While I was there, I saw two policemen putting handcuffs on the guy who drove the truck to the dispensary a few days earlier. His face was all bloody and he appeared intoxicated.

The insurance agent called me on the hotel office phone with updates a few times each day and finally we got approval for the plane to land. This island only had a short airstrip that was rarely used, so news spread fast that a plane was going to land. The hotel got someone to drive us and acquired a gurney from somewhere to move Ed from the room to the truck. This was a newer truck than the one we rode in when Ed was first injured. I expected to ride in the cab with our bag, but everyone who worked at the hotel wanted to go to the air strip to see the plane. It was a challenge to make sure I didn't get left behind. One guy rode in the bed of the truck with Ed after deciding to load the gurney back there too in case it was needed to get him into the plane. He held onto the gurney during the entire ride to make sure it didn't fall on Ed's face.

The plane was equipped with a hospital bed and lots of modern equipment and supplies. The doctor took charge immediately. The plane had 12 seats and three crew members – a pilot, a copilot, and a mechanic. I'm not sure what an airplane mechanic could do once we were in the air, but I tried not to think about that. One of them told me the flight would be about four hours and asked if I had brought any food. When I said no, he gave me a paper bag with a container of Jell-O, a banana, and a Coke.

The flight was uneventful, and it was close to midnight when we landed. An ambulance, a fire engine, and a few police cars, all with their lights flashing were waiting to meet the plane. The uniformed men on the tarmac asked me what happened to Ed, obviously assuming it was something life threatening. They almost seemed disappointed when I told them my husband hurt his leg. Thankfully it was a short ride to the hospital. The doors to the Emergency Room were blocked by armed guards. Once inside, we were left on our own with staff who did not speak English except for one nurse who said, "Doctor comes here." So, we waited.

The doctor who was called in from home turned out to be an orthopedic traumatologist who spoke excellent English, which was a relief. He ordered an MRI which was done immediately even though it was the middle of the night. Ed's room had a couch where I could sleep so I was able to stay with him. We were exhausted.

All the prescribed drugs and supplies were provided by an independent pharmacy located across the street. At different hours of the day and night, a young man knocked on the door of Ed's room and handed me a paper listing in Spanish the items that Ed needed. It always had a total amount in US dollars at the bottom, which I paid him in cash. He retrieved the items from the pharmacy and delivered them a short time later in a plastic grocery bag. This included everything from syringes to IV bags to pills and miscellaneous supplies. Each time a nurse came in, she took everything out of the bag and did whatever needed to be done with whatever was inside. It was a very strange system.

We didn't recognize the name of the doctor who was ordering all this stuff and Ed was complaining about feeling woozy. He didn't have any pain, and no one ever explained what they were giving him or why. After three days, I told the young man that Ed did not want anything more from the pharmacy. I just said "No Farmacia. No Farmacia." He stopped coming.

When the doctor Ed had seen in the Emergency Room came to explain that the MRI revealed a torn meniscus that required surgery, Ed said he preferred to have it done at home so he could continue with follow up care and the physical therapy he needed. The doctor agreed, called the travel insurance company, and spent half an hour making arrangements for Ed to go home on a 6:00 am flight the next day, insisting that he travel first class because he couldn't bend his leg. The travel insurance covered Ed's ticket and I paid the difference between first class and coach fare so I could sit with him.

All this time I had been ordering guest meals by filling out a form every day, so I rarely left his room. Now I had to figure out how to pay the bill, get transportation to the airport and have Ed ready to leave by 4:30 am. I went down to the lobby of the hospital and asked each person at every desk I saw for someone who could speak English. When a young man from the accounting department greeted me in English, I nearly kissed him. He gave me instructions for the hospital Wi-Fi system, arranged for a big taxi to pick us up in the morning, and showed me where to go at the end of the day to pay the bill. My hero!

All this time, our big suitcase was still at the hotel on Santa Cruz Island. When it became clear that we wouldn't be returning, the hotel staff agreed to ship it to the hospital in Guayaquil, but there was only one flight per day and they had missed it the first day we were at the hospital. On the second day, they got the suitcase onto the flight, but it was delivered to a cargo center near the airport. They told me I could take a taxi and pick it up, but I was promised it would be delivered to the hospital and I stood my ground. They finally agreed to send some-one to get it and the day before we left, two people delivered our big suitcase to Ed's room. We finally had clean clothes to wear.

The accounting office had everything ready when I went down-stairs that night, and I paid the bill with a credit card. On my way back to Ed's room, I passed an area that held several wheelchairs. I took one, hustled it onto the elevator, and kept it in Ed's room overnight. It was one less thing to worry about.

The next morning, the staff understood we were leaving, and they did everything they could to help us. Our taxi was waiting when we got outside. When the driver opened the trunk, we saw that the taxi ran on natural gas and the tank took up most of the space. Ed needed the whole back seat to put his leg out straight. Somehow, we managed to get the big suitcase in the back with Ed and the overnight bag in the front seat with me. Good thing it was a short ride.

At the airport, the gate agent got a wheelchair for Ed and because we were flying first class, she gave us a pass for the lounge where we could have breakfast while we waited for the flight. The day before we left the hospital, Ed figured out that he could move sideways by using a different set of muscles on the outside of his leg. He was able to walk to the restroom in the lounge on his own but only sideways in one direction which meant sometimes he walked in circles to get where he was going. He drew some strange looks but at least he could move on his own.

When we reached the gate, I started to relax for the first time since Ed fell. We were going home, and soon this would all be over. Then the gate agent came on the loudspeaker and called Ed's name, asking him to come to the desk. She told us that our luggage had been selected for narcotics inspection and I should follow her downstairs.

I left poor Ed in his wheelchair at the gate while I followed the agent down into the bowels of the airport. She led me into a huge room with a long aluminum table at the far end where a bright light shone down on our big suitcase. It was the only one in the room. Lined up along the walls were men dressed in camouflage with the words "Anti-Narcotics" on their uniforms. Most of them had leashed dogs at their feet. That was when it hit me that the big suitcase had been out of our possession for five days and anyone could have put something in it without our knowledge. I envisioned myself being hauled away to a prison somewhere in Ecuador never to be heard from again. The man explained in English that he was going to search the bag. He went through every item out one at a time and checked each pocket of every piece of clothing. He found nothing. He put it all back in the suitcase and said, "You may go". I don't ever remember feeling so scared or so relieved when it was over.

Back home, additional scans revealed that Ed had torn his quad tendon completely off the bone. He did not have a torn meniscus. Ed's knee was repaired by the same surgeon who reconstructed my knee after the snowmobile accident in Yellowstone. We now have matching scars on our right knees.

CEREMONIES AND CELEBRATIONS

NEW FRIENDS IN DUSSELDORF

The first year we lived in Germany, we went to Dusseldorf for Fasching, the German version of Carnival. It was supposed to be one of the best places in Germany to celebrate the holiday before the beginning of Lent. We enjoyed a lovely train ride along the Rhine River, then checked into our hotel and set out to find a place to eat.

After wandering through the streets in the dark, we found a large brewery near the river that served food. Several of the people inside were already in costume even though the festivities didn't start until the next day. There were no empty tables, so we asked a group of three women if we could join them. They didn't speak English but were very friendly and we noticed by the number of tick marks on their cardboard coasters that they were on their fourth beer.

The one who did the most talking was actually from Poland. The volume of beer she had consumed added to her speaking German with a Polish accent as well as a lisp made for challenging conversation. We had a great time talking with these women and enjoyed the food and the beer. When it came time to leave, we paid our respective bills and went outside together. That was when we realized that we had taken a very roundabout route looking for a restaurant and didn't know how to get to our hotel. Our new friends were kind enough to walk us to a main street we recognized. After assuring them that we could find our way from there, they kissed us goodbye on each cheek and we wished each other well.

The next morning the streets were filled with people in the most unusual costumes I've ever seen, ranging from elaborate to ridiculous. Beer flowed everywhere despite the early hour. The giraffes and the clowns had their own portable bar that they pushed around town.

My favorite was the guy inside a shower on wheels that he rolled down the street. He was doing fine until someone tried to climb in with him.

In the afternoon, we secured a spot along the street to watch the annual parade. Almost everyone around us had brought empty bags and we soon found out why. The people in every float, truck and car that paraded by as well as those who marched on foot all threw candy out to the crowd. Lots of candy. We're talking German chocolate here. At first, we started catching it but soon our pockets were full. It was great fun.

During the parade, we stood behind a very friendly group who had brought along a small cooler and were drinking ice cold limoncello from small plastic glasses. The man doing the pouring spoke excellent English and told us he was a policeman in a town just across the border in Belgium. He invited us to drink with him but only after making sure we weren't driving. Once Ed assured him our hotel was nearby and we had traveled by train and not by car, he began pouring for us and didn't stop until the parade ended.

In the afternoon, we enjoyed a boat ride on the river where we met some more friendly people and enjoyed some more local beer. In spite of their gruff outward demeanor, Germans really do know how to party.

JULY 4TH ON KODIAK ISLAND

The second week of our Alaska camping tour began with a flight to Kodiak Island on the 4th of July. The town of Kodiak isn't very big, but it's beautiful and the people are very friendly.

Ed has maintained his membership in the American Legion as an Army veteran and we sometimes stop at a Legion when we're traveling in the US. His membership enabled us to gain entrance to the American Legion in Kodiak and we were treated like celebrities. People kept bringing us food from their potluck dinner, pouring drinks, and asking about our trip.

That night, we boarded a ferry back to the Alaska mainland. It didn't get dark until midnight, but we were able to see the red, white, and blue fireworks in Kodiak from the ferry. It was the most patriotic July 4th either of us could remember.

SUPER BOWL PARTY ON THE CRUISE SHIP

The Super Bowl was televised for us on the ship, but it didn't start until 1:30 am so we went to the Super Bowl party on the outside deck before the game. Our French chef admitted he didn't have a lot of experience preparing typical football party food and he even asked the passengers for suggestions.

The party turned out pretty well except for the chicken wings. I'm not sure where the chef got them, but the wings were so tiny, they must have come from baby chicks.

VOODOO CEREMONY IN TOGO

After five days at sea crossing the Atlantic, we were ready for some action and got more than we bargained for. We had signed up for an excursion to witness an authentic voodoo ceremony. The bus trip to the village of Sanguera took about an hour. Getting off the bus was like stepping into the pages of a National Geographic magazine.

The voodoo chief came out to meet the bus and performed a "libation ceremony" that involved dumping various liquids on the ground while muttering words that we couldn't understand. We were at the back of the group, so it was hard to see what he was doing but it sounded impressive.

When we walked into the center of the village, some of the local people were already dancing to a constant drumbeat that continued to get louder and faster. The dancing and chanting and yelling increased in intensity the longer we were there. Some people in grass skirts and painted faces were stumbling around in trances.

The guide on the bus insisted that everything was genuine and the ceremony was authentic. It was absolutely wild. The only time I got nervous was when the guy who kept slashing at a stick with a big ceremonial knife got close to me.

CEMETERY IN BORA BORA

On our tour of the island, someone on the bus asked the guide about what appeared to be graves above the ground next to some of the houses. The guide explained that when people die here, the family members put them in above-ground tombs next to the house where they lived. Relatives have picnics and family gatherings near the grave so the departed can still participate.

The island had a cemetery but the guide said if you're buried there, it's because you were a bad person and nobody loved you.

FIREWALKERS IN FIJI

Fiji is made up of 330 islands. The international date line runs through one of them where it's possible to straddle the line and have each foot in a different day. Our tour guide told us this proves time travel is really possible. We docked in Suva, which is the capital and the largest city in the South Pacific. This is where missionaries and settlers arrived and also where a tribe of cannibals lived. Fiji has a scary past.

We had never been to Fiji before and I'd always been fascinated by the firewalkers. Now we had the chance to see some in person. The bus ride to the cultural center took about an hour. On the way, our guide tried to recruit volunteers for firewalking. He didn't get any.

So here's the story of the firewalkers (condensed version). All firewalkers are members of the Sawahu tribe from the island of Benga. Long ago a warrior named Tui went out to hunt eels but found instead a tiny man who was a spirit god. This tiny man gave Tui power over fire. They went back to the village and the tribe dug a big pit and then filled it with white hot fire. The tiny man jumped in and told Tui to follow him, promising he would not be burned. Tui did as he was told and was not burned. Members of this tribe intermarry, so all can claim they are direct descendants of Tui and all are firewalkers. Firewalkers can also heal burns. Our guide said he tried it once and burned his feet. A firewalker just ran his hands over the soles of his feet and the burns were gone.

As we entered the stands to watch the firewalkers, we were each given a bottle of Fiji water. I had seen this in the grocery store at home, but never realized it actually came from Fiji.

After we were settled in our seats, the tribal priest appeared and began chanting over the fire, which had been lit four hours earlier. Then some tribesmen came down the hill and removed the wood from the fire and set it aside. They used long poles to turn the rocks hot side up and pack them together. Then they lined up and took turns walking over the hill of the hot stones.

Lots of chanting and yelling made this a very noisy, elaborate business. They mostly walked on their heels without letting their toes touch the coals. At the end of the ceremony, I wasn't 100% convinced it was real but it was very entertaining.

Our guide told us on the way back to the ship that two of the dancers we saw were his sons. They have regular jobs. Employers in Fiji support firewalking, so these men are allowed to take time off work, come and entertain us at the cultural center by walking on hot coals, then go back to work. Pretty amazing.

NATIVITY SCENE IN PERU

On our tour of Arequipa, we stopped to see a sprawling nativity scene that overlooked a lovely valley. Just like this archway, many of the buildings here are constructed of white volcanic stone that is found everywhere in this region.

In the US we're accustomed to nativity scenes that have camels and donkeys, but over the years we've celebrated the holidays in different countries where all kinds of nativity scenes are on display: A stable with salamis and bottles of chianti hanging from the eaves in Italy, a stable with monkeys and parrots in Costa Rica, etc. In Peru the animals in the nativity were mostly llamas. I guess it makes sense when you think about it.

FINDING FIREWORKS IN NEW ZEALAND

On the ship, we learned that our overnight in Auckland happened to be the same evening as a light show in the wharf area followed by fireworks. Oddly, the taxi driver who took us to the aquarium earlier in the day knew nothing about this. The light show included twelve different elaborate displays spread out over several blocks and we walked through all of them.

The fireworks were scheduled to start at 7:30 pm and we spent most of the hour beforehand trying to figure out where to stand. We knew they were going to be set off from a barge in the bay but there was water all around us and way too many bays. People were walking in every direction so it was impossible to follow the crowd. Signs were posted with arrows for fireworks but they all led to dead ends.

Earlier in the day, we had passed an interesting little public library in a shipping container with some silly looking chairs nearby that were low, deep, and hard to get in and out of. We were almost ready to give up on the fireworks when we saw the library again. The overhead door had been closed and locked but the chairs were still there. It gave us time to rest our feet and decide which way to go next.

All of a sudden, the fireworks started and we had a perfect view without leaving our chairs. What luck!

SOMBER COMMEMORATION IN DRESDEN

Over Presidents Day weekend we took a train to Dresden, which is known for porcelain factories and fine ceramics. It's located in the former East Germany where accents are very different from those in Bavaria. Ed had a much easier time understanding the people there than I did. He grew up in a Pennsylvania Dutch home where the dialect of German spoken was totally different from the German I learned in high school.

We had no idea when we picked this weekend to visit Dresden that it was on the anniversary of the WWII bombing. An estimated 25,000 people died when the city was heavily bombed for three days in February 1945. Over 1800 bombs were dropped in just 25 minutes. Each year at 10 pm on February 13, church bells all over the city ring to honor those who lost their lives that night.

When we heard the bells, I opened the window of our hotel room which faced a pedestrian only street lined with stone buildings. It's impossible to describe the sound of those bells echoing off the walls throughout the city. We put on our coats and went outside. The bells rang for 25 minutes to mark the duration of the bombing.

Large sections of the square outside the Frauenkirche cathedral were blocked off and filled with lit candles. We lit one and went inside the church to join the silent line of people walking through the exhibit of photographs from that night, then went upstairs to attend the church service. Elderly couples held each other and cried while grandparents quietly told their grandchildren what it was like that night when they were only children themselves.

A church has stood on this spot for over 1000 years. Two days after the bombing, the burned out building collapsed completely and it remained a pile of rubble until 1994 when rebuilding began. All the blackened stone that could be used was added to new stone and serves as a reminder of the church's sad history. It was completed in 2006.

February 13 in Dresden was a night I will always remember.

DANCING AT THE CHRISTMAS MARKET IN BERLIN

One of the best Christmas markets in Berlin was in Gendarmenmarkt Square across the street from our hotel. A stage was set up at one end where an oompah band was playing. When they started playing "Rock Around the Clock", we looked at each other and smiled. We couldn't resist. There was enough space in front of the stage for us to dance the jitterbug and that's exactly what we did. All alone. When the song was over, we realized that a big group of Germans had surrounded us, applauding and yelling, "Sehr gut!"

We visited Berlin a few times after that, but none of our memories of the city are as special as this one. Every time we hear that song, the memories of that Christmas market come back to us.

FLYING SUGAR ON QUEEN'S DAY IN AMSTERDAM

When we planned our first visit to Amsterdam to see the blooming tulips, we had no idea that our stay in the Netherlands would coincide with Queen's Day. This annual celebration commemorated the Queen's official birthday on April 30 which was celebrated in the Netherlands each year until 2013. In 2014, following Queen Beatrix's abdication, it was replaced with King's Day, which falls on April 27.

Queen's Day was one big party all over the city. Almost everyone we saw was dressed in orange and carrying a can of Heineken beer. The color orange is the symbol of the Dutch Royal Family. It goes all the way back to William of Orange, who was crowned Prince of Orange in 1544.

Obviously, we weren't prepared for this and had to stop at one of the street vendors to buy an orange scarf, orange hat and some orange beads. The canals were packed with boats, and the sidewalks and bridges were full of revelers all wearing orange.

At lunchtime, we stopped at a food truck to get a Dutch pancake which is kind of a combination of a crepe and a popover. Ed ordered his with a thick coating of powdered sugar on the top. As we stepped aside to find a place to sit down and eat, a sudden gust of wind came up behind Ed. The powdered sugar shot right off his pancake onto the front of my black coat. I could see it coming, almost in slow motion. I tried to dodge it but couldn't get out of the way fast enough.

I wore that powdered sugar all day.

BAPTISM IN FINLAND

During a Baltic cruise stop in Helsinki, we visited Uspenski Cathedral on top of a hill near the harbor. The area around the front door was roped off so we couldn't enter the main part of the church, but from the side entrance we were able to watch the baptism ceremony of a baby boy about eight months old.

The baby seemed fascinated by everything the priest said and did. It was a rare opportunity to witness what is normally a very private family event.

SINGING WITH LOCALS IN IRELAND

We had time for a pub crawl during our visit to Killarney with friends from Denver. The small bar we stopped in was celebrating the birthday of an elderly regular whose son came by to play his accordion for the occasion. The guest of honor's favorite song was "3 6 9 The Goose Drank Wine" better known as "The Clapping Song" by Shirley Ellis. This man walked around the pub with his pint, repeating the lyrics over and over. He stopped at our table and got us to sing "I've Been

Working on the Railroad" with him. I had the feeling he thought that was the only song Americans know.

There weren't a lot of people in the pub but the ones who were there all knew each other and were very friendly. If we hadn't bought tickets to an Irish folklore show that evening, we would have stayed until closing.

BIRTHDAY CELEBRATION IN ICELAND

When Iceland Air began nonstop service from Denver to Reykjavik, we took advantage of a special offer for a three-day package. While returning to our hotel after dinner one evening, we witnessed a wild birthday celebration on the street. A group of women on their way out of a bar were walking close together in multiple lines of four with a large balloon between each person. If I'd had a balloon handy, I would have joined them.

Evidently the idea was to stay together and keep the balloons in place as they walked. They were giggling so much, I didn't hold out hope that the balloons would last long, but they sure were having fun.

UNEXPECTED CHURCH SERVICE IN ITALY

The cathedral on the main square in picturesque Amalfi dominates the town. We climbed the 62 steep steps to reach the main entrance where a sign was posted indicating that a service was taking place. It said visitors were welcome to attend the service but if not, we should wait until it was over.

We had attended services in many other European churches during our travels and decided to go in. We sat at the back and watched as the priest sprinkled incense and we listened to his prayers. It wasn't until he moved away from the flower arrangements that we realized there was a casket behind him. We were attending a funeral service with only a small number of mourners.

When the service ended, six tall swarthy men carried the casket up the aisle, one slow step at a time. Each one in turn glared at us. It was clear we didn't belong there and everyone in attendance knew it. Visions of mafia danced in my head. Others waiting in the pews turned to look at us as well. Not wanting to call further attention to ourselves, we remained at our seats and tried to look very solemn.

The family was not fooled by this. The heartbroken young widow (we assumed) could barely walk up the aisle behind the casket. Her father and mother (we assumed) walked on either side, holding her by the arm. All three stared at us. It was getting uncomfortable. We stayed in our places until the last mourners left and then walked around the inside of the church for a while before showing our faces at the door. We stepped outside just in time to see the hearse pull away and drive down the pedestrian-only street. All the mourners had departed.

The next time we see a sign about a church service going on, we'll make sure we know what it's all about before we decide to participate.

WEDDING VOW RENEWAL IN SORRENTO

Our plans for a return visit to Italy were already underway when my romantic husband suggested we renew our wedding vows in Italy since we would be there very close to our 25th anniversary. A lovely idea, but how would I go about arranging it?

A hotel in Sorrento advertised weddings and receptions on their website, so I sent an email asking if we could have a vow renewal ceremony there. The hotel staff put me in touch with a local officiant who spoke excellent English. She sent me a copy of a vow renewal ceremony she had used before so we could review it and make any changes we wanted. It was beautiful just the way it was. She even added a lovely poem for the end of the ceremony, and provided a beautiful certificate written in Italian calligraphy on parchment.

We renewed our vows at sunset on the terrace of the hotel overlooking the sea and fell in love with each other all over again. The hotel arranged for a lovely private dinner inside afterwards. It was perfect.

The following day we took the certificate into town to find an Italian frame for it since Sorrento is famous for inlaid wood. An open door in a small building along a narrow side street revealed two older men sitting around a big room filled with pieces of wood and an assortment of projects in varying degrees of completion. It wasn't the kind of place we had in mind, but we stepped inside.

One of the men spoke some English so we handed him our certificate and asked if he had a frame that would fit. He read it and looked back at us with a big smile. Italians are such romantics. Then he went in the back of the workshop and reappeared with the perfect inlaid wood frame we were hoping to find. We watched while he meticulously matted and framed our certificate, wrapped it in padding and brown paper, then tied it with a string so that it would make it safely home.

Our vow renewal certificate still graces our front hall.

CULTURE AND CUSTOMS

ROMANIAN TOUR GUIDE'S NARROW ESCAPE

While living in Germany, we booked a two week private tour of Romania and Bulgaria. Since the fall of Communism in 1989 and 1990, we had been curious about the countries that were "behind the iron curtain" and closed to visitors for so many years. Romania was the only country where the events during the fall of Communism turned violent.

On our first day in Bucharest, our guide took us to the place on the main square where he and his friends participated in the Romanian Revolution in December 1989 that ended the 42 years of Nicolae Ceauşescu's communist rule. Riots, street violence and murders by secret police peaked in the capital city and the huge crowds protesting government policies were surrounded by police as they jeered Ceauşescu while he was giving a speech. Our guide feared for his safety and fled home. A friend called later to ask if he'd heard that many in the crowd were killed by police, including some of their friends. Until that phone call, he had no idea that he had barely escaped with his life. Ceauşescu and his wife got away through a nearby hotel to a waiting helicopter on the roof. They were later arrested in the countryside and executed.

Our guide became very emotional standing on the exact spot where he could have been murdered himself had he not left when he did. This man lived through horrors that we couldn't even imagine. As hard as it was to talk about this, he said it was important for him to share his story with us.

VISITING GYPSIES IN RURAL ROMANIA

Visiting the home of gypsies was the only part of our guided week in Romania that I was uneasy about. The gypsies we had encountered in Rome and Vienna were pushy tricksters and thieves. I mentioned this to our guide at dinner the night before the scheduled visit and he explained that the family we would be visiting was part of a community that was making an effort to break away from the traditional gypsy way of life and earn an honest living from making copper pots and other items to sell. I agreed to go.

The family lived in small village out in the countryside. They kept a large fire going behind the house and demonstrated their skill in heating and molding copper and other metals to make their wares. I couldn't help keeping my purse very close to me the entire time I was there, but it turned out to be a nice visit. Their twelve-year-old son was learning the copper trade and I bought a small copper dipper with a long handle that he had made himself.

The wife showed me a large stack of linens she was accumulating for their very young daughter who would soon be married. By the time we left, we started to look like gypsies too!

This was a tight community of people who lived in all kinds of homes, from shacks with a horse and wagon outside to lavish multi-story estates. Everyone stared at us as we drove by. Ed was interested in one particular large house with a unique design that he could see from down the road and asked our guide if we could drive closer to it. He was a bit reluctant but finally agreed.

Ed took a picture from the car which was gradually being surrounded by gypsies. One asked what we were doing there. Our guide replied that he was the driver for an architect and his wife, and they admired this house very much. The gypsy accused him of making up stories about the people in the community and then going back to the city to say bad things about them. Even though we couldn't understand a word they were saying, it was obvious that the conversation was turning into a heated argument. Our guide kept trying to assure the gypsies we were only admiring the house and we would leave immediately without saying a word to anyone.

They let us go.

LIFE AFTER COMMUNISM IN BULGARIA

In Bulgaria, our big burly guide also talked openly about the changes in his country. He told us that only about half the people feel they are better off since the fall of communism, especially the older ones who still have no idea how to find work on their own. Under communism everyone was given a modest place to live and a job. They could earn enough to buy food although selection was minimal and shortages were common. He jokingly said, "Everyone had a job but nobody worked."

Now people rummage through trash bins and rely on family members who are able to find jobs and earn money. Much of the landscape looked like it hadn't changed in many years. The cities seemed more prosperous and the outlook there was brighter. He believes things will gradually improve as younger people make up more of the workforce but expects it will take a long time.

The churches and monasteries here are magnificent and we really enjoyed our visit here. One day we stopped in a small coffee shop during one of our long drives. I admired the spoon that came with my coffee and asked our guide what the words on it meant. He said it was just the name of the shop and told the shop owner how much I liked the spoon. The shop owner gave me two of his spoons to take home.

LOOKING FOR FAMOUS PEOPLE IN POLAND

The NATO summit in July 2016 was scheduled to start in Warsaw the day after we arrived. Although the meetings were primarily held at the National Stadium, the Presidential Palace was also expecting dignitaries and was closed to the public with no tours until after the summit ended. However, it was possible to peek through the windows of the palace into rooms prepared for formal meetings and dinners with flags, centerpieces, and place settings.

On the main streets throughout the historic city center, we looked closely at every official-looking black limousine and SUV that drove by, searching for a famous face. Our walk back to the hotel was long but it enabled us to see more of Warsaw. The Tomb of the Unknown Soldier was particularly impressive. The city showed off its finest parks and gardens for this event and we were happy to have been there in time to enjoy it.

CUSTOMS AT HOME IN COLORADO

I joined a writers group in Denver just before their annual retreat and was delighted to learn that a space had opened up due to a cancellation. The retreat was held at a resort with rustic cabins at some hot springs high in the Rockies. I joined a carpool with the women who would be sharing their cabin with me. I was looking forward to a great weekend to learn more about the craft of fiction writing and make some new friends. The hot springs nestled among gold aspen trees and thick pines looked inviting and relaxing.

As we checked in and picked up our cabin keys, one of the women I rode with stunned me by asking, "At what time are bathing suits optional?" I began to wonder what I'd gotten myself into. After all, I really didn't know any of these people.

As it turned out, that weekend was the beginning of lasting friendships with women writers who taught me so much and continue to help one another succeed in publishing their work. I didn't bump into anyone without a bathing suit the entire weekend.

FEELING AT HOME IN HAWAII

When we docked in Honolulu towards the end of our world cruise, everyone felt like we were home after five months at sea. We had a very brief face to face meeting with immigration authorities who looked at our passports and gave us a little slip of paper to prove we were cleared to re-enter the United States.

After a short stop in a drugstore for toothpaste and a greeting card, we went to Starbucks and used their super speedy free Wi-Fi. Compared to the Wi-Fi on the ship, it was fantastic. We made some phone calls, sipped our respective beverages, and just enjoyed being back in America. I didn't expect to feel this way. It was kind of weird because it didn't look anything like home. It just felt like it.

PUERTO RICO AFTER DARK

The walking tour of Old San Juan that we had booked was more like a steep hike. The guide led us up one big hill after another until we reached El Morro, the huge fortress overlooking the city. Construction was started by the Spanish in 1539 with walls up to 20 feet thick made from limestone and sandstone blocks with rubble sandwiched in between. The views made the climb worthwhile. The fort, the castle and city walls that make up the UNESCO World Heritage San Juan National Historic Site were really impressive. We were the last group of the day to go through and the sun was setting when we reached the final viewpoint at the top.

The Spanish flag still flies at the top along with those of the US and Puerto Rico. The guide took us around the outside of the fortress and then through the tunnels that led to the dungeons. I was quite far behind the group and Ed was quite far behind me with a sore knee. The voices of the people in the group grew more faint as we walked and I started to worry that the iron gate at the entrance to the tunnels had been padlocked after the group went through and the gate at the exit would be padlocked before we reached it.

The guide wasn't very conscientious about keeping a head count so he may not have noticed that we were so far behind. With no shortage of things to start worrying about, I started yelling down the long curving tunnel, "Wait! Don't lock us in!" I had visions of getting trapped there all night with the rats and big black iguanas, and soon I started to run. Eventually we made it out to the plaza where the rest of our group was wandering around. No one missed us.

On the way up to the fortress we had passed some interesting cafés and Ed suggested we stop somewhere for Sangria and tapas. It sounded like a great idea. We were wiped out. The guide suggested a place that sometimes has flamenco shows on Thursday evenings in addition to good Sangria and tapas, and he gave us directions. It took us a while to find our way back through the city, but the place our guide described turned out to be located only a few blocks from the ship.

The wonderful entertainer who played the Spanish guitar on stage stopped by our table and told us he was 80 years old and once performed on the Ed Sullivan Show. Not only did he play the guitar well, but he also sang beautifully and was a good comedian.

Words cannot describe those flamenco dancers. Their huge, ruffled dresses and fancy footwork were unbelievable. I have no idea how long the show lasted, but we sure had a good time. Maybe the pitcher and a half of Sangria had something to do with it. The food wasn't great but it didn't matter.

We spent most of the next day telling everyone we knew what a good time we had. A man from the walking tour stopped us in the hallway and said, "I remember you from the San Juan death march last night. Where did you go when you left the tour?" When we told him, he was sorry he didn't go with us.

AN AFTERNOON IN LIVERPOOL CATHEDRALS

Our city tour took us to two of the main churches in Liverpool, England. The Liverpool Cathedral was built in the early 1900s but it appeared much older. The organ has over 10,000 pipes and the Gothic arches are enormous. The altar was carved into a wall of sandstone, then painted. Lots of atmosphere there.

In stark contrast, the Metropolitan Cathedral of Christ the King Catholic Church was very modern with lots of light. Building of this church began in 1962 and was completed in 1967. It holds 2,300 people.

The thing that struck me about both these churches was large non-religious gift shops and cafés inside. Churches used to be just for worship, but evidently now you can attend a service, pick up a birthday gift and eat lunch with friends all under the same roof in one trip. Maybe generating revenue this way is probably what enables them to keep the church running when the number of worshippers decline. Maybe stores and restaurants inside churches have become more common than I realized, but this was the first time I'd seen them on such a large scale.

As one would expect, the Liverpool tour included sites frequented by the Beatles. We drove by many of the places mentioned in the familiar songs that our guide played for us on the bus as we went along. Our stop at Penny Lane was my favorite, even though it looked like all the other streets in the neighborhood.

The entire tour was terrific.

BEAUTIFUL SINGING IN QAQORTOQ, GREENLAND

Qaqortoq was a real treat. The steep hills covered with brightly colored houses were unlike any other place we'd been in all our travels. Our tour was supposed to be two hours of walking through the town, but when we got off the ship, the excursions staff just told us to "walk that way" because a concert was starting at the high school in ten minutes. We had some trouble finding it but the walk through the town was so interesting, we were glad we made the effort to get there.

Five men sang to us from the depths of their souls. They had the most beautiful voices. Occasionally one would explain that the next song is about summer, or this song is about love. The last one they sang was about peace. It was all in their native language of Inuit, so I didn't understand any of the words, but it was very moving just the same.

Only one store in town was open, a small grocery that had mostly packages of frozen fish and unfamiliar meats. Across the bay was the fur house where furs and sealskins are processed and tanned. Importing these things into the US is illegal, so the excursions manager warned everyone not to buy anything made from marine mammal products. He also warned us about the fish market. They sell whatever they can catch, and many of the items for sale are not the kinds of things we're used to seeing. In other words, if you have a weak stomach, don't go. The fish market was closed anyway because it was Sunday so there was no decision to make.

Although we ran out of things to see here, I just couldn't get enough of those colorful houses and the amazing people who live in them.

VIKINGS IN NEWFOUNDLAND

To say that there's not much in L'Anse Aux Meadows would be a vast understatement. There are exactly 19 residents in this village. One is a school age child who travels 40 minutes each way to go to school in the nearest town that has one. Residents are not permitted to sell their property here. When the owner dies or chooses to leave the village, their house is bought by the park system, which will eventually own everything. Why did we stop here, you ask?

At the northernmost tip of Canada on the Atlantic coast, L'Anse Aux Meadows is the site of the first Norse settlement in the Americas. Leif Eriksson crossed the Labrador Sea from Greenland and landed at L'Anse Aux Meadows 500 years earlier than Columbus came to North America. The site was uncovered in 1960 and became a UNESCO World Heritage Site in 1978.

Norstead is a recreated Viking village, where local people (from miles around evidently) dressed as Vikings offer living history inside the various buildings. It was really very well done. One of the buildings contained a wonderful recreation of a Viking ship. I hadn't thought about it before visiting here, but the Vikings evidently brought women. I guess they needed them to make little Vikings since they planned to stay.

LEGEND OF THE BAOBAB TREE IN TANZANIA

The ruins at Bagamoyo date back to the 13th century and consist of two mosques and 30 tombs. These are the oldest mosques in Africa. Bagamoyo was also the last place that the people living in Tanganyika saw of their homeland before being taken to the slave markets in Zanzibar. The name Tanzania comes from the combined names of these two lands.

Behind the ruins stood a giant baobab tree that is over 500 years old. According to an African legend, if you walk all the way around the tree, it will add a year to your life. So of course I did that. Just as I came back around to the front, our guide ran up to me and said, "No, no, Madame! You have walked the wrong direction. Now you have taken a year off your life!" He took my hand and walked me all the way around the tree the other way to correct my error. I had no idea how important it was to walk in the right direction. I think I'm even now.

GHOST TOWN IN CHILE

The caliche mine at Humberstone is located in the Pampa region of the Atacama Desert in Chile. At its peak, this mining town had 3,700 inhabitants including 500 schoolchildren. It was built in the 1930s and when the mine closed in 1960, time seems to have stopped. The hot, dusty, and dry location helped to preserve the buildings of what had been a very prosperous town. It became a UNESCO World Heritage site in 2005. This place is literally in the middle of nowhere and it gets no rainfall. Ever.

The Humboldt current keeps all the moisture offshore so there is a constant fight over meager existing water supplies between the mining companies and the needs of the people in this area. Trade with China has become so essential to the economy here, that English is no longer the second language. It's Chinese.

This region also holds one of the largest accumulations of naturally occurring sodium nitrate in the world. Nitrate salts bind together in mineral deposits called caliche ore which was mined in Humberstone. Some of the salt from the mines in this area is shipped all the way to the northeastern US for road salt in the winter. Imagine that.

The buildings we walked through appeared as though people still lived and worked in them. So many of their belongings remained behind; desks and books were still in the school classrooms and the shelves of supplies in the general store looked like they had just been stocked. This community in the middle of the desert even had a theater. It seemed like a pretty nice place to live, as long as you didn't need much water.

We walked several blocks through the town and could easily see where UNESCO has made a difference. Many of the buildings that were weakened by earthquakes over the years have not yet been restored. Our guide gave us a stern warning stay away from those. The restoration work here will continue for a very long time.

CULTURE AND HISTORY IN PERU'S CAPITAL

Our eight hour tour on a bright December day took us to see the "Highlights of Colonial Lima". This city of ten million people was founded in 1535 by Francisco Pizarro. A quick summary of interesting facts our guide told us on the bus: Over four thousand varieties of potatoes are grown in Peru. They come in every shape and color, including blue, yellow, red, pink, and even bright purple. Ladies sell quinoa for breakfast on the streets of Lima. 80% of Peru is Catholic. Peru still has bullfights and matadors; it's part of the culture.

The bus ride from the port city of Callau to Lima took about 40 minutes. People smiled and waved to our bus as we drove by. The bus let us off at Plaza Major which was one of the most beautiful city squares we had ever seen. The crown jewel here is the massive cathedral. It's so big that it was impossible to get it all in one photo.

Lima was one of those places where I wished I could bring home all the colorful items on display in the shops. We settled for just looking. After a very informative tour of the square, we had some free time. It wasn't nearly long enough to see everything, but we really enjoyed our day here. We headed straight for the chocolate museum that had a lovely shop in the lobby. The aroma was heavenly.

We had seen police in various places around the square but we had become accustomed to that in South America and didn't think much about it. The side streets leading to the square were blocked off with barricades but we didn't think much about that either. A fellow passenger asked me if I had seen the demonstration and I said yes, thinking he was talking about the chocolate making demonstration in the museum. He was talking about the demonstration of protesters. Down the block, the number of police in riot gear had grown and the chanting of the crowd got louder but the police held them back, away from the square.

We hoped it wouldn't get out of control and hurried over to the presidential palace where the changing of the guard was just beginning. I had expected to see men in fancy uniforms yelling orders, marching around, and taking up their new places at the gates. Not here.

The official band came out and marched right up to the fence to play for the crowd. It was a really big band — three tubas! As long as the demonstrations didn't get any closer, we wanted to stay for the entire ceremony. They were still playing a half hour later when it was time to head back to the bus.

The street we had to cross to get back to the bus was blocked by another demonstration. This one by Santa and his elves on motorcycles zigzagging all over the streets. It was hard to find an opening to run across to the other side.

Lima was an unexpected delight in many ways. We'd love to go back there one day.

ANCESTORS IN PAPEETE, TAHITI

Most of the tours offered here involved going to beaches, so we hired a taxi for the day to take us around the island. Along the way our driver told us about the first place he was taking us to called Marae Ta'Ata, an archaeological site with ruins from the first ancient buildings on Tahiti where it is believed the people worshiped their gods. When we arrived, he told me it was important to put my hands on the stones so I could feel the "mana" of his ancestors. I did.

HORRORS OF WWII OFFSET BY PEACE AND CALM IN JAPAN

Since our first two cruise ports in Japan were places that were heavily bombed in WWII, most of the excursions offered here related to war monuments and museums. We chose to set off on our own in search of today's rebuilt Nagasaki while still paying respect to its past.

Nagasaki is not a huge city and it was easy to get around on their transit system. We stopped at the ATM in the cruise terminal building to get a supply of Japanese Yen, picked up a good map and headed to the tram stop about eight blocks away.

The tram system in Nagasaki was simple. Everyone got on at the back door and off at the front door. We paid at the box next to the driver who sat on the right hand side of the tram. He wore a white glove on his left hand, the one he used to feed the money into the box. The box spit out change and transfer tickets, and the driver was very helpful. Except for the very first tram we rode, we were the only non-Japanese aboard. The trams were old but quite efficient and they ran every ten minutes.

At the Peace Memorial we didn't go inside the war museum. The photos displayed outside near the hypocenter of the atomic bomb were hard enough to look at. Much of the city was completely destroyed. I had to keep reminding myself that Pearl Harbor happened first.

We got back on the tram to visit Sokufuji Temple, a Zen temple built by a Chinese monk named Chaonian in 1629. There were several interesting temples in the city, but this one was the easiest to reach. Unfortunately, it wasn't open. Even the outside of it was quite impressive yet very peaceful and tranquil. I could feel myself relax when we entered the grounds. A groundskeeper was meticulously arranging the gravel in the zen garden with a tiny rake. I could have spent the rest of the day here.

After a short walk through the little cemetery on the hill above the grounds, we went out through a narrow walkway where we were pleasantly surprised to find restrooms that were open, clean, and very convenient.

From our balcony on the ship at the end of the day, we enjoyed a performance by the Nagasaki high school band, cheerleaders, and flag twirlers. They played Japan's national anthem along with several familiar numbers. At the end, they all lined up on the pier and waved goodbye as we sailed away. It was a heartwarming end to our day in Nagasaki.

SAD MONUMENTS IN HIROSHIMA

In the Peace Park, we spent some time at the Atomic Bomb Dome, which was registered as a UNESCO World Heritage Site in 1996. It's essentially the shell of a large dome topped building that was left standing after WWII.

In some ways, this was more moving than the pictures we saw of the atomic bomb destruction in Nagasaki. Again, I reminded myself that Pearl Harbor happened first, but it didn't help much, especially when I saw parents trying to explain to their school age children what had happened here.

MORE JAPANESE CULTURE ALONG WITH SOME CONFUSION

When we arrived with another couple by train from the port in Kobe, our guide for the next day and a half was waiting for us outside the Kyoto station. Thom was a graduate student from the Netherlands who spoke excellent English. He had spent a semester abroad in Japan and fell in love with the country and culture. He'd been living in Japan for four years and although young, he proved to be very knowledgeable.

Kyoto was the imperial capital of Japan for over a thousand years. It is the cultural and artistic heart of the nation, best known for its Buddhist temples, Shinto shrines, beautiful gardens, and historically priceless buildings. Our first stop was the Higashi Hongan-ji Temple originally built in 1602 then burned in a fire and reconstructed in 1895. After a short visit there we took the subway to visit Nijo-jo castle. Just before we entered the castle, we realized that it was past time to make it to the Miyako Odori performance of Geishas and Maiko (Geishas in training) which started at 12:30. The tickets we had purchased online months ago included a tea ceremony which started an hour earlier.

The geisha performance was supposed to be fantastic but reviews of the tea ceremony were not particularly good — no participation, just observing from your seat in a large theater. I had told Thom we felt our time would be better spent elsewhere so we planned to skip the tea ceremony. He thought I meant we were not going at all and wiped it from his radar. The geisha performance was the highlight of our time in Kyoto and we didn't want to miss it. Since we were on the opposite side of the city, we had to go by taxi and needed two of them since there were five of us. Miraculously, we arrived in time and were each given a little bag with a sweet in a box and a plate from the tea ceremony we didn't attend. Our seats were in the last row of the balcony — the only ones available at the time I booked — but they were great.

This performance is only open during the month of April and goes back to 1872 on the occasion of the Kyoto World Exposition. Musicians playing traditional Japanese instruments sat on both sides of the theater, along with a singer. Kimono clad women danced through four seasons with changing scenery and unique music. It was magnificent. The traditional theater normally used for this was being renovated to make it earthquake proof, so this year the performance was held in a more modern venue. I couldn't imagine it being any more impressive.

To make up for his misunderstanding, Thom offered to take us to a private tea ceremony conducted by a friend of his at 4:30 and we agreed. Big mistake. During lunch, I asked the price. $150 per person. We couldn't justify spending that on an hour of tea drinking, even though I knew there was more involved. Thom called his friend but it was too late to cancel. We compromised by agreeing to pay what we felt it was worth afterwards and Thom knocked some money off his guide fee. It was awkward but we managed to get through it.

After lunch, we took a combination of bus and subway to Ginkakuji Temple, another World Heritage Site in a part of the city built in 1482 by Ashikaga Yoshimasa, a Shogun. It was at the top of a long hill filled with historic houses and old shops known as the Philosopher's Walk. The highlight of this area was the Shogun's house and garden. Gardeners come through daily to re-rake the zen garden, and trim and manicure the gardens. I wished we could have stayed longer, but it was time to head downhill and get to the tea ceremony on time. I was surprised at the number of people we saw on the streets in kimonos. For some reason, I thought this was something people only wore on special occasions. Here, even the bunnies wore them.

After another ride on a crowded bus, we walked several blocks to the tea house. Thom is a typical Dutch man, tall with long legs that go twice as fast as ours. He was hard to keep up with and he kept saying it's just a few more blocks. We had to stop at an ATM because the tea master only accepted cash. I wasn't sure exactly what to expect at the tea ceremony but what happened wasn't anything close.

Thom introduced us to his friends who gave us each a pair of brand new tabi-socks in a cellophane package along with a ceremonial fan. While we changed our footwear in the "welcome room", we were told a little bit about the house. The tea masters bought this three-story tea house from a Japanese businessman who had it built for his geisha. The relationship fell apart, she found a different patron, and he sold it to these two tea masters.

They led us upstairs to the tearoom. I had told Thom earlier that none of us were able to sit or kneel on the floor, so they prepared the room with small stools for us to sit on. These tiny stools tipped very easily. It was hard to concentrate on the ceremony for fear of falling over.

Words cannot describe the excruciating detail that these two men went through to tell us about their tea ritual. We were there for three hours. They explained that the tea they were serving was very thick warrior tea. It tasted like liquid spinach, only worse. When asked what I thought of the tea after my first sip, it was difficult to come up with a response that didn't insult them. All I could say was that it tasted healthy. The ceremony went on and on. It was clear these two men relished everything about it. All I could think about was getting off the tippy stools and going to the hotel to get some sleep.

The most interesting part of the experience was the tea house bathroom. Japanese toilet seats are all heated, even in the train station, and automatically cleaned after each use. This bathroom was the most modern one I had ever encountered. As soon as I opened the door to go in, the light gradually came on and the toilet lid slowly opened by itself. I could hear it whirring and clicking while I was using it. As soon as I finished, it sprayed cleaner and flushed automatically and the lid closed while I washed my hands. There were several buttons on the wall to make adjustments to all these features. The entire toilet system seemed to be electric. There was no handle to flush manually that I could see. I have no idea what the Japanese do if the power goes out.

Finally, the evening came to a close. We thanked and paid our hosts and took the subway to our hotel without getting lost while Thom headed home to Osaka on the train.

Our second day in Kyoto started with news from Thom that there had been a 5.7 magnitude earthquake early that morning in Kobe where our ship was docked. The early morning train to Kyoto from Osaka ran late because of this. The Japanese engineers were checking all the tracks methodically, creating delays and cancellations. We agreed it would be best if we left Kyoto earlier than planned to make sure we didn't miss the scheduled departure of the ship. It was hard to leave the tranquil beauty of the gardens we had visited that morning, but we were worried about the train situation.

When the subway train arrived, it was completely full, so we waited for the next one which was also full, but the pushers made room and we got up close and personal with our fellow passengers. I now understand the stories I had heard about crowded Japanese trains. Some of the subway cars were designated for female passengers only to minimize problems with male passengers who have roaming hands.

We were able to get tickets for the Kobe train scheduled to leave in ten minutes and dashed to the platform. Our guide was heading home again, so he rode with us as far as Osaka. It was a good thing we caught it, because the next one had already been cancelled. The train was crowded but after a few stops we all found seats.

At the Kobe station, we found a taxi to take us to the port. Nobody there knew anything about an earthquake. No one we talked with on the ship had felt anything during the night and the ship sailed on time at 2:00 pm with no mention of anything out of the ordinary. It was all very strange.

Kyoto is a beautiful city filled with history and culture. We barely scratched the surface and hope to return one day.

INTERVIEWED IN HONG KONG

Our plan was to buy tickets for the Hop On /Hop Off bus that included the ferry to Hong Kong from Kowloon where our ship was docked. That part went smoothly. It was a short but beautiful ride across the bay. Soon after we boarded the double decker bus, we realized we were on the green line that went out to the beaches and not the red line that wound through the city of Hong Kong. We stayed on the bus and it turned out to be a great way to see the area outside the center of the city while getting a better feel for the way people live here.

We got off at Stanley Market and were approached by some very polite schoolboys who were taking a survey. They worked in teams of four, one snagging someone to interview, one to ask the questions, one to record the answers, and one to hand out a thank you note and appreciation gift which was a foil packet of Mr. Brown's milk tea mix.

Their teacher hovered nearby while they asked questions about where we were from, when we arrived, why we came to Hong Kong, how long we were staying, what we liked about it, etc. They all spoke excellent English and were delightful. If we had gotten on the right bus, we never would have met them.

MAKING NEW FRIENDS IN VIETNAM

We didn't expect Hanoi to be a very friendly city but we were pleasantly surprised. On the crowded sidewalk after dinner in the city, I asked to take a photo of a cute little girl whose mother nodded enthusiastically and stepped aside. I thanked them both with a nod and a smile and we moved on. The little girl immediately brought her two friends over so I could take her picture with them, so I did. Then the whole family wanted to get in on it and have their picture taken with us. Then the grandmother wanted her picture taken with Ed. Then some other people wanted us to take their picture and they started lining up. Then some other Vietnamese started taking pictures of us taking pictures. None of them said much but they all laughed a lot.

The entire experience was fun but a bit bizarre.

BRITISH CULTURE IN TASMANIA

Tasmania always sounded to me like a very wild and exotic place. While there, we learned it was founded as a penal colony with 300 inmates from Britain. Much of the capital city of Hobart was built by convicts with sandstone from nearby cliffs.

Tasmanians boast that they have the clearest skies, the purest air, and the cleanest water in the world. That's really saying something. 100% of their power is hydroelectric. There is almost no flat land here. It's also an expensive place to live. A small two bedroom cottage made of sandstone goes for around $700,000 US.

Hobart has a very British atmosphere. There are lawn bowling clubs and badminton clubs and lots of pubs. At one point there were 137 pubs within a one kilometer radius. Their tasty fresh water and local hops and barley make for very good beer.

Our kind of place.

LEARNING THE CULTURE OF BRUNEI

The only thing I knew about Brunei before coming here was that the Sultan of Brunei was a very rich man. We had booked a half day tour titled "Brunei Culture and Visit to Water Village". The entire day was very strange.

The Sultanate of Brunei is actually located on the island of Borneo. All its wealth comes from oil and natural gas. Brunei adopted strict Islamic Sharia law in 2014 which allows punishment such as stoning for adultery and amputation for theft. I made sure that my hands were always open and visible whenever we were off the bus just in case someone of authority might get the wrong idea.

Our daily newsletter on the ship probably offered the best description of Brunei: "This tranquil (and somewhat solemn) nation is the realization of a particular vision: a strict, socially controlled religious state where happiness is found in pious worship and mass consumption."

The first thing our tour guide said in her nice welcome speech was "My name is Evie and I am BBC." I thought wow, we have a reporter for a guide. No. BBC stands for Brunei Born Chinese. The people who are born here enjoy very generous support from the government and most have a very high standard of living. Those who were not born here live very differently.

We learned from fellow passengers later that our guide was much more open about life here compared the other guides. Most people own two cars. That's two per person, not two per household, which explained why we saw so many houses that looked like they had parking lots for driveways. The typical house here would qualify as a mansion in the US.

Gas is very cheap and there is no tax. There are very few taxis here because tourism is not promoted. There are not many public buses either because everybody drives cars. The buses they do have run at the whim of the driver. If he's in a good mood, he's on schedule. If not, he drives when he feels like it. Our guide actually said that.

All this government support sounds like a great thing, but Brunei is realizing that the people have no motivation to work, so entrepreneurship is almost nonexistent. The city almost felt eerie because there were so few people outside, even in residential neighborhoods. All I could think about was that if the oil ever runs out, these people will be in big trouble.

We were able to see a portion of the Sultan's Palace from a distance and learned that it contains 1,788 rooms including 257 bathrooms, a banquet hall that can be expanded to accommodate up to 5,000 guests, and a mosque with space for 1,500 people. The palace also includes a 110-car garage, an air conditioned stable for the Sultan's 200 polo ponies, and five swimming pools. In total, the palace contains 2,152,782 square feet of floorspace with 44 stairwells and 18 elevators. It's unclear how many people live there but it sure seems like a lot of house.

On the way back to the ship, we passed a beautiful golf course that was designed by Arnold Palmer. Our guide said not many people use it because the monkeys come and snatch away the golf balls.

THE GRAND AND MYSTERIOUS
SHWEDAGON PAGODA

Our ship arrived in the country of Myanmar late in the day and we chose a tour to see the temple that evening. The 2,500 year-old Shwedagon Buddhist Temple covers twelve acres. Spectacular doesn't begin to describe this place. The 325 foot gold dome was visible from the bus as we approached. It's plated with 8688 sheets of gold and is studded with more than 7000 diamonds and precious gems like rubies, sapphires, topaz along with a massive piece of emerald. Its dome is crowned with a 72 carat diamond. Tourists aren't allowed to get anywhere near the dome for obvious reasons but we admired it from afar and tried to interpret the map.

We went in through the foreign visitor's entrance, took off our shoes and socks, and put them in laundry baskets that were labeled for our tour, then waited for the tour guide to put a red dated sticker on every person's shoulder. She gave us each a packet of wet towelettes to use at the end of the tour before we put our shoes back on. We had been told before departure that our shoulders and knees had to be covered so we were prepared for that, even though it was 102 degrees that day. After passing through the metal detector, we took a long elevator ride up to the entrance. It seemed like we went up about six floors but there were only two stops, top and bottom.

The temple is an enormous complex surrounding the dome, filled with individual altars, pagodas, Buddha statues and lots and lots of gold. I had never seen anything like this. For the next hour and a half, our guide walked us through the entire temple which seemed to be laid out similar to a shopping mall although that was probably not the intent.

Several extended families wandered through various sections of the pagoda and we saw lots of smiling children. Some people were at prayer in front of an altar, some walked from one altar to the next and some sat on the floor in groups talking and laughing. Silence was not required here.

Our guide explained that people donate money to have a statue or an altar or a side pagoda built. I can't imagine what some of these things must have cost. Donation boxes were everywhere, many of them labeled for specific purposes like maintenance, gold plating, electricity, and other things.

Because there's no roof over the temple complex, it's completely open to the weather. We were so glad to have come in the evening so we didn't have to walk on the hot tiles during the day. The wet wipes the guide gave us really came in handy at the end. The bottoms of our feet were black.

FROM BUDDHIST TEMPLES TO HINDU TEMPLES

In Mangalore, India we visited the massive Gokarnanath Temple, dedicated to Hindu deities. We had to remove our shoes in the parking lot as soon as we got off the bus. It was a good thing we were there early in the morning before the sun heated the walkways. The temple was gorgeous and encompassed several buildings.

Although I couldn't quite grasp the meaning the various Hindu statues and why they are worshipped, the whole complex was very impressive and very different from the Buddhist temples we had visited. The main temple was divided into different sections for different gods whose names were very difficult to remember and even more difficult to pronounce. Each section contained an elaborate statue guarded by a priest whose job seemed to be receiving gifts from worshipers which were mostly food or flowers for the god and putting a colorful spot on the forehead of each person.

In one section the priest had two bowls of powder on the table. He gave some gift givers yellow spots on their foreheads and some got red spots. No matter how many times I watched the process, I couldn't understand the system and lost count of the number of individual gods inside this building. The priest next to the lion god called Ed over to him and touched his ponytail. Then he just nodded and that was the end of that. No colorful spot on the forehead for Ed.

When we returned to the main entrance, I'd never seen so many shoes in one place. Big piles of them were everywhere but somehow, we all managed to find our own. By this time we had learned to carry wet wipes with us to clean off our feet in case the guide didn't offer any. On this tour, we had one of those guides.

While we were putting our shoes back on, I watched an Asian man screaming at a bus driver who had just backed the bus over a big pile of flip flops. The sandals were mangled, broken, and completely messed up. I felt sorry for the people coming out of the temple after walking barefoot on hot stones in the sun only to find that their footwear had been run over by a bus and rendered useless.

FAMILY LIFE IN ZANZIBAR

80% of Zanzibar is Muslim and almost all the people here wear traditional clothing, especially in the city. Our guide was very open about the customs and culture of his people. He has two wives, one with three children and one with two. The wives keep separate huts and he alternates between them. When he returns home at the end of each day, he places his walking stick above the door of the hut where he plans to spend the night. This way all five children know to go to the other wife's hut to sleep.

The law allows up to four wives but most men can't afford more than two. His grandfather had 28 children. It's still considered a symbol of manhood in their culture. The more children you have, the greater man you are.

The children are only required to go to primary school. Girls as small as five wear cream colored head coverings and blue robes. Girls who go to secondary school wear white and black. Those thick head coverings and heavy robes had to be miserable in the heat. There are over 100 children in one classroom and they walk as far as 5 kilometers to get to school.

We forget how lucky we are to live in the United States.

UNAPPRECIATED PERFORMANCE IN HUNGARY

Behind a lovely palace in the town of Tihany lies a beautiful garden surrounded by benches. After paying my entrance fee to visit the inside of the palace, I was given a pair of soft wooly slippers to wear. Evidently this prevents someone's street shoes from scratching the wood parquet and polishes the floors at the same time. They were very slippery especially on the stairs, but I managed to stay upright.

In the music room on the second floor, a young woman was playing the piano like I've never heard it played before. She was in a world of her own as if she could feel every note. There were about ten or twelve young people seated in the room listening and a middle-aged woman standing by the window. When the music ended, I was ready to applaud but no one did. I quickly realized that this was a group of students and the one who had just played clearly fell short of the high standards demanded by the instructor. The poor young woman was scolded severely and had to repeat the same section over and over again because it simply wasn't good enough.

I was convinced that if she could overcome that kind of criticism from her instructor, she was destined for stardom.

CRAMPED AT THE CZECH OPERA

Our German friends invited us to spend a weekend with them in Prague during opera season. Prague was only two and half hours by car from our German apartment in Amberg. The best part of seeing a performance in Prague was the screen above the stage that ran translations of all the lines into Czech and English. We thoroughly enjoyed Turandot, the story of the emperor who decreed that his daughter will only marry a suitor of noble blood who can correctly answer three riddles. It was especially entertaining because we could understand everything.

We had bought tickets online for four seats in a box on one of the lower balconies. I had never sat in a box before and am not likely to again, at least not in Prague. The only seats with a clear view of the stage were in the front row of the box where our knees were smashed against the half wall. We kept rotating seats so no one would have to spend too much time with cramped legs or too much time not seeing the stage. We enjoyed it but all four of us limped out of the building when it was over.

MOVIE MAKING IN PRAGUE

On a later trip to Prague we toured the castle and grounds and then went out through the back gate intending to walk through the gardens on the other side of the hill. A block past the gate, we noticed a large gathering of people dressed in 1940s clothing. Then we saw men in German WWII uniforms and cars from the same era. As we came closer, we realized these were actors in a movie that was being filmed on the square nearby.

A woman was running past storefronts while a man hollered "Halt! Halt!". She looked over her shoulder and ran faster, then she crashed into a mattress that was against the wall. We assumed she was off camera at that point. This short scene was filmed over and over while we watched. We kept trying to get closer to the action, only to be told to move back behind the cars.

Finally I approached a woman who appeared to be in between tasks and asked her what the movie was. "Anthropoid," she said, and pointed to the tag on her jacket. I wrote it down and we bought the DVD after we got home.

The scene we watched during the filming had been reduced to a split second and then cut to a closeup of the woman we saw running who now lay dead on the street. It was exciting to catch a glimpse into how movies are made.

"LA FABULEUSE" IN SAGUENAY, QUEBEC

Saguenay was founded as a French colonial trading post along the St Lawrence. Except for a few Inuit and Cree villages, there are no towns due north between Saguenay and the Arctic. It didn't just rain the day we were here. It really poured.

The main event in Saguenay was "La Fabuleuse", an extravagant stage production that chronicles the history of the city. It didn't sound overly exciting, but we were amazed. This place survived a huge fire, a landslide, and a terrible flood. The stage was filled with more than 150 volunteer performers who played up to 12 roles each, 20 professional stage technicians, 25 support staff, six live horses, a pig and a flock of geese, antique cars, a gigantic water basin, light shows, music, and spectacular special effects. They must have closed all the businesses in town during the performance so that everybody who lived here could be on the stage. It was quite a performance.

BAGPIPES IN JORDAN

The ancient city of Jerash began as a village settled by the Greeks and was later built into a city by the Romans. It is considered one of the greatest classical cities in the world but was partially destroyed by a violent earthquake in 749 AD. The Jordanians rebuilt parts of it with new stone rather than restoring it with original existing stone, so it does not qualify as a UNESCO World Heritage Site.

Jerash is enormous, and it was impossible to see it all in one afternoon. The city had two theaters, a long shopping street, and countless buildings and plazas with decorative columns. After our orientation tour, we had some free time to explore on our own. I kept to the main street while Ed hiked over to the second theater off the beaten path. Very few people wandered that far. For some inexplicable reason a man in traditional Arab clothing was playing bagpipes on the stage of this ancient theater, accompanied by a drummer who handed Ed his drum as soon as he saw him.

Ed joined right in and picked up the beat. Then the bagpiper started playing "Yankee Doodle". Ed stopped the music long enough to hand his phone to the only other tourist there, so he could take a video. It was like a bizarre scene from a Monty Python movie.

PIANO PLAYER IN SYDNEY

We started our first day in Sydney at the Queen Victoria Building across the street from our hotel. It was a beautifully preserved old building with stained glass windows, wrought iron railings, a big clock, and a lovely rotunda. It was filled with shops and cafés, all of them busy.

A grand piano in the middle of the second floor was available to anyone who wanted to play it. We were lucky enough to hear a young Asian man play fabulous classical pieces with no sheet music. He had so much talent and was in his own world the entire time he played. I wondered what his story was. He was barefoot and had a hole in the front of his T-shirt. Maybe he was hoping the right person would come along, hear him play, and offer him a job. I hope someone did.

DANCING AT THE SYDNEY OPERA HOUSE

During our first visit to the city, it wouldn't have mattered what was playing at the Sydney Opera House. The important thing was to see a performance in this famous venue. We were so fortunate. "The Merry Widow" turned out to be the best ballet we'd ever seen. The performance was absolutely mesmerizing — the dancers, the costumes, the set, everything.

The grand finale of the evening happened along the waterfront as we headed back to the hotel. A man with a saxophone started to play the beautiful Elvis tune, "I Can't Help Falling in Love with You" as we walked by. We put our arms around each other and started a long slow romantic dance on the walkway without saying a word.

TERRIBLE TOURS, TERRIFIC TOURS AND SOME IN BETWEEN

LONG AGO WE LEARNED THAT IT'S BEST to expect the unexpected when we travel. A tour that sounds great on paper can turn out to be awful. Towns we hesitated to visit and tours we weren't sure we wanted to take sometimes brought pleasant surprises. The other people on the tour can make it wonderful or make it awful and there is no way to predict how it will unfold.

Here are the stories of the worst tours we've taken, followed by the best. The ones in between are just that - in between.

TERRIBLE TOUR IN GUATEMALA

Our six hour tour to the old city of Antigua wins the second prize for the very worst tour ever. (The first prize goes to the one in Brazil where our boat got stuck.) Our guide was very proud of his country, but he didn't have a clue how to herd 26 people around the crowded historic center of a UNESCO World Heritage Site. It took over two hours to get there even though it was only 65 miles away. The roads were hilly, curvy and in very poor shape.

The day before the tour, the lecturer on the ship showed a picture of Antigua's new bus parking area. It was landscaped, level, and had a new restroom building specifically for bus passengers. Our bus didn't park there. Instead we parked on top of a hill in an empty gravel lot, much farther away from the center of town.

We must have walked ten blocks before we came to restrooms at a church where we paid $1 for two people. We weren't permitted to go inside the church. Our guide said there wasn't enough time, yet he was busy talking to the townspeople he knew while the rest of us waited to get the tour started.

The most photographed place in Antigua is a lovely arch topped by a clock tower. If you stand in the right place, you could see the nearby active volcano through the arch. Our guide didn't take us there. He said there wasn't enough time. Instead he took us to a jade jewelry showroom and told us it was run by his friend who would make us a good deal. It seemed we had enough time for that.

The vendors on the streets were pushy and followed us around no matter how many times we said no. Hundreds of people from the ship descended on this little mountain city at once and the locals were trying to make the most of our visit. The sidewalks were packed, no one knew where they were going, the groups got mixed together, and the tour guides were hard to follow. Several people got separated from their group and got lost. It was awful. Of the two hours of free time scheduled, we ended up with only 40 minutes and had to choose between going to the market or eating lunch. The guide said we would stop for a food and restroom break on the way back to the ship, so we opted for the market. The bus never stopped on the way back.

The streets were made of very rough cobblestones that were uneven and spaced far apart due to the eruption of the nearby volcano about a year and a half ago. It was a city full of potential broken ankles but the guide kept walking fast without ever turning around to count the people or to make sure that we could all keep up with him. I don't even have any decent photos. The whole day was absolutely terrible.

The following day, the General Manager on the ship told Ed that he had over 50 people in his office complaining about this tour. I was surprised it was only 50.

PANAMA HATS, COFFEE, AND A BUS ACCIDENT IN ECUADOR

Our tour from Manta took us to the colonial hill town of Montecristi, "the birthplace of the Panama Hat". It was the longest two hour tour we'd ever taken.

During the entire half hour ride to Montecristi, the guide talked about nothing except panama hats — how they are made, how to select the best quality, how he could help us negotiate with the vendors, etc. When we got off the bus at a small courtyard where hats were being made, we heard the same thing all over again from the hat people. It starts with the toquilla straw plant which only grows in this region and does not survive when exported. The wicker is soaked, strung, and dried before it is woven. It is backbreaking work.

Everyone gasped when the guide said we would be spending an hour here. One long table displayed a wide selection with price tags starting at $250 per hat. Our guide said you're not just buying a hat, you're buying "a piece of art". It takes two to three months to make one hat by hand from start to finish. The material is delicate and the making of hats is affected by the weather and humidity. All of this still wasn't enough to convince me to take one home. We wandered away.

After looking at more hats than we could count out in the main square, we had another half an hour before it was time to go back to the bus and I was ready for a good cup of Ecuadoran coffee. At the first café we stopped in, the woman held up a jar of instant Nescafé. I shook my head and started to walk away. She went out to the sidewalk with me and pointed to a restaurant down the street where I could get fresh brewed coffee. That place had no customers, just some women in the kitchen chopping things presumably in preparation for lunch.

I called out, "Cafe con leche?" and the response was enthusiastic nodding of heads. We sat down and listened to the chattering and rattling of pots and pans in the kitchen. Then one of the women appeared with a cup of steaming coffee and a full cup of hot milk. I mixed them together and it was delicious. Ed had an Inca Kola which was not so delicious.

Back on the bus, the first thing the guide wanted to know was how many of the 40 of us had bought a hat. There was one. The bus had just started to pull away from the curb when we heard a bang and some crunching. The driver had cut the turn too hard, scraped a pole and the side window at the back of the bus shattered, covering four passengers with broken glass. It took a while to make sure everyone was ok, get the passengers reseated and the glass cleaned up. It was a mess.

When the bus returned to the port area, the driver had no idea where to go and took a few different roads, turned around and drove back out again. Finally, he dropped us off at the right place. We were glad to have returned from this tour unharmed and hatless. When we told the General Manager on the ship about the bus accident, he hadn't heard. The tour company never reported it.

NO RESTROOMS IN LOVELY AREQUIPA

Arequipa is a beautiful old city high in the Andes with stunning architecture, wandering llamas and many colorfully dressed indigenous people. It sounded great. Unfortunately our tour guide was very young, inexperienced, and untrained. She didn't seem to know much, so she kept repeating things. The most bizarre part of the bus trip was the announcement she made about restrooms. During our 2 ½ hour drive, the bus never stopped. She said there would be no restrooms in Arequipa unless we went into a restaurant and then we might be able to use one as a customer. Otherwise, we should all use the tiny restroom on the bus at the bottom of the stairs by the back door before we got off. Most guides discourage the use of the bus restroom because the plumbing is often inadequate. Not this one.

Because the bus was full, people scrambled out of their seats while the bus was still moving and lined up in the aisle to use the restroom before it was time to get off. Ed and I stayed in our seats. It was amazing that no one fell or got injured standing around as we drove those winding mountain roads. Most tour guides want you in your seat with your seat belt buckled for the entire trip. Not this one.

As we got off the bus, the guide gave us each a map and sent us off to look around on our own. That was the extent of the "walking tour". We started looking around for a restroom first, On the far side of the square off a side street, we found a church cloister that had been converted to shops and cafés. It had a public restroom that charged $1 for the two of us. Before we left, a different tour guide brought her group from the ship to the same restroom and told the attendant who had just taken our money that these were cruise ship guests and they should enter free.

ACCIDENTAL ADVENTURES • 273

When I told our guide about this later, she had no idea where this restroom even was. We normally give our guides a tip when the bus brings us back to the ship. Not this one.

STRANGE TOUR IN GASPÉ, ONTARIO

The more I learned about Canada during our morning tour of the area, the more impressed I was. Gaspé is another city along the St Lawrence that I had never heard of. Propellers are made here for green energy windmills. There are 25 salmon rivers in this area and Jimmy Carter used to come here to fish.

This is another place where the faint of heart cannot survive. Up to 15 feet of snow falls every winter but last year, the schools were closed for just one half day all season. We were there on October 3 and at noon the temperature had only reached 36 degrees. Gaspé is located at the northernmost point of the Appalachians. It's possible to hike from here all the way to Florida. I don't recommend it.

Lobster was so plentiful here in the 1930s and 1940s that only poor people ate it. Kids who had meat in their school lunches were considered rich. The prison only served lobster and the inmates always complained. Hard to imagine.

Our afternoon tour was called Perce and UNESCO Geopark. During the bus ride, the guide rarely spoke and when she did her accent was so thick, it was hard to understand her. Everything we learned about Gaspé came from the guest lecturer on the ship, not the tour guide. UNESCO is usually an indication that a park or historical site is worth seeing. This one was a rare exception. It was so strange, I'm not sure I can describe it.

When the bus arrived at the Geopark, the people seated on one side of the aisle were directed to get on a smaller shuttle bus waiting nearby, but the guide didn't say where it was going. Those of us on the other side of the bus were instructed to enter the "Tektonic Building". Everyone was to meet in town at the Information Center at 3:45 pm but we were still unclear about what would happen in the meantime.

The guide got on the shuttle and the rest of us wandered toward the building. It didn't seem to have much going for it. After we stood around for a while, a woman passed out cards with pictures on them. She said they were to be used for turning on different exhibits. After we had used all the cards and watched three movies, then we could go back out.

The woman with the cards led us into a big room with various lighted exhibits about geology and formation of the earth. When we heard the siren and saw smoky fog coming from the corner, we were to head over to the benches to watch the next movie, which lasted about three minutes each time. The whole thing was very strange.

After we finished with all of that, it was our turn to ride the shuttle which took us to the top of the mountain above the city. A spectacular view awaited us from the glass floor of viewing platform high above the town and the shoreline. Ed ventured out onto the glass, but I stopped at the edge of the metal floor and tried not to envision myself tumbling into the treetops below. The most interesting part of the tour was seeing Perce Rock where Jacques Cartier planted a wooden cross when he claimed this land for France in 1534.

When we learned that the next shuttle wasn't going to leave for another fifteen minutes, we decided to walk down the mountain into the town. The sign on the trail said the distance was 1.7 but it didn't say 1.7 what. We assumed since we were in Canada that it was kilometers. After we'd covered that distance and more, we decided it must be in miles. By the time we reached town, we'd walked almost five miles. Fortunately, the trail was well maintained, all downhill and the views were beautiful. It turned out to be the best part of the day.

When we finally reached town, we had less than a half hour before the bus came to take us back to the ship and we really needed to find something to eat. There wasn't enough time to sit in a restaurant and order something. The only open café didn't have anything quick but we managed to get some chocolate bars there.

The bus was 20 minutes late because the bus company had arranged to take another group of people unrelated to the ship around while we were at the Geopark. Some people had left some belongings on the bus not knowing that other people would be sitting in their seats. They were not happy. The guide was totally useless and didn't say a word the rest of the trip.

By the time we got back to the ship it was almost dark. When we returned to our stateroom, a box containing a bottle of tabasco sauce was sitting on the door handle. No note. There was a message on the phone from a new friend who thought we might like this type of tabasco sauce. Ed called him back and left a message saying he was mistaken; we really didn't use tabasco. He took it back to the friend's stateroom and left it on his door handle. A while later, the friend called again to say that bottle of tabasco sauce had been all over the ship and he would find someone to give it to at the veterans get together the following day. It was a bizarre ending to a very bizarre day. We learned the next day that none of the veterans were interested in the tabasco sauce either.

SKIPPED TOUR IN PHILLIPSBURG, ST MARTIN

At 7:30 am when our ship docked in Phillipsburg, I looked at the weather forecast. It said, "82 degrees — Feels like 91". That day neither of us had the energy or the motivation to go out in the heat for a three hour tour of another Caribbean island we had never heard of. They were all starting to look alike and there was nothing unique about this one.

In the afternoon, I overheard some people complaining at the excursions desk that the tour bus they were on that morning was so dilapidated that all the seat backs were broken. When people sat down, they all went backwards. The air conditioning on the bus didn't work and the windows didn't open. This was the tour we didn't take. Good decision.

WALKING TOUR IN MOZAMBIQUE

During our walking tour of the capital city of Maputo in 97 degree heat, our guide told us it was absolutely forbidden to take a photo of a government building or any private residence or any people directly. Most of his descriptions ended with, "Do not take photographs here". He said it was only allowed to take photos of buildings of cultural significance but in Maputo there weren't many of those. He said taking forbidden photographs would result in "trouble". He didn't elaborate on what this trouble was, but we sure didn't want to find out. It was a rough looking place. Amazingly, the train station here was once voted among the top ten beautiful train stations in the world by Newsweek magazine. It was the only beautiful building in the city, except maybe the new bank which was ultramodern and not in the photography-approved category. The train station was empty, but outside the streets were very crowded with people who didn't look like they could afford a train ticket even if they had someplace to go.

Pedestrians clearly do not have the right of way here. Nobody on our walking tour got run over, but a few of us came close, including me. Locals on the sidewalk didn't exactly push us out of the way, but they didn't make it easy for us to pass each other either. Many streets didn't have sidewalks, even though we were in the main part of the city. We walked down several streets that had piles of rubble where the buildings had fallen in. People were sitting around at the edges of the rubble but no one appeared inclined to clean it up or fix anything.

Maputo was in some of the scenes from the movie, "Blood Diamond". A few of the blocks had buildings that looked a bit like New Orleans but were still very run down. This is the country where, not long before we visited, a mound of garbage collapsed after heavy rains and killed 17 people. Now that I've been through the outskirts of the city, I have no trouble believing this.

As we made our way to the market, the guide reminded us that the people here have very little money and try to sell whatever they can. Unemployment is over 50%. Most don't have steady jobs so selling things that they can carry is their sole source of income. One guy had a pile of trousers over one arm and shirts on a hanger in the opposite hand. Another had buckled belts hanging over both arms. Very few people had white skin here, so we were prime targets. Anytime someone came up to us to sell something, Ed answered him in German which usually sent the person scurrying away. We were afraid that buying one thing from one person would bring on a mob in no time.

This warning in the ship newsletter about souvenirs in Mozambique was enough to deter me from buying anything even if I saw something that I wanted to bring home with me. "In order to reduce the number of large insects and spiders which might be brought back on board, we ask you to declare any souvenirs to Security at the gangway as you return. For your own comfort, these items will be collected, inspected and then delivered to your stateroom." Good thing we read the newsletter before we headed out.

SHUTTLE BUS ADVENTURES IN CHINA

Sanya, a city on an island off the coast of China, offered a shuttle bus from the port to a department store and shopping area near the beach. Because the bus was run by the Chinese, the ship had no control over the schedule. As it turned out, there wasn't much of a schedule at all.

By the time we got off the ship, one of the two buses at the end of the gangway was already almost full. Ed got on and the door closed immediately behind him. A Chinese man pushed me toward the next bus and didn't understand when I tried to tell him my husband was on the other bus. Meanwhile, Ed was trying to get the Chinese driver to let him off because I wasn't able to get on with him. The driver finally understood and decided there was one empty seat I could have so we were able to ride together.

The bus let us off in front of a large hotel and drove away. We had a map but no idea where we were on it. A Chinese woman holding a sign with our ship's name on it appeared out of nowhere and told us how to get to the department store and the ATM because of course we wanted to go shopping and we would need Chinese cash. She said the shuttle bus would return to the same spot. Then she melted away into the crowd without saying when.

We wandered through some shops until we found the department store. It was filled with designer clothing, Rolex watches and western brands. There was a "gourmet supermarket" on the top floor. We looked in the window and saw lots of American items — Cheerios, Pop Tarts, Blue Diamond Almonds, etc. I guess those things are considered gourmet in China. We didn't go inside.

Sanya attracts a lot of tourists from Russia because it's so close to the border. Some of the store signs were in Russian. At the beach there weren't many people in the water, probably because of the warning signs about the strong currents. Interestingly, some of the bars along the beach had signs posted in multiple languages that said singing was not allowed. It must be a problem when the Russians start drinking.

When we returned to the hotel for the shuttle bus ride back to the ship, we assumed the bus would come about every half hour as our cruise ship shuttles typically do. This one didn't. An hour and fifteen minutes later more people had gathered in front of the hotel than would fit on one bus and it still hadn't come. The Chinese woman with the ship sign magically reappeared and people immediately started telling her she'd better get another bus. She didn't. Fortunately, Ed and I were able to escape the chaos and get on the bus.

PROTESTS AND POVERTY IN NORTHERN CHILE

The contrast between southern and northern Chile was mind boggling. Our morning tour in Valparaiso took us through this port city outside of the capital of Santiago. Before we left Denver, we met some people from Chile who were considering buying our house. The husband told us how beautiful Valparaiso was, filled with wine bars, cafés, green parks, and colorful buildings. They ended up buying a different house from ours, but I wish I could remember when he said he left Chile, because Valparaiso was nothing like he described.

In 2010, an 8.8 magnitude earthquake off the coast of Chile destroyed many of buildings in Valparaiso that have yet to be repaired or rebuilt. Social unrest and protests have made the city unsafe with most areas becoming seedy and covered in graffiti with words like "Death to the Rich" and "Kill the Police".

A handful of buildings around the square remained unscathed and this is where we were taken. Although it was Sunday, a small market was set up but most of the stands offered flea market items, except for one that sold chocolates and another that sold bottles of wine. Only Chilean wine is sold in Chile. If you want to buy wine from another country, you have to leave Chile to get it. Our guide warned the group not to wander away from the square because the surrounding streets were not safe. Packs of stray dogs roamed around the area but they didn't bother anyone as far as I know.

When we got back on the bus, the guide said we were going a short way up the coast to the resort town of Viña del Mar, which was "just like Miami Beach". After what I had just seen, I had trouble envisioning this. As we drove, we could see Valparaiso across the bay. The city looked like it was sliding down the hillsides a little at a time.

Viña del Mar is evidently where the other half lives. It was lovely but such a stark contrast to Valparaiso a short distance away. We spent a lot of time at a small museum that had artifacts from Easter Island and some very tiny restrooms. There wasn't much else there.

We passed a lot more blight on the way back to the port. I kept thinking that if these people haven't been able to clean up the devastation in the ten years since the earthquake, when will they? Our bus passed several people selling items spread out on blankets lined up along the sidewalks block after block.

The guide said the average income here is about $400 a month, which is also the average rent so they sell belongings in order to buy food. It's got to be a horrible way to live. Sooner or later they'll run out of belongings to sell and then what will they do? It was one of the most depressing tours we'd taken since boarding the ship.

We weren't sure if we would be able see Santiago the next day because of the protests and social unrest but the tour left on time as planned. During our hour and a half bus ride from the Valparaiso to

Santiago, our excellent guide Max talked openly about the protests that started in late October 2019 over an increase in subway fares. You wouldn't think that would be a big deal, he told us, but so many people already didn't have enough to live on and then had to struggle even more to scrape together enough money to get back and forth to work. He said groceries, prescriptions and education costs were extremely high here.

We passed a lot of farms and orchards where produce was grown for export. The valley between the two cities was green due to irrigation from aquifers but the hills were already very dry and it was only late spring there. Santiago relies on the snow melt from the Andes for their water so they already had most of what they were going to get for the year. The riverbeds were almost dry as well. We saw one that had a few trickles but that was about it.

The bus let us off on the Plaza de Armas main square where we began a walking tour of downtown. The buildings here were protected by a heavy police presence so there was no graffiti. The large subway station at the opposite end of the square was closed, as were many others. It had been filled with dirt and rocks dumped by protesters so it could not be used. The fare increase prevented them from riding the subway, so they made sure nobody else could either.

Outside the Supreme Court Building a protest was getting underway and gathering strength quickly. Max said they were protesting
pension cuts. A poster hung at the second floor level showed a man
with a red eye. This had become a symbol of police brutality because
they aim rubber bullets at the eyes of protesters who then become
blinded and wear eye patches. When Max told us that if the police
showed up "there will be problems", so we took a few quick photos
and he herded us away.

By this time, we were ready for a restroom break. Max led us over
to the Cultural Center, a modern building constructed in 2008 for the
arts, theater, dance and music classes and events. Much of it was
closed due to the social unrest but we were able to go inside. In the
past, temporary exhibits like King Tut and the Terra Cotta Warriors
had been brought here but not recently. The only activity we saw appeared to be some kind of lunchtime exercise class. I couldn't really
figure out what they were doing.

Max was an exceptional guide and a very honest and straightfor-
ward one. The sadness he felt when he talked about what the protests
have done to the city that he's lived in all his life was very evident. I
found myself wondering how I would cope if all this happened in my
home city and I had to sell my belongings to buy food. I couldn't
imagine it.

STUNNING SCENERY AND BUS TROUBLE IN SOUTHERN CHILE

Near the tip of South America we enjoyed a beautiful tour of Tierra del Fuego National Park with a wonderful guide. The ragged mountain peaks, glaciers, and dense forests in this region were absolutely stunning.

At our last stop along the Beagle Channel, the main attraction was the location of the southernmost post office in the world. Several people on the tour bought postcards and stamps in this tiny building and sent them with the rare "bottom of the world" postmark.

When it was time to leave, we piled back on the bus and crawled our way out of the small, congested parking lot. There wasn't room for the bus to get enough momentum to make it up the steep hill to the main road. We started up the hill a few times but had to keep backing down to make room for a vehicle coming from the opposite direction. Then the guide explained the problem: our bus had no first gear.

When we finally made it to the top of the hill, we passed another tour bus with mechanical issues. The driver was opening one bottle of drinking water after another and pouring the contents into the overheated engine. Luckily our bus made it back to the city with no further problems. We never heard what happened to the other bus.

HIGH TECH RESTROOMS IN PICTON

Picton was as far south as we went in New Zealand on our world cruise before heading north again, and it was getting dark quite early, even on sunny days. I really wanted to take one of the tour boats across the sound to hike through the forest a bit but none of the boats were scheduled to return before our ship left. One that really sounded interesting followed the mail route to deliver small cargo and mail to the homes and businesses around the sound that are only accessible by boat. The route varied every day. The problem with this one was the same; the return time was between 5:30 and 6:00, and we had to be back on board by 5:30.

We bought tickets for a tour boat that was only out for about three hours in the afternoon to pick up and drop off hikers. It was a relaxing boat ride that included a bit of wildlife and ended with a spectacular sunset.

Our tour boat didn't leave until 1:30 so we had time to walk around town a bit. One of the things I really loved about Japan, Australia and New Zealand was the abundance of clean public restrooms. We had visited several over the past few months, but none were as high tech as the ones in Picton. They appeared to be brand new.

Red and green lights on the outside indicated which ones in the row of four were available. When I slid the door open, the inside lights came on and a male voice told me to close the door all the way and push the button on the wall to lock it. After I did that, elevator music started to play. Then the voice told me that the door would automatically unlock after I washed my hands, or ten minutes after I had entered. I could also unlock it manually if I chose to do so.

The entire experience was very interesting. Our tour was too.

NICE LOCALS AND PUSHY LOCALS IN THE SOUTH PACIFIC

Our tour stopped in a fishing village that offered small shops, a nice view of the sea, a beach, and a restroom. I ended up in a long conversation with a man selling souvenirs. Some of these people are really pushy but this guy was soft spoken and very nice. I told him that his island was very beautiful, and we were enjoying our visit here. He said when he was younger, he wanted to travel and see other places but now he realizes that he loves it here too much, and no longer wants to leave. This village was having their weekly fish fry that evening and the people were busy setting up a bandstand and grills. This man asked me if I could stay and share some of their local fish, but I said unfortunately we were only here for a short time (like 10 minutes). I wished him well and we said goodbye.

Ed had an entirely different experience with a really grisly looking guy on the beach who wanted Ed to shake his hand. It was filthy. I'd never seen my husband shy away from shaking anybody's hand until that day. This guy wore torn shorts, a dirty shirt and had lots of tangled hair past his shoulders, a long matted beard, and no teeth. It must have been long time since he'd gone anywhere near a bar of soap. He kept asking if Ed wanted to take his picture, so that Ed would be obligated to give him money. I walked away when that part of the conversation started and finally Ed got away too. I couldn't get the hand sanitizer out of my purse fast enough for him.

DIFFICULT PASSENGER IN ARGENTINA

We signed up for an overnight excursion to Iguazu Falls and attended a briefing where everything about the tour was clearly explained. On the way to the Buenos Aires airport, a woman in the tour group began causing one problem after another and didn't quit until after we returned to the ship the following day. She needed a walker and ignored the advice that this tour was not appropriate for anyone with mobility issues. She insisted that the guides (one who accompanied us from the ship and a local guide at the falls) enable her to take the included speed boat ride in the afternoon, even after they explained to her twice that it involved 92 steps down to the boat dock and back with no railing! She argued that she could go if someone would carry her walker for her.

We boarded the speed boat in the middle of a crowd of people. It seemed like a fairly new boat but the seats were very low, narrow, and every one of them was filled. We had to put our life jackets on and buckle them before getting in. The seats were so close together that it was hard to move our arms once we sat down.

The guide had told us that we would see the falls from above in the afternoon. The boat ride would give us an entirely different perspective of the falls from below. He stressed that it was essential for us to take our rain ponchos with us on the boat. In the middle of the hot humid rainforest, I wasn't anxious to put mine on any sooner than necessary. I waited until we got close to the falls and by then it was almost too late. We were packed in too tight and there wasn't enough time. Each person was given a rubber bag for cameras, shoes, and any other belongings we brought that we didn't want to get wet. The guide announced when to take our cameras out and when to put them back in and seal the rubber bag again while I tightened my life jacket.

We bumped over rapids as water poured from the falls into the boat, onto our heads and down our backs. We were soaked in no time. One guy did nothing but bail water from the bottom of the boat. It's hard to describe how impressive these falls were. The roar of the water when we got up close was unbelievable.

Luckily, we had clear skies with no afternoon rain showers. We were already wet enough. It took a while to dry off, gather our things together, return our rubber bags, climb back up the steps, get back on the jungle truck and then walk to the park entrance to wait for the bus.

Our dinner at the hotel was wonderful except for the woman with the walker who was behind me in the buffet line. She kept telling me to explain to her what each dish was, as if I worked there. I just pointed to the little sign in front of each item and suggested she read it.

Iguazu was a hard place to reach but well worth the effort. The falls were spectacular and all too soon, it was time to head to the airport for our flight back to Buenos Aires to meet the ship. We ate our box lunches on the bus like school children. Everyone was happy except the woman with the walker, even though I had seen her in the morning on one of the walkways overlooking the falls with our guide who was carrying her walker for her. If the guide hadn't been willing to do that, she would have taken the trip and not seen the falls at all. Despite the generosity of the guides, she repeatedly complained to them that she wanted a refund for the boat ride they didn't "let" her take. She had a very hard time getting through the airport when we departed Iguazu as well as after we landed in Buenos Aires. When she asked another passenger to carry her bag, I felt sorry for her because she was having trouble breathing, but she never should have signed up for this tour. It wasn't safe for her to go and it made everything more difficult for the guides.

There were others with mobility issues who shouldn't have gone either but they didn't complain quite as much. Some people seem to accept their physical limitations and stick to what they can handle but this group did not. Because of all this, we were delayed leaving the airport. The bus took us directly back to the ship and we missed our city tour of Buenos Aires. This would have been a fabulous tour without the difficult people. Maybe we should have asked them to refund our money for the city tour they caused us to miss!

Some of the passengers got together to complain to the General Manager about how physically demanding the tour was. Either they didn't read the description or didn't listen to the briefing, or they ignored what they were told. We kept our distance from this group and never heard how it turned out. If I reach the point in my life that my health prevents me from getting around, I truly hope that I have the grace and dignity to accept it and not make others suffer because of it.

RUDE PASSENGER IN BERMUDA

Outside the terminal, we were directed to a taxi van for our tour of the Crystal Caves. About 35 people went to see the caves, four to a taxi. We spent 15 minutes waiting for our fourth person who never showed up, so a staff member from the excursions desk rode with us as an escort along with a man who was traveling alone to make four passengers.

In 1907, two teenage boys were playing cricket and saw their ball disappear into a hole. They went in after it and discovered this cave. It's 1500 feet long and 186 feet deep. The lower 60 feet of the cave are under crystal clear water. It was a great tour.

Outside it was noticeably warmer than when we had gone in an hour earlier. The woman we had waited for at the pier took a later taxi instead of the one she should have been in (ours). Our taxi driver was still expected take her back so we waited another 15 minutes for her tour to be completed. We all walked across the parking lot together to the taxi. When the driver opened the back door, she got in and sat just inside the door where no one could get past her. She acted as if it was her own private taxi and the rest of us didn't exist.

We all managed to get in and she started talking about wanting to go to St George's on the other side of Bermuda. The driver told her it would be a long taxi ride and he would have to drop the rest of us off at the ship first. She said he could just take her to a transit stop where she could catch a bus to St George's. He advised her to get exact change from a store before she got on the bus. Since it was sunny and hot, the driver went out of his way to take her to a bus stop that was shaded and near some businesses. She had no clue how obnoxious she was.

We were happy to see her get out of the taxi and didn't run into her again.

AMARULA FROM THE SHIP TOUR

We learned by accident that it was possible to tour some areas of our Viking ship that were typically restricted to the crew. Tours were limited to eight passengers at a time and were not offered very often. The Beverage Manager took us through the wine storage room which was immense. One of the other couples mentioned how much they like Amarula which I had never heard of. It's made with sugar, cream and fruit from the marula tree which only grows in one place in the entire world, a small region of South Africa. The marula tree bears fruit only once a year and elephants come from miles around to eat it. It doesn't require fermentation but evidently contains something intoxicating because the elephants are often seen laying down near marula trees.

We went on to see the laundry where massive machines swallow up clean tablecloths and napkins and spit them out on the other side, impeccably pressed and folded. We also met a man whose job it was to press shirts one at a time the old fashioned way, standing at an ironing board.

The food storage areas consisted of multiple rows of refrigerators, freezers, and storerooms filled with vast amounts of produce and supplies. Stacks of 50 lb. bags of flour from France and sugar from Germany lined the walls. All of this was connected by a long wide corridor known as I-95, named after the busy freeway on the east coast. The tour was fascinating.

Back in our stateroom a bottle of Amarula was waiting for us. The label had a little story about the marula tree and a picture of an elephant laying on the ground next to the tree. It tasted a bit like Baileys only lighter.

IMPRESSIONS OF CHINA

I didn't really know much about the Forbidden City before coming to Beijing. This palace complex was home to emperors and their families for over 500 years and was also the center of political and ceremonial activity. It consists of 980 buildings covering more than 180 acres and was constructed by over a million workers from 1406 to 1420. The name Forbidden City comes from the law stating no one could enter or leave it without the emperor's permission. 24 different emperors, their families and their concubines lived here. The furnishings and contents of the buildings were moved to a museum in Taiwan many years ago where they remain today. It was impossible to cover it all in the short time we were there. Even though we weren't able to go inside any of the buildings, it was still an impressive sight. Long lines greeted us at the entrance even though we arrived very early.

We passed through several gates, around courtyards, over bridges and across open squares. Visitors enter at one end of the complex and leave from the other. Only one way traffic is allowed, so everyone walks in the same direction which is a very good system. It would have been impossible to get through otherwise. It's huge and well-guarded with cameras everywhere.

The bus then took us to Tiananmen Square, one of the ten largest squares in the world, where we saw the Monument to the People's Heroes, The Great Hall of the People, and the Gate of Heavenly Peace. It took a long time to walk through even a small part of it. Soldiers and cameras were everywhere here too. We had no trouble because we were with a guide, but China is not a place I'd feel comfortable navigating on my own.

Our guide told us that he had just completed college the year before the pro-democracy demonstrations in 1989 but he said no one really knows very much about the incident. Websites like Google and Wikipedia are banned in China and much information is blocked. Then he changed the subject and explained that until recently, every family was permitted to have only one child. The government has realized that there are too many older people and not enough younger ones to take care of them. Now families that already have one child are permitted to have another. Our guide has one son who is just finishing college and so he hopes that his son will give him two grandchildren one day. He stopped short of discussing anything controversial like mandatory abortion laws.

Our guide also told us that the average apartment building is 35 stories, but many go up to 50. Any building with less than six stories is not required to have an elevator. After three days in China, I still couldn't quite grasp how so many people can live in these gigantic high rise apartment buildings that all look that same. Some appeared to be in the middle of nowhere. I would have trouble finding my way home.

China surprised me in some ways. Yes, the authorities here really want to know exactly who you are, where you're going, what you're doing, and they make sure everyone understands who is in charge. Despite all the security, people on the streets were friendly. They often smiled at us and sometimes held up their babies, so we could take photos of them. Older women whispered to each other while pointing to Ed's long white ponytail.

It's an amazing country and I'm glad we had the opportunity to see it.

LEARNING ABOUT "THE TROUBLES" IN NORTHERN IRELAND

In Belfast, our tour guide spent a lot of time explaining "The Troubles". I only remembered that Catholics and Protestants were killing each other beginning in the 1960s, but I never really understood that these were fueled by historical events and not religious conflicts. Descendants of the Catholics who were kicked out of England during the religious wars of the 1600s are now the Nationalists who want to see Northern Ireland unite with The Republic of Ireland and become independent from Great Britain. The Ulster Protestants are now Unionists who want both Northern Ireland and The Republic of Ireland to go back to being part of the United Kingdom. The division between these two groups is about 50/50. Between the late 1960s and 1998 when the Good Friday Agreement was signed, 3500 people died fighting about it. During the Troubles, Northern Ireland was ruled by paramilitary loyalist groups fighting British troops and each other for control.

Our guide was excellent and she did not shy away from discussing this. When she was a child, one person a week died as a result of hunger strikes in the Crumlin Road Prison. Until it closed in 1996, women and children were held there for stealing bread.

Despite the cease fire and 1998 peace agreement, the Troubles continue to flare up. The paramilitary groups have now become the politicians.

The "Peace Wall" area of Belfast looked in some places like the border between Israel and Palestinian territories. Tall fences and barbed wire divided neighborhoods with narrow gates for people to slip in and out. Signs and elaborate graffiti covered the fences and the surrounding buildings. We were permitted to look around at the wall but had to stay within a block of the bus. It wasn't safe to go any farther.

Sadly, our guide said the people in Belfast continue to tell each other to pray for peace but get ready for war.

LEARNING ABOUT THE SHETLAND ISLANDS

Many cruise ships end up missing the port in the Shetland Islands because of the frequent rough weather in the north Atlantic. Our ship was among the lucky ones. We had booked an independent full day tour with Grant, a delightful young man who taught us so many fascinating things about his homeland. Before stopping here, I knew very little about the Shetland Islands.

There are five times more sheep than people in the Shetlands and it rains 260 days a year. The culinary delicacy here is mutton soup. Grant said you just put dried salted mutton in a pot of water and "boil it up". Sounds delicious, doesn't it?

Our tour was so interesting that nobody minded the constant rain. Our first stop was at an overlook area amid some houses so Grant could explain the lay of the land. He asked us to move away from a certain house because his friend lives there. If his friend hears him talking to a tour group, he opens the window and yells, "Rubbish! He's feeding you rubbish!"

Even though the Shetlands are part of Scotland, the Shetland dialect sounds more Scandinavian than Scottish. Grant deliberately spoke with a Scottish accent so we could understand him, but it's not the way his family talks. He's the youngest of six. His three sisters all work in social services, one brother is in construction and the other is a paramedic.

Grant told us that he remembers very deep snows as a child. When his father opened the back door in the winter, the snow that was packed against it filled the doorway and fell into their kitchen. Regularly. During the winters, he always got two or three weeks off school until the town could get enough snow cleared for the children to go to school again. Now the light snow they get is gone in two or three days. He remembers many people in the town engaged in the sport of curling on the lakes in winter when he was small. Now the lakes never freeze. This has all happened in the last 20-25 years. The impact of climate change is a big concern in the Shetland Islands.

One of the most interesting stops on the tour was the Croft House Museum, a 19th century Shetland croft house, which was lived in until the late 1960s. The man of the house was typically a fisherman, seaman or whaler. His wife and family worked the land while he was away at sea. The house had very thick walls and small windows.

A typical family that lived in a two room house like this included grandparents, parents, and children. Each bed in the house was surrounded by wooden walls with a sliding door that could be closed for privacy. Behind the house, we were treated to a close look at some adorable Shetland ponies.

Our last stop was the 4000 year-old Jarlshof settlement with Bronze Age and Iron Age ruins. Archaeologists have submitted this to UNESCO so it is likely to become a World Heritage Site before long. Grant explained that while funding is badly needed to explore and preserve it, once UNESCO takes over, his tours will be conducted from the outer edge pointing at things instead of walking through them as we were able to do during our visit.

SINGING TOUR GUIDE IN THE FAROE ISLANDS

The Faroes are home to 22,000 people and 70,000 sheep. After lambs are born and before they are slaughtered for food, the number of sheep goes up to 140,000. The word Faroe means sheep. Small wonder. The capital city of Torshavn is very modern and filled with brightly colored buildings. Faroese would be a tough language to learn.

There are no trees here. Early wooden structures were made from the wood of shipwrecked boats long ago but now timber is imported. They had no written language until the late 1800s. Surprisingly, they don't get much snow here even though the Faroes are about halfway between Iceland and Norway. The gulf stream warms the ocean water enough to just bring rain. Lots and lots of rain.

The highlight of our tour was a stop in the village of Kollafjordur to visit an old Faroese church with a turf roof. It was one of nine churches built on the islands between 1830 and 1850. Our guide sang to us in Old Norse while we sat in this beautiful place — a fisherman's song asking for God's protection before heading out to sea. It brought tears to my eyes even though I couldn't understand any of the words.

NORWAY IN A NUTSHELL

Our three day "Norway in a Nutshell" tour included a boat ride up the Sognefjord, a 12 mile long, high altitude scenic train ride from Flam, and then a ride on the main train line to Oslo. We had planned to add two nights at a hotel in Oslo and return to Bergen on the train at our own expense. Our ship was scheduled to dock in Bergen for three days, so this was perfect.

When the tour company asked which hotel in Bergen they should deliver our package tickets to, I explained we would arrive by cruise ship at 8:00 am the morning of the tour, not realizing that the fjord boat was scheduled to leave Bergen at 8:00 am that day. There was no way we could swing this. The tour operator was able to rearrange things into a revised two day tour for us without Oslo for the same amount of money we had paid. He e-mailed all the tickets and I printed them at home.

Our Viking ship arrived at the Bergen port in the pouring rain. Ed was catching a cold and not feeling well. There was no shuttle bus because Bergen is relatively small and there were no taxis on the pier either, so we walked to the train station. Luckily, I had a good map. It took about a half hour.

We were able to get right on the train without waiting but a young woman was sitting in our reserved seats with food and electronics spread over four seats in a small section designated as a quiet area. It was kind of like first class but not quite. Anyway, I showed her our tickets and she said nobody pays any attention to the seat numbers on this train and we could sit anywhere. A well-dressed woman on the other side of the aisle spoke to her in Norwegian for a few minutes. I don't know what she said, but it was enough to make this young woman pack up and vacate the car.

We got off the train in Voss where we had two hours before catching the bus up the mountain. We looked around in a few shops and went down the street to see the old church. In 1023, King Olav came to Voss to convert people to Christianity and built a large stone cross and a wooden church. In 1277 the wooden building was replaced with the stone one that is still used today. It was open but people dressed in black were getting out of their cars and going inside. Rather than risk a repeat of our Amalfi experience by barging into another funeral, we just walked among the orate stones in the cemetery outside and admired some of the nearby houses.

In a nearby cozy café, we enjoyed some delicious soup and crusty bread served in an interesting double bowl. Back out in the rain, we made our way to the bus station and found the bus to Gudvangen. It was pretty empty, so we made ourselves comfortable in window seats until departure time. All of a sudden, a big group of elderly people with suitcases and umbrellas came from the direction of the train station. All of them boarded the bus and some of the local people had to be turned away to wait for the next one. The woman who sat next to

Ed spoke excellent English and told him she lived on a farm near Lillehammer where the Winter Olympics were held in 1994. Several guests stayed with her during the Olympics.

Most of the passengers got off the bus at the sprawling Stalheim Hotel at the top of the pass. This particular hotel dates back to 1885, but there has been one at this spot since about 1700 when royal mailmen stopped here to change horses. The woman next to Ed said she had never stayed here and just decided to go. She sure picked a wet weekend.

This was the most thrilling bus ride of my entire life, through the mountains on a narrow road with hairpin turns that didn't look like they could possibly accommodate our big city bus. Poor visibility, wet roads, 18% grades and no guardrails made it even more harrowing. The road from Voss to Gudvangen holds the record for being the steepest road in Norway and that's really saying something.

A handful of people stayed on the bus for the wild ride down to Gudvangen. Believe it or not, the bus driver stopped twice on this road so we could get a good lock at the waterfalls and raging rivers. At the end of the ride, we complimented him on his driving skills and walked down the street to board our fjord boat for the two hour ride to Flam.

I never expected to see such a modern elegant boat. Since there were only about ten other passengers, we had plenty of room to walk around and take photos. Long waterfall ribbons covered the mountainsides above picturesque villages. The mountains seemed to rise straight up out of the water.

The historic Freitheim Hotel in Flam offered an amazing dinner buffet with local fare like filet of whale. It definitely did not taste like chicken. New items kept coming out of the kitchen and it was impossible to taste everything.

The next morning after breakfast, we walked over to the train station to take the Flamsbana scenic train 12 miles to Myrdal. It was a beautiful ride even though the pouring rain continued. The train went through 22 tunnels and stopped at the Kjosfossen waterfall for five minutes so everyone could get off and take photos. At Myrdal we changed to the Oslo-Bergen train and enjoyed every bit of the surrounding beauty before arriving back in Bergen.

On the Bergen train, we overheard a conversation behind us between two Americans and an accompanying Viking representative. It appeared that a group of people bound for our ship had been in Oslo and were getting instructions on where to go when the train arrived in Bergen. I whipped my head around and asked if we could hitch a ride on their bus to the ship since it was raining so hard. He didn't appear to believe me when I said we'd been passengers on the ship since London. He said he'd go check with his colleague but he never came back. We followed the Viking people outside to the bus and climbed on. There were plenty of empty seats in the back. As we arrived at the ship, the same Viking representative came up to us and said, "So, you made it, huh?" We just smiled and said yes, thank you very much.

Although we had a few hiccups in planning this trip, it was a wonderful taste of Norway and I wouldn't hesitate to do this tour again if the opportunity came along. Especially in sunny weather.

EXCELLENT GUIDE IN NEW YORK CITY

By the time we got off the ship in New York the skies had opened up and it began to pour but it really didn't matter. Our Manhattan Highlights tour guide was terrific. He knew every inch of Manhattan and was highly skilled at keeping everyone together as he herded us through the crowds.

The most memorable stop was at the September 11 memorial. We stood in the middle of the newly built transit station and shopping mall and looked up through the narrow glass at the top where we could see the new One World Trade Center building.

Our guide said, "Imagine yourself dashing through here on your way to work or stopping to get a cup of coffee. You hear a deafening sound and you look up to see a big building crashing through the ceiling above you."

Standing on that spot listening to those words made the events of September 11 seem more real than all the news clips on TV.

MEMORABLE PEOPLE
AND ACTS OF KINDNESS

DURING OUR MANY TRAVELS OVER THE YEARS we encountered many people who went out of their way to offer help when we
needed it, directions when we were lost, and genuine kindness that
comes from the heart. This happened over and over, no matter what
part of the world we found ourselves in. While it was important to
trust our instincts about strangers and avoid situations that didn't feel
right, meeting local people always enriched our travel experiences no
matter where we went.

On the streets of Xian, a Chinese man in a military uniform came
up to us and put his hand out for Ed to shake. He smiled and said a
lot of words we didn't understand. The photo I took of the two of them

shaking hands is one of my favorites and it reminds me why we travel. This is the beauty of going out on your own in a strange country.

NEW YORKERS REALLY ARE NICE PEOPLE

When it was time for lunch on our second day in the city, we started looking for a good New York style deli to get a corned beef sandwich. While we were standing on a street corner trying to decide which direction to go, a tall man in a suit asked us if we needed any help. I was shocked. I didn't think New Yorkers did that. He was on his way back from Ben's Delicatessen with a container of chicken soup in his hand. It was only a few blocks away and he highly recommended it. He gave us directions and went on his way. We found it with no trouble. The corned beef was perfect and so were the crispy pickles that came with it.

HONEST PIZZA SHOP OWNER IN ROME

After an exhausting morning at the Vatican Museum beginning at 8 am standing in a line that stretched around the block, we were hungry. We headed south toward the Trastevere neighborhood and stopped in a small pizza shop. It had only five seats at a counter along one wall and a glass case with a few different kinds of pizza in it along the opposite wall. It smelled wonderful and there was room for us to sit down. An elderly man occupied one seat and a friend of the pizza shop owner stood at the counter chatting. The pizza was cheap and delicious.

Many Italian men are handsome but I've seen few as good looking as the one who stood behind this counter. Thick dark curls rested above large bedroom eyes and his warm smile made me feel like I was the most welcome customer ever to walk through his door. Ed paid for our lunch and insisted it was time to tear myself away from this guy and head to our next stop. We left.

The friend of the pizza shop owner caught up to us at the end of the street and said, "Please! You must come back. The change was not

310 • KATHY FRONHEISER

correct." Back at the pizza shop, the handsome owner who spoke no English explained through his friend that Ed had given him a 20 Euro bill and he only gave him change for 10 Euros. He was so terribly sorry.

When traveling, we always carry a few gold dollar coins with pictures of past presidents on them for tips or gifts for friendly children. On that day, we happened to have one with Abe Lincoln on it. Ed gave it to him and explained all about Honest Abe. When he heard his friend's translation, tears welled up in his eyes and his voice cracked when he said "Grazie. Grazie", over and over.

We tried to return to this place on subsequent visits to Rome but were never able to find it again.

WARM WELCOME IN ANZIO

During WWII, my Dad fought with the US Army at Anzio beach, not far from Rome. On rare occasions, he talked to me about this and after he died, I wanted to visit Anzio. I had read about the small museum there and took along a photo of my Dad in his uniform, hoping to match the insignia on his sleeve with pictures that might be displayed there.

Trains from Rome to Anzio only ran once an hour and the ticket line was long. We managed to figure out how to get our tickets from the machine in the station, finished our transaction, plucked two tickets out of the tray, and caught the train just before it left.

When the conductor came through and looked at our tickets, he explained that I handed him return tickets from Anzio back to Rome. Did we also have tickets from Rome to Anzio? In our haste to catch the train, we didn't wait for the machine to spit out the other two tickets. We assumed the ones we had were round trip. He thought for a minute, handed back our tickets and asked us to please buy two tickets from Rome to Anzio when we got back to Rome.

I glanced out the window when the train slowed down just as we passed a large sign that said "Anzio" and we got off at the next stop. It turned out the sign was on the road and we got off one stop too early for the museum. We sat in a small coffee shop opposite the station and waited an hour for the next train. Like all coffee in Italy, it was delicious.

The museum near the beach had only a few rooms. We stood in the entry trying to determine if we needed to buy a ticket or make a donation to go inside. I held my Dad's 8 x 10 photo in my hand. An elderly man with a cane walked up to me, pointed to the photo, and said, "Tuo padre?" (your father?). When I responded, "Si", he asked "Americano o Brittanico?" (American or British?) When I responded "Americano", he grabbed my hand, shook it and said "Liberto Roma! Grazie! Grazie!" He may have been old enough to have been a child during the war or heard stories about it from his family but it was clear he was grateful to soldiers like my Dad. He led us over to a desk where a kind man asked me to sign a register and then told me to wait. This was in 2004 and they had just celebrated the 60th anniversary of the battle. He gave me a commemorative medal and a certificate with much gratitude for my father's service.

I was overwhelmed.

HELP IN BUCHAREST

On our first day in Bucharest, our guide recommended a restaurant for an early dinner at the end of an afternoon of touring. We had already checked into our hotel and he explained how to get back there after we finished eating. The food was excellent, and they served very tasty lemonade by the pitcher.

By the time we paid our bill and got ready to leave the restaurant, we had completely forgotten which way to go. Our best guess was completely wrong. We came upon a park with children playing and parents sitting on benches that looked quite safe although there were three big scruffy men in uniforms with lettering that looked like some variation of the word "Security" on the back.

Fortunately, I had picked up a card from the desk of the hotel before we left that had the name, address, and phone number on it. I gave it to one of the security guys and tried to ask for directions but of course, none of them spoke English and my knowledge of Romanian was and still is nonexistent. They each looked at the card and shook their heads. One took out his cell phone and called the hotel to get directions, then motioned for us to follow him.

All three guys walked us over to the hotel, which wasn't far away. We just couldn't zero in on it by ourselves. They were very kind, shook our hands and said a bunch of words that we couldn't understand. As I watched them walk away, I thought how threatening they looked but they were really very nice and couldn't have been more helpful.

HONEST HOTEL EMPLOYEES IN JORDAN

One morning after we were all assembled on the bus after breakfast, our guide asked who was in Room 234. Silence. After all the hotel rooms we'd stayed in during this trip, it was pretty hard to remember room numbers from one hotel to the next. He asked again and still no one responded. Then he said, "The person in Room 234 left $250 in cash behind." All of a sudden six different people said, "I think I was in Room 234." Everyone laughed. Our guide admitted that he had already obtained the name of the guests in 234 from the hotel and returned their money. They had no idea they left cash behind.

The people who work in Jordan hotels certainly are honest. There are many places in the world where these people would never have seen their $250 again.

TORN PANTS AT THE CASTLE IN JORDAN

While everyone was snapping pictures at a viewpoint opposite the Crusader's Castle at Kerak, one woman in our group accidently dropped her cell phone while trying to get a good shot. It fell through a fence onto the roof of a building below. Our Tourist Policeman sprang into action and climbed down to retrieve it for her. It wasn't easy to reach and he tore his pants in the process. When he handed the phone to her, she told him if he took his pants off, she would sew them for him. The expression on his face was priceless.

When I took the photo of the man walking across the hills near the castle, I thought how timeless the scene was. Someone like him could have stood on that spot hundreds of years ago and not looked any different than he does today.

US AID FOR THE TOWN OF KERAK

American foreign aid enabled the town of Kerak to install metal posts at the edge of the sidewalks along the curbs. Our guide explained that it seems like a small thing but the town was so congested because of the constant heavy traffic on the narrow streets that they had gridlock all the time. Cars parked on the sidewalks because there was no room on the street. He said, "Before, the sidewalks were full of cars and the streets were full of people. It's so much better now."

It was so nice to hear about something that is actually done with all the money we send to other countries and to know that it makes a difference in the lives of everyday people. He truly sounded grateful to America for this.

GENTLE TAXI TOUR DRIVER IN THE SEYCHELLE ISLANDS

We rented a taxi van with a friend from the ship and her 94-year-old mother to spend four hours driving around the island from the city of Mahé. The driver took care to make sure "Mama" was settled and comfortable in the front seat after every stop before getting behind the wheel. If the walk at a particular stop was too far or she wasn't up to getting out of the van again, he stood by her open door and talked with her. He was soft spoken, kind, and gentle. Exactly the kind of tour guide we were hoping to find.

The driver spoke excellent English and we learned so much from him about his homeland. There are 115 individual islands in the Seychelles but only three are inhabited. One of the uninhabited islands is home to the black parrot, the only place on earth where this bird can be found. Unemployment here is less than 4%. Children start school at four years of age and continue free public school through the 12th grade. If people have to leave their jobs in order to care for aging parents or sick family members, the government pays them while they do so. Ninety percent of the food is imported, mostly from South Africa, because this island is very hilly and the clay soil makes it hard to grow anything. Even so, 25 varieties of bananas grow here and even more varieties of mangoes. They have wind turbines and desalinization plants. Rising sea levels have made it necessary to begin relocating people to Mahé from one of the other islands because it will soon become inhabitable. Pirates are a problem here too. The driver knew of several fishermen who took their boats out to sea one morning and never came home. In spite of their problems, the people of Seychelles love their home and welcome those who visit it with open arms.

TRUSTWORTHY GUIDES IN COSTA RICA

Several years ago, we took an overnight flight from Denver to San Jose, Costa Rica and rented a car to drive to a time share we had reserved in Quepos. Since we couldn't check in until mid-afternoon, we stopped at a small national park and hired a guide. We had read that car break-ins were common in Costa Rica so we weren't totally surprised when the guide told us to take everything out of our car and leave it inside the park office. It was more of a shack than an office, with only one young woman working there. If we had stopped to think about this, we would have taken one look at this shack and these strangers and driven away. Instead, we reminded ourselves that this was a national park and the guide wore his license certification card on a lanyard around his neck. We took all our luggage out of the car and left it in the corner of the shack.

Then the guide told us there was another entrance to the park down the road and he suggested we leave the car there while we walk through the forest. It would be closer to the more interesting parts of the park. So here we were, newly arrived in a foreign country and not only did we hand over all our belongings at the direction of a stranger but we let him in our car and followed his directions down a dirt road to an unmarked park entrance.

We walked down the trail for a while until he suggested a short cut that went through dense forest and tall banana plants. It was beginning to feel like we were in one of those movies that motivate the audience to warn the people on the screen and shout, "No! Don't go in there!" We would never have found our way out alone. If anything bad happened, no one would have ever found us.

As it turned out, our guide was kind, courteous and very knowledgeable. He pointed out many things we would have overlooked, including the leaf-cutter ants at our feet and the sloth in a tree. When we returned to the shack, all our belongings were right where we left them, untouched.

During the same trip, we had arranged for a guided walk in the Monteverde Cloud Forest. We thought we had left in plenty of time, but the roads were poorly marked and very muddy because of a bad rainstorm the previous night. It was slow going, especially when we came to dead ends and had to turn around.

We finally found the entrance to the forest, only to learn that our tour had already left. Don't worry, the man in the office told us, it was still possible to catch up to the group. A big shirtless guy appeared with a bandana around his head and a machete hanging from his waist down to his knees. He slung a chainsaw over his shoulder and said, "Follow me. I take you to your guide."

Although we wondered what this guy was going to do with the chainsaw, we followed him down the trail into the forest, trying not to think about the possibility that he could be chopping up Americans who would never be found. It wasn't long before we caught up to the guided group, and the man with the chainsaw went off to clear the storm debris from the trail ahead.

The tour was wonderful and once again we were so glad that we trusted a stranger.

NICE PEOPLE IN MOMBASA

Mombasa is not a place where one would expect to encounter friendly, helpful people but we found some. The traffic in Mombasa was unbelievable. Lots of tuk-tuks roared around with noise, dust, and pollution everywhere. We slid past the tour guides trying to snag cruise ship passengers getting off the shuttle bus and walked toward the entrance of the old city.

At a gift shop owned by a man from India we had a very interesting conversation. He came to Kenya as a boy with his parents and grandparents and spoke excellent English. His grandfather was an engineer hired by the British to help build the railroad between Mombasa and Nairobi and on to Uganda. The shopkeeper said he sent his children to college in England and they never came back. He misses them but he understands.

He was very interested in our cruise around the world and said we must have lived very good lives to have received this gift. We bought a few trinkets from him and he asked how we were going to spend our day. We explained our plan to visit the fort and then walk down to the church. He took us outside, down to the corner and flagged down a tuk-tuk to take us, making sure the driver knew exactly where we wanted to go.

Titus, the driver of our tuk-tuk, also spoke English and wore white gloves. He only charged $1 for the ride. It wasn't as scary as I expected even though the tuk-tuk was pretty flimsy and the traffic was heavy. He asked how long we would be at the fort and when we said only about ten minutes, just long enough to walk around the outside a bit and take some photos, he offered to wait for us.

Just as we arrived at the fort, a tour bus from the ship pulled up and people we knew were shocked to see us climbing out of a tuk-tuk that they weren't brave enough to ride in. We later learned that two friends from the ship also went out on their own. Each hired a tuk-tuk and they raced against each other on the busy streets. I don't remember who won the race, but they said, "It was a hoot!" We weren't quite that brave.

A man selling jewelry and souvenirs outside the fort had a bracelet made of wooden beads that caught my eye. When I asked the price, he said $2 so I bought it. He said, "The peoples with no legs makes this for you." Then I noticed a small sign indicating the proceeds were for the handicapped.

We climbed back into our tuk-tuk and asked Titus to drop us off at the church. A woman in a uniform next to a gate blocking the drive said we would have to get permission to go into the church from someone in the building at the back. If we were permitted to go in, it was not allowed to take photos there. We said okay.

Before leaving Titus, we took his picture and he said, "May I give you my e-mail? Perhaps we can communicate." I said sure. He waited until we walked over to the building where an elderly man offered to take us inside. He told us that the church was "fairly new". It was built in 1923. He also said it was fine to take photos. As we entered the church, Titus waved goodbye and drove off.

On the shuttle bus return trip, the young guide on board asked how we enjoyed our visit to Mombasa. When we told him about the man from India in the shop and his grandfather, he said there were many engineers from India who came to Kenya in those days, arranged by the British settlers who needed the railroad. Many were killed by man-eating lions. When no more were willing to come from India, they had to get engineers from England. I hope they got hazard pay.

NEAR CATASTROPHE AT THE OLD FORT

Near the ruins at Bagamoyo, we stopped at the old fort on the coast where slaves were held until they were loaded onto sailing ships. The pits and chains were sickening. The fort wasn't big enough to accommodate all the people on our vans, so we didn't see a lot, which was okay. It was a depressing place with a very bad atmosphere.

The stone steps to the upper level were steep and uneven. Several people from our bus who had mobility issues were really struggling here. It was hot, crowded and very hard to see the steps. There was no railing either, so everyone tried to keep one hand on the wall as they went down. The elderly man in front of us stumbled suddenly and Ed grabbed his arm just in time to stop him from falling. The man was badly shaken and Ed kept telling him, "I got you. I got you." That man would have taken everybody on the stairs down with him if he'd fallen. Clearly this is a place where bad things still happen.

Every now and then, Ed became the kind stranger offering help when it was needed.

LYING DOWN WITH FRIENDLY GERMANS IN SINGAPORE

At the end of a lovely day exploring Singapore on our own, it was getting dark and time to head over to the "Supertrees" for the evening light show at the Gardens by the Bay. A walkway high above the ground winds around and connects enormous artificial trees that are lit up at night. We got in line for the elevator that goes to the top of the tallest tree, but then learned the wait time for the elevator was a half hour and we could only stay on the walkway for 15 minutes. The young woman selling tickets candidly told us the best place to see the lights was from the ground anyway.

The base of each of these trees was surrounded by a very deep bench so it was possible to lay on your back and watch the lights without straining your neck. There weren't many empty spots on the benches and people were starting to sit on the ground. We found one spot next to a group of young German women from Berlin who squeezed together so both of us could fit in next to them. It seemed like a perfectly normal thing to do, lying on our backs side by side close to strangers watching the colors change on the trunks and branches of countless trees, all choreographed to music. It was fantastic.

FLAGS IN JAPAN

At the port in Kagoshima, locals lined the pier waiting for our cruise ship to dock. They called to us with loud Hellos waving their arms and waving flags.

One man stood out from the crowd. He had flags for all the countries that our passengers were from. I'm not sure how he got this information, but his flag count looked accurate to me. While we waited for the shuttle bus, I showed him the photo on my phone of the flag collection Ed put together of all the countries we've visited together over the years. This man was thrilled. He had found a fellow flag lover.

He didn't speak English, but he made it clear that he wanted us to stay put while he ran up the hill to his car. He came back with a brand new flag of Japan wrapped in cellophane and presented it to Ed with a bow. His wife and I both took a picture of the two of them with Ed holding his new Japanese flag. Ed gave them some chocolates we had brought from the ship. We tried to carry on a conversation, but it was difficult. A few words back and forth with much bowing was all we could manage. We said goodbye when the next shuttle bus came and headed into the city.

When we returned that evening, the man with the flags was waiting for us. He held out a yellow bag for Ed, then ran to get a young woman who worked in the port building to translate for him. Inside the bag was a flag with two big fish and some small fish hanging from it. The woman explained that this flag was for children's day that is celebrated in Japan once a year and the big fish represent the parents. I told her to tell him that we have two grandsons who will be interested in this flag. He was delighted. Then he showed us the sumo wrestler candy he had put in the bag for us to enjoy. This sweet man would have had no idea what time we were coming back, but he was there waiting for us. We were really touched by this.

Many locals were out on the pier to see the ship sail away at 9:00 pm. Ed went back outside after dinner to talk with them and offer chocolates from the ship. Our new friends were still waving flags and saying goodbye until we were out of sight.

FINDING SUSHI IN KAGOSHIMA

Since Kagoshima was our last stop in Japan, Ed wanted to have real Japanese sushi in a place that specialized in sushi and not in a regular restaurant. This wasn't as easy to find as one might think. We tried to follow the directions that a young man on the street gave us, but it didn't work out too well.

While we were trying to figure out where we went wrong, a Japanese woman walking by heard us speaking English and kindly asked if she could help. We told her we were looking for good sushi. She thought for a minute, walked us over to a bench in an arcade and told us to sit down and wait while she went to find out.

When she came back a few minutes later, she knew where to go and walked with us a few blocks, then down an alley to a little place called Kirin-Sushi. The door was locked and the sign said it would open at 5 pm, which was in only five minutes but she banged on the door until the manager opened it. They talked back and forth, then she told us that all of his tables were reserved but we could go in and sit at the counter. We said that would be fine and thanked the nice lady who went out of her way to take us there.

Ed said it was the best sushi he'd ever eaten.

WELCOMING PEOPLE IN AUSTRALIA

According to our Oceania ship itinerary only one day was scheduled for Sydney. This was our first visit to Sydney and one day wasn't nearly enough. We decided to fly from Townsville and spend three days in Sydney until ship caught up with us even though that meant missing Brisbane.

Townsville was one of the most welcoming places we'd ever visited. It seemed like the entire city was out to greet us, hand out maps and organize shuttle bus passengers. Everyone was so friendly, asking where we were from, how long we were on the ship, whether we had been to Australia before, etc. We had some time to walk through the town before heading to the airport.

Evidently it was unusual for anyone to be pulling a suitcase down Main Street. Several people smiled at us when we passed by. One local asked if we had bought so many souvenirs in Townsville that we needed to buy a suitcase to put them in.

When Ed spotted a little pie café, he wanted to go inside and see all the flavors of dessert pies not knowing that in Australia, pies are usually main dishes like beef and bacon pie, chicken pie, vegetable pie, etc. There were a few dessert pies, but not many. We were able to get the last lemon tart for Ed and a square vanilla fluffy thing for me. When we finished eating, we asked the woman behind the counter for directions to the closest taxi stand. She offered to call one for us so we wouldn't have to walk any farther with our suitcase.

The taxi driver was from Fiji. He was fascinated by our trip around the world and had a million questions about where we'd been and where we were going. He had traveled all over the western US with his extended family. They rented a twelve passenger van so they could all travel together and really loved the United States.

I don't remember any of the sights in Townsville but I will always remember the nice people that live there.

RIDING WITH LOCALS IN FRENCH POLYNESIA

I had never heard of Nuku Hiva before we visited, but a lot happened there. Robert Louis Stevenson landed here in 1888. Herman Melville deserted his whaling ship and hid among the native people here which inspired him to write his novels. The earthquake in Japan that caused the Fukushima disaster in 2011 created a tsunami that reached Nuku Hiva, bringing four separate nine-foot tsunami waves per hour all day. This is also where the fourth Survivor episode was filmed during the first season on CBS.

The ship only offered one excursion here, a drive across the island to visit the scenic Taipivai Valley. Only about 2,500 people live here and there are no tourist services to speak of. At the pier, it seemed like every local who could play a musical instrument or perform a native dance came to entertain us when we got off the tender boats. The arrival of a cruise ship is clearly a big deal on this island.

We toured the island in privately owned four-wheel drive vehicles. Five caravans of 15 cars with four passengers in each vehicle bumped over dirt roads along the edges of steep cliffs. It was crazy. Evidently before the ship arrived, the word went out that if you have an SUV or extended cab pickup, you can earn some money by driving tourists around in your vehicle. I'm sure the cruise line's corporate office breathed a big sigh of relief when the last tour ended without incident.

Only one guide spoke English. Whenever our caravan stopped, he gathered everyone from the cars and told us all kinds of interesting things about the place where we stood. He was a retired teacher from France who had settled here many years ago. Not many cruise ships stop here, and he was honored to be asked to provide us with a tour of his island home. There wasn't much local industry other than small farms. A supply ship comes every two or three weeks.

French Polynesia impressed me with the way they maintain traditions and ensure that each generation knows about their ancestors. The people here are not wealthy but they are very rich in culture and history and are happy to share it with those who come to visit.

On the way back to the ship at the end of our full day tour to the valley, we saw a small bed and breakfast with an open restaurant on the front porch. We stopped for a cold beer and sat outside next to a long table of locals. Some of them were eating a strange kind of puffy pizza. Three of them played stringed instruments and they sang several songs. They were delightful. I went inside to order a second round of beer and asked the server if these people come here often and sing. She said, "No, they are here for you." Then I realized that except for this long table, all the other customers were from the cruise ship.

I gave a bag of wrapped chocolates from the ship to the woman at the end of the table. They passed the bag around quickly and everybody took one. I went over to one of the musicians before the bag reached him and told him in French that the chocolates were for everyone and we loved their music. They laughed and began to sing a song about chocolate. Everyone was having such a good time.

They all waved to us when we left. I'm convinced that island people are the happiest in the world. The old saying that money doesn't buy happiness is absolutely true.

COINCIDENCE IN AMERICAN SAMOA

On our way through the town of Pago Pago, we ran into some friends from the ship who were looking for the American Samoa National Park Headquarters. The map indicated it was farther down the street, so we went along with them in search of it. Our friends had national park passport booklets with pages stamped at the various national parks they have visited around the US. The stamp from American Samoa is quite coveted because this place is so hard to get to.

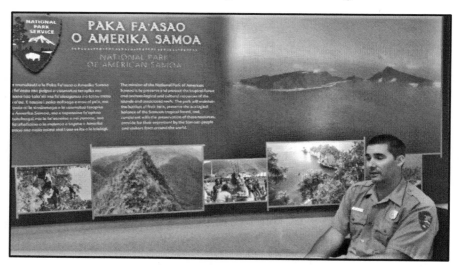

We found the park headquarters with no problem and the ranger there was very nice. It turned out he met his wife at a deli in Denver where she sold cheese and he sold wine. This deli was in our neighborhood not far from our house and we had shopped in it. It is a small world indeed.

TICKET SHORTAGE IN RIO DE JANEIRO

On our way to Sugarloaf Mountain in a terrible downpour, our bus driver dropped us off a few blocks from the train station where we waited while our guide picked up the tickets. We were at the tail end of the group and when we reached him, he had no tickets left. That was when he realized that he had given tickets to two people who were not in our group. He was two tickets short. The train whistle blew and it was time to leave.

The sommelier from the ship was on the tour with us as an escort and he ran back to the ticket office to get two more tickets. They held the train and once we got our tickets, we ran down the platform and hopped on just before the doors closed. He remained our hero for the remainder of the cruise.

HELPING LOCALS IN TONGA

On our second world cruise we stopped again in Nuku'alofa, the capital of Tonga. It was the day after the eye of a cyclone passed over the city. The island was spared from the most damaging effects of this storm, which had been elevated to Category 3. It suffered erosion and road damage at the opposite side of the island from the port, but there were no deaths or injuries here. Two other groups of Tonga islands nearby didn't fare as well.

Ed had decided before we docked that he wanted to help these people, who hadn't completely recovered from the impact of a strong cyclone two years earlier. He tried to organize a group from the ship to help get the roads open and do what he could for people whose homes were damaged. When it didn't seem possible to get this together, he set out by himself to do what he could. I love him so much for this.

He found a taxi at the pier and told the driver he wanted to go where there was storm damage to help clean it up. The driver said if that's what he wanted to do, there would be no charge for the ride. Ed worked all afternoon alongside the locals who shared their beer and their smiles while clearing branches and debris from the road leading to a village at the other side of the island., One of them drove him back to the ship at the end of the afternoon.

Ed came back dirty and exhausted but glowing with the heartfelt reward that comes from giving help where help is needed. I hope the people he spent the day with will remember him. He will certainly remember them.

FRIENDLY FARM AT IOWA HIGHPOINT

The Iowa highpoint was my favorite because it was on the Sterler family farm. The day we stopped there was hot and humid, with grasshoppers everywhere. We parked on a rural dirt road and just as we were walking up to the house to ask permission, Mrs. Sterler opened the screen door and said, "Well, it looks like we've got a couple of highpointers here. It's out by the silo next to feed trough. You'll see it when you get back there. Thanks for stopping by."

We signed the register that was set up next to a basket of Iowa highpoint commemorative key rings with a sign that said, "Help yourself". The farm is now Hawkeye Point park and boasts a picnic area under the grain bin shelter and a silo with an observation deck. I'm glad we visited when the Sterlers were there to greet us.

MT RUSHMORE ENCOUNTER

Many years ago, we took our kids on a camping trip to Mt Rushmore in South Dakota. After supper, we followed the crowd back to the monument to see it lit up in the dark, and the kids wanted to stop for ice cream. I told Ed to go ahead and take them while I stopped in the gift shop. Ed and I always walk very close together, especially in crowds. I leaned my head on his shoulder and said, "Where do you want me to meet you?" When he didn't answer, I looked up at his face. It wasn't Ed. The stranger didn't say anything. He just smiled.

THE PEOPLE OF AFRICA

The sheer number of the animals we saw on safari was mind blowing, but what impressed me most about Africa was the people.

In Tanzania, our guide took us to a remote Masai village where the chief honored us with a visit inside his hut and the women of the tribe taught me to dance with them. We were the only visitors at the time and were treated like royalty.

The school children were adorable. I didn't realize that in African schools, the boys sit always together on one side and the girls on the other. Masai all have closely cropped hair and I couldn't tell the difference between the young boys and young girls. They were all dressed the same. Our guide tactfully pointed out that I was sitting with the boys when I should have been on the other side of the teacher with the girls.

Many of the children we saw in the larger towns wore school uniforms, but as our jeep passed through small villages, most were dressed in rags and their families had little more than a fragile roof over their heads. They often ran toward the jeep to smile and wave, laughing and playing as if they were the happiest in the world and had everything they could possibly want.

The person I remember most of all was the woman walking not far from the road with a water jug on her head. We hadn't passed any signs of civilization for quite a while and there was nothing ahead of us that I could see. I watched her for as long as I could, wondering where she had come from and where she was going. Before taking time off work to travel to Africa, I sometimes spent hours writing and rewriting a document, agonizing over finding the right words. All that seemed so meaningless after encountering this woman who probably spent every day of her life on this path just getting water for her family.

SHOPKEEPERS IN BENIN

Motorcycles and small motor scooters were the primary mode of transportation in Contonou, the largest city in this west African country. It wasn't unusual to see a father driving a motorcycle, with two children behind him and a mother at the back, sometimes with a baby in front of her, all on one motorcycle the size of one that would hold only two adults in the US.

Many people seemed to earn their living by walking along the street with whatever they could carry and sell to people stopped at traffic lights. Everything from bed sheets to pineapples. I was amazed by the size of those stacks of merchandise that people could carry on their heads. I never saw anything fall off or even shift around. The bus dropped us off at a sprawling market. It was terribly hot here and sometimes one of the shopkeepers stood next to me waving a fan back and forth to keep me cool while I was looking at the items they had for sale. The official language in Benin is French. Many of the shopkeepers didn't speak English, so I brushed off my high school French and had some interesting conversations.

The one I remember most was a young shopkeeper who looked to be no more than fourteen. We had a nice conversation in French and then she walked toward me and asked if I would push my hat back from my face. She stared at me and said she had never seen anyone with blue eyes before.

CONVERSATION WITH A BEDOUIN

As our bus traveled to the vast desert at Wadi Rum where Lawrence of Arabia was filmed, our Jordanian guide explained that in the past it had been common for men to have more than one wife. Because of the high unemployment now, most men have only one unless they are wealthy.

When we reached Wadi Rum, Ed chose to ride a camel across the desert while I rode in the back of a pickup truck with two women from Wisconsin. I'm not sure which one of us was safer. We met up again at a large Bedouin tent made of very heavy woven fabric. Local items were for sale at good prices. I bought a pretty purple scarf and sipped some delicious hot tea.

I approached one of the Bedouins who was standing alone and asked if he spoke English. He said he spoke a little, so I asked him how many people live in this camp. He said no one lives there; it's only used as a business for the tourists. They all live in a village down the road. I asked about his family. He appeared to be in his early 30s. He told me he has six children, which seemed like a lot considering how young he looked. When I asked if he had more than one wife he said, "No, Madame. Only one wife. These are modern times!"

LIFE IN LITTLE PETRA

On the day we visited Petra we had also booked a short tour of Little Petra, just five miles down the road. After walking miles through Petra all day, we questioned the wisdom of having added another tour but we were so glad we did. Little Petra was built around the 1st century AD by successful merchants from the main city of Petra and was used as a stopover for visiting traders. Near the entrance we passed a few Bedouin camps that looked like they could be dismantled in short order if the occupants suddenly decided to move on.

Very few people visit Little Petra, but it's worth making the time to see. The people who live there must be very tough to live in such a harsh environment. It's too bad we weren't able to communicate with any of them. They must have amazing stories to tell.

The approach to the Little Petra took us through a very narrow canyon, similar to Petra, but this one was only 1200 feet long instead of two miles. In some places it was so narrow that we had to walk single file so it was a good thing there were no crowds here. At one narrow point, some young boys blocked our way and started singing with their hands out, hoping for tips. Our guide shooed them away.

Inside a cave not far from the entrance, a young man with dark curly hair sat at a table. It looked like he had set up housekeeping with a little kitchen arrangement in the front and a bed on the raised area at the back. I never knew there was such a thing as a furnished cave. It wasn't exactly plush, but it definitely had a lived in look.

Once I was directly in front of the cave, I could see that there was a young blonde woman in local dress sitting opposite him at the table. We walked by again on our way to the exit and I waved to them. Both smiled and waved back. I wondered about the circumstances in their lives that brought them together here and later regretted not stopping to talk with them.

THE LAST DAY OF EVERY CRUISE

In the morning of our last day of each cruise we took, I never wanted to open the drapes. Seeing our final port would make the end of the cruise real. But as the saying goes, all good things must end someday and each of them did. There were always teary goodbyes with friends that last morning and promises to see each other again. When our turn came, we got off the ship for the last time, grateful for all the fabulous experiences we had, the amazing places we visited, the friends we made, and the knowledge that the world really is filled with warm wonderful people.

COVID-19 BRINGS OUR TRAVELS TO AN EARLY END

Our Viking world cruise began in August 2019 with dreams of sailing all the way around the world for eight and a half months. When news of Covid-19 broke in early 2020, we expected that our scheduled ports in China and Hong Kong would be cancelled but thought the cruise would continue. It didn't take long for most of the other ports in Asia to be cancelled as well. As we sailed northward from Tasmania, we received frequent updates, and none were encouraging.

After a lovely day in Brisbane with friends, our ship headed east to New Caledonia — two days out, two days in port and two days back. I suspected this was to give the cruise line and the captain time to make new plans. There wasn't much to see in New Caledonia but at least we can say we visited the island where McHale's Navy, the 1960s sitcom, took place. I was surprised to learn that French is the official language there.

We sailed up the east coast of Australia as rumors flew about what would happen next. No one on the ship was sick but the captain admitted that the virus was severely affecting our options. This no longer resembled the cruise we had purchased, and we still had two months left with no clear itinerary. When the cruise line offered passengers a refund for our remaining unused days if we wanted to go home, we decided to take it and got off the ship in Darwin with eight suitcases.

We flew from Darwin to Sydney to San Francisco to Chicago and landed in Allentown, PA exhausted but healthy and relieved to be back in the US. Several people we knew who stayed on the ship kept in touch by e-mail and wished they had gotten off when we did. We clearly made the right decision. Even though the cruise ended much differently than we expected, the six months we spent on the ship were wonderful and we had no regrets.

OUR ACCIDENTAL ADVENTURES RIGHT HERE AT HOME IN 2020

WHEN WE RETURNED TO THE US AFTER living in Germany, we found Denver had become crowded, expensive, and the altitude was beginning to aggravate my health issues. Before leaving on our world cruise in 2019, we sold our house in Denver and planned to live in a brand new independent living retirement community near Allentown, PA where Ed grew up. When people on the ship asked where we lived, we jokingly said we were homeless.

The day after we arrived in Allentown, we noticed that the corner of our large hard sided suitcase was cracked. The luggage was brand new and this trip was the first time we had used it. We decided to take it back to the airport the following day and file a claim.

The Allentown airport is small and minimally staffed by the airlines. The airline counter was empty. We waited around and then noticed two ticket agents sitting at a table near the windows. They told us that the ticket counter wouldn't be open for another three hours. They were just waiting to be notified when the next flight would be landing. We told them we had just arrived from Australia the day before and could they please take care of our damaged luggage? One reluctantly stood and took a look. We hadn't removed the airline luggage label so she could clearly see we had indeed just arrived the day before.

She asked if we would be willing to accept a replacement. We expected to fill out forms, take it to a luggage repair shop for an estimate and then wait for a series of next steps. Instead, she wheeled our suitcase through a doorway behind the ticket counter and returned with a brand new bag the same size and style as ours. It still had the labels and tags from the manufacturer on it. No paperwork, no signatures, nothing. We thanked her and hurried away with our new bag, hoping she wouldn't change her mind before we got out the door.

The following day, we returned to the same counter at the airport to request a refund for a future flight that had been cancelled. We thought we'd have better luck in person since the phone lines were so busy. Our luggage issue was resolved so smoothly, so we thought maybe our ticket issue would be too. We weren't quite so lucky this time. The same woman told us to take care of it online. They weren't set up to do refunds at the Allentown airport.

While we were there, a young college student trudged in with several cloth shopping bags filled with his belongings. He explained that the college was closing because of the virus and he had to fly home on short notice. He didn't have a suitcase. The ticket agent went in the back and wheeled out our old suitcase and gave it to him. He was thrilled and we were happy to see that our suitcase got recycled.

We knew that our new retirement apartment wouldn't be ready for move in for months after we returned from the cruise. Before we left, we had arranged to rent one in a similar independent living retirement community owned by the same parent company until the new one was ready. All our furnishings had been moved from Denver to a storage unit in Allentown before the cruise, so all we had to do was hire a mover to deliver it. Nothing could have prepared us for the complications ahead.

Because we returned to the US two months earlier than expected, the only available apartment in this community was 880 sq ft. and it wouldn't be ready for three weeks. We had downsized considerably, before and after our earlier move to Germany, but not enough to fit into a place that small. It never occurred to us that the promised apartment wouldn't work out. Initially we thought we could try to make it work and take just some of our things out of storage, but the next day we both knew it wasn't feasible. We got our deposit back and began looking for a place to live.

We had reserved our room at a hotel online while we were still on the ship and prepaid for three weeks. It turned out to be nothing like the photos. It was sprawled out over a large plot of land near the intersection of two freeways. It had fallen into disrepair, barely achieved the lowest standards of cleanliness, and attracted some unsavory characters who often banged on doors in the middle of the night.

The room had a small counter height refrigerator but no microwave so we had to go out each day for prepared food. We stayed at this hotel just long enough to use up the prepaid charges and moved to a more modern extended stay hotel as the impact of the virus worsened.

This new hotel was well prepared to deal with all the Covid guidelines that initially were all quite a shock but have since become commonplace. The registration desk required my signature on a document stating I had no symptoms and had not been out of the country in the past two weeks. This was true. We were in the bad hotel for three weeks before coming here. A line of tape kept each guest six feet from the desk and from each other. The door from the lobby was locked all the time so only guests with key cards could enter.

Housekeeping staff did not enter guest rooms. When we needed fresh towels, we brought the used ones to the office, dropped them in a bin and a gloved masked employee handed us fresh ones along with soap, shampoo and toilet paper whenever we needed it. We changed our own sheets and took those downstairs as well. A vacuum cleaner was kept by the elevator for guest use and spray sanitizer with rags was available upon request. We had a full-sized refrigerator and a microwave but the cabinets and drawers in the kitchenette were empty so we managed with the paper plates and plastic flatware.

After declining the offered apartment at the retirement community, we began our search for another place to live in earnest. Everything we looked at was too old, too dirty, had no garage or no laundry in the unit, or wasn't available for another six to eight weeks. One complex we stopped in had no vacancies but they recommended another unrelated one designed by the same builder. It was a little farther out of town than we would have liked, but we went to see it anyway.

The woman in the leasing office there was very nice but she had nothing available. The next day she called and said she had a cancellation. We couldn't get there fast enough. She showed us the floor plan, explained the details, and then apologized for not being able to take us inside because it was an eviction. She drove us past the building in a golf cart but didn't stop. It was a three story townhouse at the bottom of a hill surrounded by woods but only a mile from a mall and major commercial area. We went back to the hotel and filled out the application forms online.

The next day, we picked up certified checks at the bank for the security deposit and first month's rent and went back. This time contractors were making repairs inside the townhouse so we still couldn't see the inside. The following day was Sunday and according to the website, the leasing office was open in the afternoon. We went over there again hoping to see the inside this time but the office was closed. We drove down the hill and got out of the car for a closer look on our own and were appalled.

The front door had been bashed and the doorway was covered with crime scene tape. Two young guys were talking in the parking lot and Ed asked them if they knew what had happened. They said the FBI had been there last week and rammed the door but they didn't know much about the circumstances. According to them, it was an okay place to live. We walked across the back of the building to the patio of the unit and found the screen door torn, trash laying around and nothing to see from the back windows except the dark side of the hill.

The next morning, we went back again and after much discussion we asked for our deposit back. By now we were 0 for 2 and getting discouraged. We went back to the hotel and started all over again, making a list of every possible house, townhouse, and apartment house in the area that could possibly be rented to us and ruled them out one at a time. By now our criteria had softened. We could get by with less, keep a small storage unit and manage with one bedroom if it had enough living space. Things were really looking grim.

We were soon to be 0 for 3. After a discouraging day of research, we looked at an apartment complex that had great reviews posted on their website. A friend's daughter lived there for a while and liked it, so we thought we'd give it a try. Just like the previous place so many things here should have been red flags, but we were getting desperate.

This complex also had several vacancies, which should have told us there was a problem here.

We were shown the two largest apartments, one vacated by people who lived here for many years. It smelled like smoke even though it was supposedly a nonsmoking property. Then we looked at a larger one on the second floor. The garage was very deep, room for plenty of storage and it had an area off the living room that was big enough for an office. We loved the size and glossed over the worn carpeting and older appliances. We took the paper application home, happy to have found a place.

A little more research revealed that good reviews on the apartment website were four and five years old. More recent reviews were harder to find and they had terrible things to say. Appliances are old and tenants can't get anything fixed; the leasing office keeps your security deposit for all kinds of vague reasons; snow is not removed well, etc. Then some comments made by the woman at the leasing office came back to us. She said the maintenance man was gone for five days to Phillies spring training and she joked that he told her not to call him. As much as we liked the space, all this gave us second thoughts. We kept looking.

Then we made an appointment at a complex across the road from one we had just backed away from. It appeared to be well maintained, fairly new and had lots of green space. It had 30 buildings with 14 apartments in each and even had model apartments to show us. There were very few vacancies here. Even though the largest available apartment was smaller than we would have liked, but we were beyond ready to check out of the hotel and get settled.

Here everything fell into place easily. The carpet in our unit was being replaced with new wood grain laminate flooring so we had to wait another three weeks before we could move in. It was worth it. We've been very happy here and plan to stay until our independent living retirement community is ready.

IN CONCLUSION

When we left our cruise in February 2020 everyone assumed that Covid-19 wouldn't last long and travel would open back up. It hasn't turned out that way, but we'll be ready to pack our suitcases when the world calms down and travel becomes safe again.

It can't happen soon enough.

ABOUT THE AUTHOR

KATHY SPENT MUCH OF HER CHILDHOOD in Cleveland, Ohio at her favorite place, the library. She read book after book about far off lands and people who lived very differently than she did. In 1988 when she met her husband, Ed, she told him that she dreamed of traveling the world. He has made that dream come true for her over and over. Writing about their memorable experiences is her way of thanking him.

In their early years together, summer vacations meant tent camping at nearby state parks. Their last three years before retiring were spent living and working in Germany which enabled them to visit the highlights as well as the hidden gems of Europe. Since retiring, they have explored exotic parts of the world, visiting South America, Asia, islands of the South Pacific, Australia/New Zealand, and spent two weeks in Israel and Jordan. In total, the Fronheisers have visited over 100 countries, several of them multiple times. Their retirement home is in eastern Pennsylvania where Kathy continues to write about their past travels and plan future ones. Their suitcases are always packed and ready for the next adventure.

Kathy Fronheiser's first book is a historical fiction novel, *The Mirror's Secret*, which you can read about on her website, www.kathyfronheiser.com. She continues to focus on additional fiction projects in between travels.

Made in the USA
Middletown, DE
16 July 2021

44028769R00197